The Illustrat

Digital Camera Handbook

Copyright © 2007 The Foundry Creative Media Company Ltd

This 2007 edition published by Barnes & Noble, Inc.,
by arrangement with The Foundry Creative Media Company Ltd

Publisher and Creative Director: Nick Wells
Senior Editor: Sarah Goulding
General Editor: Nigel Atherton
Specialist Editor: Joël Lacey
Designer: Mike Spender

With special thanks to: Chris Herbert, Penny Brown and Polly Willis

ISBN 13: 978-1-4351-0063-3
ISBN 10: 1-4351-0063-8

Printed in China

1 3 5 7 9 10 8 6 4 2

The Illustrated
Digital
Camera
Handbook

General Editor: Nigel Atherton

Authors: Nigel Atherton, Hannah Bouckley, Ian Burley,

Steve Crabb, Jamie Harrison, Joël Lacey

BARNES
& NOBLE

NEW YORK

CONTENTS

INTRODUCTION

The year 1839 was a good one in the history of communication. Two men, Louis Daguerre in France, and William Henry Fox Talbot in England, both announced that they had managed to solve a problem that had been vexing scientists for centuries: how to record an image, and make it permanent. Thus photography was born.

At the time it was a crude, slow and highly toxic activity, but as the years went by, pioneers found ways to make it easier: glass plates, pre-coated plates, flexible film. However, by the first decade of the twentieth century the last big, revolutionary development in photography had already been achieved, with the invention of colour – though it would be decades before it was good enough and accessible enough to really take off.

Nothing really dramatic changed much after that, except that cameras got smaller and more automated, lenses improved, and film and print quality got better. Scientific breakthroughs were about small, evolutionary improvements in quality. That was until about ten years ago. There was no 'eureka' moment in a bathtub, no falling apples, no specific date on which digital photography was invented, but somehow, gradually, as if by stealth, the world was introduced to the idea of a still camera that did not use film.

The first 'digital cameras' were actually video cameras that took still photographs, and the quality was terrible. A few were sold to specialist markets, where the need for instant pictures outweighed concerns about the quality, or the astronomical cost, but they barely showed up on the public radar until the dying days of the twentieth century. Even then, they were very expensive, and inferior to film cameras in virtually every respect. But that didn't stop the early adopters from latching on to them with enthusiasm. Manufacturers kept plugging away, the quality got better, the prices fell lower and lower, until a point came, around 2003, when the general public suddenly realized that here was a viable alternative to their old film cameras which offered not one, but several huge advantages.

Firstly, people could see the pictures they had taken straight away, and that was a revelation. If the picture was no good it could be re-shot. If someone blinked it could be taken again. Suddenly, the nail-biting 'will they/won't they come out' trip to the photo processors was no longer necessary. Instant pictures meant instant gratification, and instant reassurance that the shot was in the bag.

If this was the only benefit of digital it would still be worth having, but there are many more. The removable card on which the pictures are stored can be reused. That means that, once you have bought both the camera and a decent sized memory card, you need never spend money again unless you want to make a print. And since the pictures can be viewed on a computer or a TV set, prints are an optional extra, not a necessity. Suddenly, once the high initial purchase has been made, photography becomes an incredibly cheap (if not free) activity.

There are still more benefits. For the hobbyist photographer, the invention of digital makes it easier than ever to tweak and enhance the photographs after they have been taken. Years ago the only way to do that was to have a darkroom. This usually entailed creating a space in the loft, the shed, the spare room or (temporarily) the bathroom, blacking it out and then juggling with trays of noxious chemicals in dim red lighting. And that was just to make black and white prints. It was expensive, time consuming and, ultimately, anti-social.

Digital photography has moved the darkroom to the home PC. Nowadays, the enthusiast can create works of art in daylight, in the corner of the living room, with no foul chemicals except for those sealed inside the ink cartridges in the printer. No paper need be wasted until the image is just right, so there are no waste bins full of test prints. And of course it's in full colour – or black and white, if that is what is preferred; changing between the two is but a few mouse clicks away.

This latter benefit, the digital darkroom, is the one which has had the greatest impact on the hobby of photography, because it gives the user an unparalleled degree of control over the final image, including many effects and enhancements that could never have been done before, even in the most high-tech traditional wet darkroom. Even relatively inexpensive printers can produce A4 or (with a slightly bigger investment) A3 prints that are virtually indistinguishable from silver based prints, and using the latest printers, they will outlast traditional prints in the archival stakes.

For anyone who remains unconvinced, the benefits still don't end there. Printing is just one method of sharing and showing pictures. With the invention of the internet, digital photographs can be enjoyed in any number of ways. They can be emailed, seconds after they have been taken, to friends and relatives all over the world. They can be uploaded to one of the numerous photo-sharing websites and sorted into albums, where fellow surfers can view, rate and comment on them. Or you can build your own image-based website, to your own design. For aspiring professional and semi-pro photographers, there is no better way to sell yourself than a business card or email containing the address of your own dot com.

Entry into this magical digital world has never been more accessible. High quality digital cameras have never been cheaper, and PCs have never come loaded with more bells and whistles. But there's a snag: there is a lot to learn. Bytes, megabytes, CCDs, USBs, RGBs, JPEGs, MPEGs, curves, histograms, layer masks, clipping paths... And that's where we come in. This comprehensive manual covers everything you need to know, from the very basics all the way to the most sophisticated techniques. Divided into easily navigable sections, you can start at the beginning and work your way through, or use it as a handy reference guide and dip in and out of it as required. However you use this book, you will find it an invaluable companion to help you get the very best from what you will soon discover – if you don't already know – is the world's most rewarding hobby.

Nigel Atherton, *General Editor*

START HERE

The Digital Camera Handbook provides a very wide range of information which can be sourced for your needs. Start here to find out where to go first.

I WANT TO CHOOSE THE RIGHT EQUIPMENT

✎ *Before you can start taking great pictures, you need the right camera for your needs.*

➲ **Go to page 14** to find out how digital cameras work.

➲ **Go to page 18** to find out which camera is for you.

I WANT TO TAKE BETTER PICTURES

✎ *Whether you're a beginner who needs some good advice or an experienced photographer who just needs to refresh the basics, everyone can use some helpful pointers.*

➲ **Go to page 34** for a whole section on taking great photographs.

I WANT TO ORGANIZE MY IMAGES

✎ *Digital photography encourages us to take hundreds more photos than we ever would with film. Keeping track of them can be overwhelming, but with a little organization, you will always know exactly what pictures are where.*

➲ **Go to page 94** to find out how to transfer your pictures to your computer.

➲ **Go to page 104** to learn more about organizing your images.

➲ **Go to page 106** for advice on creating a photo library.

➲ **Go to page 108** for archiving advice.

HOW DO I SHARE MY PHOTOS WITH FAMILY/FRIENDS/COLLEAGUES?

✑ *One of the many advantages of digital cameras is the ability to share your pictures with the whole world, should you wish, or even just your loved ones.*

⟳ **Go to page 112** for more information on sharing images.

⟳ **Go to page 116** to learn about sending pictures by email.

⟳ **Go to page 120** to find out how to use an online sharing website.

⟳ **Go to page 122** for advice on making a web photo gallery.

I WANT TO KNOW MORE ABOUT SCANNERS AND PRINTERS

✑ *It's easy with digital photography to forget about printing your photos and keeping physical copies. There are many options for doing this, however, and the satisfaction of creating an album of beautiful shots shouldn't be forgotten.*

⟳ **Go to page 124** to learn more about printing at home.

⟳ **Go to page 134** to get advice on using laboratories to print your photos.

⟳ **Go to page 138** to get the basics on scanning your images.

⟳ **Go to page 348** to find advanced information on printers.

⟳ **Go to page 350** for a more in-depth look at scanners.

I NEED SOME INSPIRATION

✑ *Beginner or professional, everyone needs inspiration. Whether it's how to get the most out of your holiday pictures, the best way to capture pets and children, or how to shoot underwater, expert ideas and advice will give you fantastic ideas for your own photographs.*

➲ **Go to page 146** for an extensive section on all sorts of different shooting projects.

➲ **Go to page 320** for a series of computer projects that will get the best out of your shots.

I WANT TO BE ABLE TO IMPROVE MY PHOTOS

✑ *Even if you are new to digital photography, you will be amazed at the small changes you can make to improve your shots. More experienced photographers will also benefit from learning about the more sophisticated software available and what it can do.*

➲ **Go to page 100** to learn the basics of cropping and rotating.

➲ **Go to page 102** to change colour, brightness and contrast.

➲ **Go to page 192** for an in-depth section on the different software available.

➲ **Go to page 244** for a section on basic image editing.

I WANT TO MOVE ON TO ADVANCED IMAGE EDITING

✑ *Once you've mastered the basics, you will be ready to tackle some advanced image manipulation.*

➲ **Go to page 290** for more about advanced image editing.

I WANT TO KNOW WHAT ACCESSORIES WILL HELP ME

✑ *There is a huge range of digital camera accessories available that*

will help you to get the most out of your camera, whatever standard it is.

- ➲ **Go to page 352** for a small section on lenses.
- ➲ **Go to page 358** for a small section on flash and lighting options in all their forms.
- ➲ **Go to page 362** for information on tripods.
- ➲ **Go to page 364** to find out about filters.
- ➲ **Go to page 368** to decide which camera bag is for you.

HOW DO I LOOK AFTER MY CAMERA?

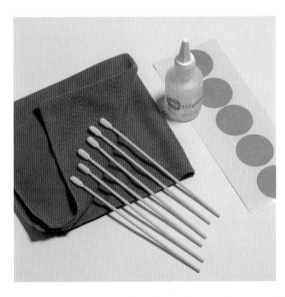

✍ *A digital camera is often an expensive investment, so the importance of cleaning it and taking care of it should not be overlooked.*

➲ **Go to page 370** for advice on maintenance and cleaning.

WHERE CAN I FIND MORE INFORMATION?

✍ *A goldmine of further information on digital photography can be found principally on the internet, an invaluable reference tool.*

- ➲ Go to page 374 for a list of manufacturers' websites.
- ➲ Go to page 376 for websites on forums, techniques, advice, news, and reviews. This page also contains websites on online printing and sharing information.

WHY SWITCH TO DIGITAL?

To take great photographs, you no longer have to be a professional photographer. Digital photography has completely changed the way we take and share photographs, and digital cameras are one of the fastest growing consumer products. But why is this? What is the advantage of digital over film?

▲ *Film cameras are slowly losing ground.*

Although digital cameras are more expensive than film cameras, the price has been steadily dropping over the last few years. At the same time, their quality and performance have vastly improved, rapidly outstripping their film counterparts. In addition, although the initial outlay may be more, you will never have to buy a roll of film again. With any standard roll of 36 pictures there are inevitably a number of failures when the prints come back from the lab – blurred images, red eye, poor composition, tilted horizons and so on. If you had the chance to look at your negatives before you sent the film away, maybe half the pictures would be rejected. If you could then erase the failed pictures and continue using the film to take even more great shots, then every picture you got back would be perfect, or at least worthwhile. Digital cameras make that a reality. The camera's built-in screen allows instant judgement, meaning that you can delete failed

▲ *More and more people are buying digital cameras as their quality improves and they become more affordable.*

pictures and continue shooting. Those pictures can then be printed or saved to a computer and the 'film' used all over again to take more photographs.

Digital cameras increase your options dramatically. In this information age of the Internet and email, photographs don't always

▲ Web galleries are a great way of sharing pictures with friends.

need to be printed. You can email the pictures from last night's party directly to you friends, or make a web gallery so everyone who was there can view them.

Another advantage is a technical one. Digital cameras are now much more advanced than film cameras, meaning that many of the problems traditionally associated with film are fixed by the camera itself, essentially now a measuring device and mini computer. There are therefore fewer failures than before, and many more chances to fix any problems at a later date on a computer using specialized computer software. This will be explored and explained later in the book. The digital age is here, and even the most amateur photographer can produce fantastic pictures with minimum effort.

◀ Digital cameras are incredibly easy to use, and even beginners can produce great quality images.

HOW DIGITAL CAMERAS WORK

Digital cameras are complex electronic devices that perform many functions and calculations every time you press the shutter button. Unlike film, the information recorded is not held as a tangible, physical entity, such as a negative. Instead it records data, a series of binary numbers that a computer can read. So how does this happen?

▼ The sensor is the digital version of a roll of film.

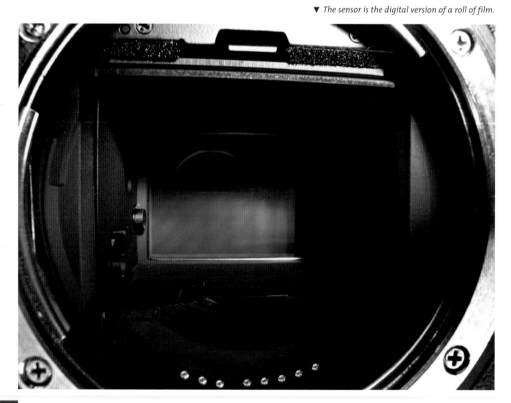

Digital Camera Handbook

When you press the shutter button on a digital camera, several things happen. The shutter opens and the subject is captured on a digital sensor or CCD (Charge-Coupled-Device) – essentially the digital version of film. The CCD is a small silicon chip holding millions of tiny light-sensitive elements, called pixels. These are arranged in a grid and receive the individual particles of light, called photons, which are turned into an electric charge by the sensor. At this time this electric signal is still in an analogue form. These signals are sent to the camera's processor, a small computer chip that turns the signals into binary code (a series of 1s and 0s) which is then saved in a format that a computer can read. The file that is created is then saved to a memory card, a small, removable storage device in the camera.

▼ Image files are stored on memory cards in the camera.

That is the basic science, but much more goes on. As you press the shutter, the lens focuses on the subject while the sensor measures the amount of light, so that the exposure will be correct. It also measures the colour of the light, so that it is replicated accurately. This process, known as white balance, is added at the processing stage. Other processes are also added to the image – sharpness, contrast correction, etc. – using mathematic formulae known as algorithms, designed by the camera's engineers.

Finally, in order to keep the file size small enough to keep the workflow and memory working efficiently, the file is usually compressed. This involves the camera processor looking for areas of similar colour and detail in the image and throwing some of that information away, thus reducing the file size. This results in a JPEG file, and when the file is opened on a computer, the computer then replaces that information and increases the size of the file again. The JPEG file is then saved on the memory card, and the camera is ready to take the next photograph.

image.JPG
2,048 x 1,536

▲ A JPEG is an image file. Clicking on this will reveal the image.

Section One: Camera Basics

ANATOMY OF A DIGITAL CAMERA

Digital cameras share many of the same functions as traditional cameras, but have lots of new features which you need to become familiar with. Here is a brief rundown of the most common features found on a digital camera.

LENS

One of the key elements of any camera, film or digital, the lens directs the light from the subject to the sensor. It is used to focus on the subject, ensuring sharpness. Most digital cameras use a zoom lens, which has several focal lengths and changes the size and perspective of the subject being photographed.

POWER SWITCH

Turns the camera on and off.

SHUTTER RELEASE BUTTON

Operates the camera shutter, a small door that opens inside the camera to expose the sensor to the image projected by the lens. Half pressing the shutter release button also operates the autofocus and initiates the light meter, which measures the light and calculates the exposure.

▲ *Digital camera front, showing the lens, flash and viewfinder.*

▲ *Digital camera back, showing the LCD screen, mode dial and various function buttons.*

Digital Camera Handbook

LCD MONITOR/MENU

Images can be composed and reviewed on the LCD (liquid crystal display) monitor. The camera's menu is also viewed on the monitor. The menu is a series of screens and sub-headings that allow you to make changes to the way your camera functions.

FLASH

Photography uses light to record the picture. If there is no light, you

▲ *LCD monitors have become increasingly sophisticated.*

cannot take a picture. Most cameras have a built-in flash to add light in the dark. The flash can also be used in bright sun to eliminate unwanted shadows.

MODE DIAL

Chooses different exposure modes or scene modes, which alter the way the camera takes the picture. You will also usually find a video mode here.

NAVIGATION BUTTONS

Usually there is a cluster of four buttons, or a rocker switch, that navigate through the menu and make changes. The arrow keys also scroll through the pictures you have already taken when used in review mode. Often the buttons will have a secondary purpose to operate other features on the camera such as the flash, self timer and macro mode.

VIEWFINDER

A small lens set into the camera to compose images without using the LCD. Many compact cameras now don't have a viewfinder, relying on the LCD monitor instead. However a viewfinder is useful in bright sunlight when it may be difficult to see the LCD clearly.

ZOOM CONTROL

Usually a rocker switch or pair of buttons that operate the zoom function of the lens. It is also often used to magnify images displayed in review mode.

TYPES OF DIGITAL CAMERA

Whatever your level of experience or your style of photography, there is a camera out there for you. There are several major categories of digital camera, although a few cross over.

CAMERA PHONES

These are a recent development but are a very popular imaging device. Image quality has been poor for a long time, but they are rapidly improving, with larger sensors, better lenses and features including autofocus, white balance and more. Camera phones are many people's first introduction to photography and encourage people to take pictures, but with a few exceptions are not used as a serious photographic tool.

▲ A hard-wearing metal body can be worth paying extra for.

ENTRY LEVEL CAMERAS

These are usually cheap and cheerful, with plastic bodies and simple controls. They often have a fixed lens with no zoom and a basic automatic exposure mode, although as prices fall manufacturers are adding more features.

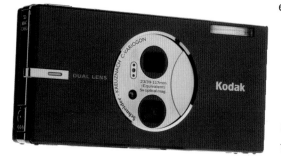

▲ Digital cameras are improving all the time.

LIFESTYLE COMPACT CAMERAS

Digital photography has freed camera designers to create much more stylish models. The smaller electronic components and lack of film chambers has resulted in some stylish and occasionally radical designs. Cameras can be the size of credit cards and come in many different colours. Lifestyle cameras vary wildly, with some models offering just basic controls to point and shoot, or more advanced exposure controls to appeal to the enthusiast.

SUPERZOOM CAMERAS

Superzooms are very versatile. They have long zoom lenses and usually a combination of exposure modes to suit everybody from the family snapper to the photographic enthusiast. Superzooms are usually larger than compact cameras, due to the size of the lens, but are still lightweight and small enough to be carried in a camera bag.

▲ *More sophisticated cameras will give you many more options.*

DIGITAL SLRS

The SLR (Single Lens Reflex) is the most versatile of cameras. Usually aimed at the more competent, enthusiastic photographer, as well as professionals, SLRs offer high quality images with lots of control. Different lenses can be used, along with a wide array of accessories. SLRs are larger than other cameras, and as you build a system with extra lenses and accessories they can become bulky and heavy to carry around. If you are serious about photography, however, the SLR is the best choice.

▶ *SLR cameras are a great investment if you are serious about photography.*

RESOLUTION

One of the first considerations when buying a digital camera should be its resolution – the amount of detail the camera can capture via its sensor. Commonly measured in megapixels, resolution has long been a competitive issue amongst camera manufacturers. There is an assumption that the more megapixels the better, but this is not always the case.

The word 'pixel' is short for 'picture element', a tiny light sensor that it is the basic element of a digital photograph. They make up an image much like individual tiles make up a mosaic. If you put a million of them together you have a megapixel. Each pixel translates to one pixel on a computer screen.

Pixels record the colour of an image as red, green and blue, commonly known as RGB. When the colours are all mixed together on a screen they form the multi-coloured image, in the same way as the image on a TV is formed.

Most cameras now offer at least three to five million pixels resolution, which indicates the level of detail a camera can capture. This is important when it comes to printing, as the more detail an image has, the larger and sharper the prints will be. For the average user, five or six million pixels will produce good results up to A4 on a home printer or from a high street laboratory.

Compacts with more megapixels are available, but they produce larger sized files, which take up more space on your memory card and on your computer's hard drive.

Digital Camera Handbook

◀ ▲ *The lower the resolution, the more pixellated your photograph will be.*

For the average home user printing 6 x 4 inch prints (the most common print size from a lab), the extra resolution would make little difference to the final print. If larger prints are needed then a higher pixel count is necessary.

Resolution alone is not the whole story, though. The more pixels that camera manufacturers cram on to their sensors, the smaller those pixel sites have to be. A smaller pixel site will gather less light than a larger pixel site given the same exposure. This means that either these chips are less sensitive or that their built-in image processors have to amplify

▲ *Larger prints require a higher pixel count to maintain quality.*

the signal from the pixel site. This also amplifies any non-image forming noise, which shows as false coloured pixels in the final image. As a general rule, therefore, cameras should always be judged by what their pictures are like, and not by how many megapixels they boast.

Section One: Camera Basics

LENSES

The lens is crucial to digital photography, as it is the means by which light enters the camera in order to record the image to the CCD. The lens is also used to focus the image so that it is sharp, and plays a critical role in determining the look of the image – the composition and perspective.

The lens is essentially a series of curved glass elements that are set into a complex mechanism. They move in relation to each other to provide the best focus for any subject at any given distance.

With very rare exceptions, all digital cameras use autofocus lenses, which automatically detect the subject and lock the focus on it. Most compact digital cameras also use zoom lenses, which offer different focal lengths (the distance in millimetres from the centre of lens to the point of focus) to allow subjects to appear closer and for perspective to change. SLRs accept different lenses, which can be changed as the situation, or personal choice, requires. Different lenses offer different focal lengths and there are four main types of lenses available for digital SLRs.

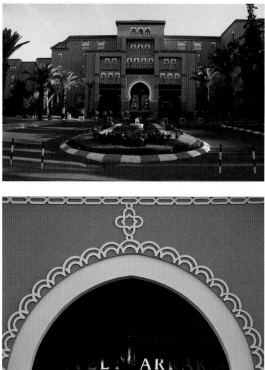

▲ *Zoom lenses enable you to focus in on a particular feature.*

▲ *A useful accessory, zoom lenses are very versatile.*

STANDARD

Offers a similar field of view as the human eye. Typically this is the equivalent of a focal length of 50 mm.

WIDEANGLE

Produces a wider than normal field of view allowing more of the scene to be captured in the frame, which makes objects look smaller (and thus further away) than they really are. They are good for capturing landscapes or buildings, and the increased perspective can be used to add drama.

TELEPHOTO

Has a longer focal length and is used to make subjects look bigger (and thus closer) than they are. Short telephoto lenses are good for producing natural portraits, while longer lenses are good for sport and wildlife photography. Perspective is decreased in telephoto lenses, making the subject look closer to the background.

ZOOM

Offers a combination of focal lengths and can stretch from wideangle through standard to telephoto. The advantage is that one lens fits all, offering versatility as well as convenience.

Most digital cameras have a smaller image area than traditional film cameras do – i.e. the sensor is smaller than a 35 mm film frame, so smaller focal lengths are needed to achieve the same effect as on 35 mm film. However, because 35 mm has been prevalent for so long, many manufacturers quote 35mm-equivalent focal lengths as a shorthand for consumers to understand the effect of any given lens.

Section One: Camera Basics

VIEWFINDERS & LCDS

Before you take a photograph, you need to compose your scene. To do this you need a viewfinder or a monitor.

OPTICAL VIEWFINDER

The most popular form of image composition has long been the viewfinder. On compact cameras this is usually a small lens fitted to a bore hole through the casing of the camera. It is usually off-centre from the lens but is also linked to it, so as you zoom the lens, the magnification of the image in the viewfinder increases. The problem with this type of viewfinder is that the image you see is not the same as the image seen by the lens, and some compositional control is lost. In addition, optical viewfinders do not show much shooting or exposure information. They are rapidly disappearing from newer digital cameras to be replaced by LCD monitors.

REFLEX VIEWFINDER OR PENTAPRISM

With SLRs, the image seen through the viewfinder is exactly the same as that of the lens thanks to a series of prisms and mirrors. Reflex viewfinders are large and bright and show most shooting

▲ *In EVF mode, the image is shown exactly as the lens sees it.*

information using LED (light-emitting diode, or small light) readouts around the outside, as well as metering and focusing points within the frame. They don't allow video shooting, however, as the mirror is in the way, and the finder goes black at the time of capture. This is because the mirror has to be lifted to allow the light waves to pass through to the CCD.

ELECTRONIC VIEWFINDER

The Electronic Viewfinder, or EVF, has gained in popularity on superzoom cameras in particular. Like a reflex viewfinder it shows the image exactly as the lens sees it, but as a video feed onto a small screen direct from the CCD. Small amounts of video footage can therefore be recorded and an array of camera data and information can also be superimposed over the viewed image. Resolution can be poor, however, and slow video refresh rates can make the view seem jerky.

▲ *Electronic viewfinders show the image on the LCD screen.*

LCD MONITOR

Arguably the most important development in digital photography, the LCD (Liquid Crystal Display) is taking the place of optical viewfinders on compact cameras. Like the EVF it offers live video feed, and screens can be large, some almost filling the back of the camera. However, LCDs are notoriously difficult to see in bright light, and by moving the camera away from the eye to a position where the screen can be seen, camera stability is reduced. This may lead to blurred photos and tilted horizons.

▼ *LCD screens allow you to see more detail but can be hard to see in bright light.*

MENU FUNCTIONS

A camera's menu is a vital element that can completely change the way your camera works. It is the means by which you can make changes to exposure, image size and much more. The more sophisticated models have extensive menus with functions you didn't even know you needed.

When you access your camera's menu, a series of lists will appear on the LCD that allow you to set up the camera exactly the way you want. This can be performed for one shot, or saved as your default for all of your pictures.

Most cameras divide the menu into three categories, or modes, with separate, more specific, modes within.

SET-UP MODE

This menu should be the first one you access after buying a camera. You can set the camera's date and time, useful so that years later you can see exactly when a picture was taken. You can also set the video output to

▲ The set-up mode allows you to change the camera's basic settings, such as date, time and language.

match the system used where you live. 'Format' lets you set the format of the pictures on your memory card and also optimizes the saving efficiency of your card for the particular camera you own.

Digital Camera Handbook

▲ *It is easy to alter the ISO speed with a digital camera.*

PICTURE/ SHOOTING MODE

This allows changes to the way the camera takes pictures, and the submenus will change the look of your photographs. Common items include image quality, to change the resolution or file type of the image; metering, which changes the way your camera measures the light; digital filters which alter the colour, sharpness and contrast of the images; exposure compensation, to make pictures lighter or darker; and white balance, which can be set to match the exposure to the colour of the light source.

REVIEW MODE

In review mode, you can change the way the camera shows you your pictures. You can usually choose the amount of time that an image is shown on the LCD immediately after a picture is taken. You could choose to display

▲ *Some modes allow you to take account of the quality of light, and you can change the settings in order to shoot either close-ups or landscapes.*

pictures as a slideshow, or a series of small pictures in a grid, called thumbnails. You can tag, or digitally pick, individual pictures as favourites either so that they can't be deleted or for printing later. You can also delete pictures you don't want.

S e c t i o n   O n e :   C a m e r a   B a s i c s

FLASH

It is unusual to see a camera without flash these days. Ideal for taking pictures indoors, or reducing harsh shadows in bright light, flash is one of the most used features on any camera. When used properly flash can vastly improve pictures, but incorrect use can completely spoil them.

There are several different types of flash, but the most common is the one built-in to the camera. Although not massively powerful, for the average snapshot they are extremely useful. When the flash is dedicated to a particular camera, the exposure and flash output are automatically set, but most cameras have a choice of flash modes and it is worthwhile exploring them.

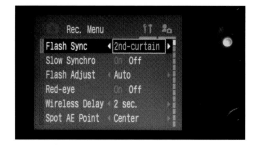

▲ *Experiment with the flash settings for different effects.*

AUTO

In this mode the camera will recognize when the flash is needed and automatically turn it on, as well as set the exposure and colour balance. This is ideal for general use, but can result in red eye.

AUTO WITH RED EYE REDUCTION

This works in the same way as the auto mode, but it will also fire a

▲ *Second curtain sync gives great shots of moving subjects.*

burst of flashes before the picture is taken in order to make the subject's pupils smaller and reduce the effect of red eye. This works reasonably well, but red eye can still occur. It also slows down the operation of the camera, as it can take a

▲ *The flash menu allows you to reduce the effect of red eye.*

second or two for the burst to fire. This can lead to the subject having their eyes closed (as the preflash triggers a blinking reaction) and less-natural facial expressions.

FLASH OFF

There may be occasions when you don't want the flash on, either for creative reasons (you may want to use the natural light) or because you are shooting candid portraits and don't want to alert the subject to your presence. There are also places, such as art galleries and churches, where flash photography is forbidden. When the flash is switched off, the camera compensates by setting a slower shutter speed to obtain correct exposure.

FLASH ON

This is the manual flash mode, sometimes called fill or forced flash. In this mode, the photographer decides whether to turn the flash on as and when it is needed. This is a useful mode if the sun is behind the subject, or if bright sunlight is causing harsh shadows. Using flash will 'fill-in' those dark areas.

SLOW SYNC

Slow sync, or synchronisation, fires the flash whilst using the same shutter speed and aperture as if the flash were not being fired. This is useful at night when a longer exposure is needed to capture the ambient light, while at the same time the flash exposure illuminates the subject. Slow sync can also be used to freeze a moving subject while leaving movement trails. Second curtain sync is another version of this, where the flash fires just before the end of the exposure. This makes movement look more natural, with a moving subject being frozen sharply at the front of a movement trail.

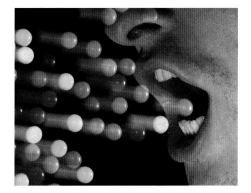

▲ *Slow sync freezes a subject and leaves movement trails.*

Section One: Camera Basics

MEMORY CARDS

Once you have taken your pictures, they need to be stored somewhere for later printing or copying to your computer hard drive. For this you need a memory card, often called a media card, and there are several different types.

▲ *Even a memory card the size of a postage stamp can hold hundreds of images.*

When you first buy a camera you will probably get a memory card with it, usually of a low capacity of 8 or 16 MB. This is enough to get you started, but will probably only allow half a dozen pictures to be stored. It is useful to keep as a spare, but you will need to buy a higher capacity card as soon as possible. There are several different types of memory card and you need to make sure you buy the right one for your camera – consult your instruction book or contact the manufacturer if unsure. Always buy the highest capacity you can afford.

SECURE DIGITAL (SD)

Currently the most popular type of card, SD is small, offers high capacity and fast write times. It is quickly becoming a standard and is compatible with other digital devices such as MP3 players, TVs, PDAs and even some microwave ovens.

COMPACT FLASH (CF)

Available in two types, Type I and Type II, Compact Flash is an older, larger but still popular type of card, especially for SLR cameras. Compact flash cards are available in very high capacities, are reliable and because of their size, less easily lost. Type I is flash based, while Type II has a tiny mechanical hard drive. Type II cards, usually called IBM Microdrives, are slightly thicker and won't fit all cameras. As flash memory capacity has increased recently, Type II cards are becoming less popular.

▲ *Buy the highest capacity memory card you can afford.*

EXTREME DIGITAL (XD)

Formed as a collaboration between Fujifilm and Olympus to replace the older Smart Media (SM), xD cards are even smaller than SD and are only used by Fujifilm and Olympus cameras. They offer a reasonably high capacity, and allow ever smaller cameras to be made.

MEMORY STICK (MS)

Memory Stick is found only in Sony cameras, and is also compatible with a wide range of Sony goods. The latest incarnation is MS PRO, which isn't compatible with older Sony cameras. MS DUO is a smaller format card for small cameras and mobile phone cameras.

CAMERA PHONES

The mobile phone industry has begun to add a camera to the phone functions, and there are very few phones available now that don't have a camera attached. Early models had very low resolution and poor control, but recent models are vastly improved, although still no better than digital cameras were about eight years ago.

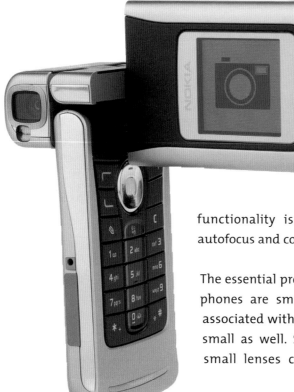

For many people, mobile phones offer their first experience of digital photography. This can lead to disappointment as the image quality is often poor, but that has changed recently with the introduction of one, two and even three megapixel models. The functionality is improving too, with better lenses, autofocus and colour controls being added.

The essential problem, however, is one of space. Mobile phones are small, and that means that everything associated with the digital camera element of them is small as well. Small chips mean small pixels, while small lenses can mean distortion problems (with

◄ *The quality of camera phone images is improving rapidly.*

squares turning out barrel shaped, for example). Perhaps the biggest problem is that taking pictures drains the phone of power – and most people still want to use their phone above taking pictures. Flash power is necessaily very limited, so chip sensitivity has to be increased and that can result in lower quality or much darker images. Whilst resolution may be on the increase, it is not clear how these other factors will be resolved.

Camera phones do, however, offer an advantage in everyday photography over digital cameras, as most people always carry a phone with them and therefore always carry a camera with them. This is transforming the way we communicate – recent world events have been captured by camera phone and sent to news agencies, offering on the spot coverage by ordinary members of the public.

Camera phones also offer a new way to share pictures, using MMS (MultiMediaSending) services such as texting with pictures. Images can also be emailed to web sites, leading to the new phenomenon of moblogging, or mobile web logging.

Camera phone images can be downloaded to a computer or a printer, either by USB cable or Bluetooth, a wireless connection system that is rapidly replacing IRDA (Infra Red Data Association standard)
as a means of transferring data.

The growing popularity of camera phones means that more people are taking more pictures than ever before, and that trend is set to rise as camera phones increase in quality and popularity.

▶ *Pictures from your camera phone can be downloaded to your computer quickly and easily via a USB cable.*

Section One: Camera Basics

THE FUNDAMENTALS OF PHOTOGRAPHY

THE AESTHETICS OF PHOTOGRAPHY

To be a good photographer it is necessary to master both the aesthetic and technical aspects of the medium. The aesthetic part is whether or not the picture is pleasing to the eye – and this is determined by several factors: the light, the choice of subject, the expression (if it is a portrait) and the composition.

▲ *Unusual architecture can make a great photo.*

The term composition refers to the elements you choose to include in the viewfinder, or on the liquid crystal display (LCD) screen, and how you arrange them. Good composition involves thinking for a moment before pressing the shutter, taking a quick look around the frame and deciding if the picture can be improved by zooming in or out a bit more, by moving the camera slightly up, down or to the side, by finding a higher or lower viewpoint, by

▶ *The right lighting is very important. Capturing the effects of a sunrise or sunset will change the whole tone of your image.*

▲ *Composition is crucial to photography.*

moving closer or further away, or by tilting the camera, perhaps to the vertical format. You make these decisions every time you take a picture, even if only at a subconscious level, but paying more attention to these processes will result in much better composition.

The other main factor influencing a picture's aesthetics is the lighting. How is the light falling on the subject – hard and shadowy, or soft and diffused? Is it a warm or cool light? From which direction is it coming – from the front, side, above or behind? If you are photographing in natural light you cannot easily change its position but you can change your position in relation to it. By moving round to the other side of a building you can shoot the sunny side or shady side, by asking a person to turn around you can get the sun behind them instead of shining in their eyes. By coming back to the same spot at a different time of day you will get a completely different type of light altogether.

▲ *Symmetry in your subject will make for an interesting picture.*

The technical aspect of photography involves setting the lens, aperture, shutter, and the various digital functions, such as resolution, compression and ISO sensitivity (the International Standards Organization setting that adjusts how sensitive the camera is to light) to obtain a good result. Modern digital cameras can control all of these technical features automatically, but these also all have a bearing on the aesthetics of the image, so if you leave all these decisions to the camera you are not completely in control over the final image. An understanding of these technical aspects can be used to create visually pleasing images, rather than just records of events.

COMPOSITION: RULE OF THIRDS/SYMMETRY

▲ *Balance your composition with different elements.*

Since the days of Ancient Rome, artists, architects and great thinkers have pondered what makes a building or a picture visually pleasing and have attempted to explain it with the use of mathematical and geometric principles. These principles can determine the ideal shape of a painting, and where the important elements should be positioned within the canvas for the most harmonious effect.

Although it may seem odd to apply mathematical rules to art there is some validity to it, which is why great artists from Leonardo da Vinci to Salvador Dalí have followed them to some extent. Even the image proportions used by most cameras today are based on the classic compositional ratios of 5:4 and 3:2. Picture frame sizes follow these ratios too.

The most useful of these mathematical and geometric principles is known as the Rule of Thirds. Imagine dividing your picture area into a grid of two horizontal lines and two vertical ones, all the same distance apart – like a noughts and crosses grid. Each line will be one third of the way in from either the top, bottom, left or right side. The Rule of Thirds says that you should place important elements of your scene on

▼ *The subject of a photo often looks better a third of the way in, rather than being front and centre.*

those lines. The real 'hot spots' are the four points where those lines intersect. So when photographing a person in a scene, rather than placing them right in the middle of the frame (which is what most amateur photographers do) you should put them one third of the way in from one side. With a landscape, that big tree or windmill should also be on one of the thirds, and the horizon should be placed on the upper or lower third.

This rule works surprisingly often, but as with most rules there is a danger of following them too slavishly so that they become dogma. If used repeatedly and relentlessly a set of pictures will eventually begin to look repetitive and boring. It is also the case that, while the rule of thirds creates a sense of harmony in your pictures, harmony is not always what you want to convey. Sometimes it is better to strive for a sense of drama, impact and discord.

▼ *Sometimes centering your subject produces the best result.*

The best way to achieve this is to deliberately break the rules, such as placing a subject right in the middle of the frame. When combined with a wideangle lens, for example, this can produce a great in-your-face effect. Centred subjects look especially effective if you introduce an element of symmetry to your composition, whether by arranging objects, altering your position or using devices such as reflections in water.

Section One: Camera Basics

COMPOSITION: GEOMETRY (LINES, SHAPES & PATTERNS)

▲ *Use the subject to guide the viewer's eyes in a specific direction.*

The eye is an undisciplined organ. Without guidance, it will wander all over the place, never entirely deciding what to settle on. With modern computer technology it is possible to track the movement of the eye and plot its course as a line. You may have seen the resulting images produced by this technology, which resemble pictures that have been scribbled over by a hyperactive toddler. This wandering is intensified when the viewer is confronted by an image whose focal point is unclear.

It is possible, and desirable, to use elements within your scene to guide and corral your viewer's eyes in a specific direction. In Western culture, where books are read from left to right, the human eye instinctively enters a picture from the left and travels across it. It would be wonderful if you could

▲ *Unusual patterns and colours create interest.*

▲ *Reflections are useful in helping to create a sense of symmetry.*

compose your shot to provide a long path, road, fence or wall running across the picture from left to right, with an interesting landmark or geographical feature at the end of it, so that the viewer's eye can follow the line through the picture and get a visual reward at the end. The human eye likes to be guided like this, and told what to look at.

Learn to look at your subject not as what it actually is, but as a series of shapes and lines. In your head, mentally draw it – a long straight line here, a big curve there, a wavy line over there – and by changing your position or zooming in or out, use those lines to guide the viewer around the image. Diagonal lines create drama, and those coming from the bottom left lead the eye into a shot. Try not to let the eye wander out the other side of the picture without resting on anything. Also,

don't forget to make the most of sweeping curves wherever you find them, which can add a sensual, feminine quality to your picture even if they are only hills, or rocks in a pond.

▲ *Sweeping curves are aesthetically pleasing.*

Repeating lines and shapes is good too. They create a natural pattern or grid which conveys a sense of order. We are not often aware of patterns in everyday life but if we look for them we find that they are everywhere; in the repeated windows on the side of an office building, the rows of apples on a market stall, the pebbles on a beach, the shadows cast by railings on the pavement – the possibilities are endless.

COMPOSITION: NATURAL FRAMES

▲ *Natural frames are all around us.*

One reason why we put pictures into frames is that the frame separates the art from its surroundings and forms a boundary that helps keep the eye within the picture. It is another eye-corralling tactic. For centuries artists and photographers have found natural elements within their scene to provide a ready-made frame for their subject and help to prevent the eye from wandering out of the picture and losing interest. It is yet another device for holding the viewer's attention, and for creating harmony within the image.

◀ *This car windscreen has become an unusual but highly effective frame for the buildings.*

The classic devices include shooting through open doorways (so that the door frame becomes a natural frame for whatever is visible though the door) as well as windows and archways (such as in a church or ruined castle). These are very literal interpretations of a frame, but

Digital Camera Handbook
Digital Camera Handbook

one of the most common devices is to photograph a landscape from under a tree, so that the overhanging branches droop down into the top of the frame from above. This gives the viewer a sense that they are peeking out into the landscape but, crucially, the branches help to prevent the eye from

▲ *Frames create harmony within the image.*

wandering out of the top of the frame. Placing the trunk of the tree down the left or right hand edge creates a frame to the side. Shooting through the boughs of a tree can create a v-shaped frame for a landmark in the middle distance.

▲ *Natural frames hold and direct the viewer's attention towards the subject.*

When you are out with your camera look for interesting and unusual ways to frame your picture, such as shooting through a car window, or using people as a frame. Try shooting through a crowd, or through the 'window' created by a hand on a hip.

Frames can also be used in portraiture. A bob haircut is among many hairstyles that provide a natural frame for the face – use things like this to your advantage. If the model is confident try placing their hands and arms in such a way that they frame the face, either in a self-consciously stylised way or, if the subject is less used to posing, in a more subtle and natural position which, nevertheless, still forms a frame.

Section One: Camera Basics

COMPOSITION: VIEWPOINT

More than 90 per cent of photographs are taken from between 1.5–1.8 meters (5–6 feet) above the ground. This is the height of the average adult's eyes. Very few people think to stoop down low or find a higher vantage point, and yet those who do are often rewarded with more visually striking and unusual results.

▲ *Remembering to look up can result in fantastic, unusual images.*

The most obvious reason for seeking a high viewpoint is to get a better view – perhaps to see over a crowd. While this is a valid reason, and is a much better strategy, on the whole, than trying to shoot through the crowd, it is not always necessary. High viewpoints provide a better view of distant landscapes, and let you see more detail in the middle distance. Try climbing a tree, a hill or even just stand on a wall or park bench. In the city head for the top of a tall building to get a sweeping uninterrupted vista of the metropolis, or find an

▲ *A high viewpoint can change your perception of the subject.*

Digital Camera Handbook

▼ Detail lost on the ground is captured here.

open window halfway up to photograph an adjacent tall building (such as a church) without having to tilt the camera upwards (which makes the sides appear to converge as if the building is falling over). Taking a high viewpoint to photograph children or animals is not generally recommended as standard practice but does serve to emphasise their smallness and add humour if used sparingly.

There are times when it is better to bend the knees and shoot from a low viewpoint. In general you'll get better results photographing children if you crouch down to their level and look them in the eye, as if you are entering their world. The same applies to pets. Getting down low means you won't get a distorted view of them (such views can give your subjects a disproportionately large head) and is much more flattering.

Landscapes, too, can be shot from ground level to emphasise the foreground. You may wish to draw attention to some flowers, or show the texture of sand, stone or cracked earth receding into the distance or perhaps you want to use a line such as a path or road marking to pull the viewer in from the foreground to the horizon. If you want that

▲ Stooping low can improve composition.

emphasised foreground to be sharp it is best to use a wideangle lens. To get a blurred foreground you will get better results using a longer focal length lens.

Many digital cameras offer an LCD screen that can tilt and swivel, making high and low-level photography much easier.

COMPOSITION: SHAPE & ORIENTATION

Just as few people think to select a higher or lower viewpoint before taking a picture, most amateur photographers keep the camera in the horizontal position for all their pictures, irrespective of the shape of the subject, and they do not think to rotate the camera 90 degrees to see if that improves the composition. There is some confusing terminology in photography whereby a horizontally oriented image is known as 'landscape format' and a vertically oriented image is called 'portrait format' – irrespective of the subject.

▲ *Landscape images are a popular option...*

This terminology applies to both the camera position and the orientation of prints, but the terms are misleading. Firstly, there is no rule that landscapes should be taken horizontally and portraits vertically. Indeed there are thousands of examples of great vertical landscapes and horizontal portraits. Do take a good look at your subject before shooting to see whether or not the shot would look better if you turned the camera. Many professional photographers shoot their subjects both ways, as it gives the client

▲ *...But portrait images can offer a new perspective.*

▲ *Landscapes often suit the subject.*

more choices in designing the layout of the page in which the photograph will be used.

Sometimes you may, for aesthetic reasons, eschew both orientations and go for a square image. Many professional medium format cameras produce square images straight out of the camera and photographers such as David Bailey are known for their square portraits of personalities such as the Kray twins. No current consumer digital camera produces square images but photographs can be cropped, if the subject looks best that way, and square picture frames are widely available.

Alternatively you can go to the other extreme and create a long, narrow letterbox shaped image – either in the horizontal or vertical orientation. This type of image, known as a panorama, is achieved either by cropping the top and/or bottom (or sides) off a normal picture, or by shooting two or more pictures of adjoining parts of the scene and then 'stitching' them together to form a seamless whole. (For more on this see pages 184 and 282).

▲ *Turning the camera gives a different focus.*

In conclusion, no one is forcing you to stick with a 5:4 ratio, horizontally shaped picture if it does not suit the subject. Don't be afraid to turn the camera or change the shape of the image altogether later on.

▼ *Panoramas offer another, striking, composition option.*

Section One: Camera Basics

COMPOSITION: WIDEANGLE PERSPECTIVE

The standard lens on a digital camera is so called because the view of the world that it produces is roughly equivalent to that seen by the human eye. In other words a subject at a given distance appears to be roughly the same relative size, and distance away as it does when you look at it with the naked eye.

This is fine for some things but sometimes you can't bring everything into the shot and you can't stand back far enough. This is a particular problem with big groups and small interiors. Conversely, sometimes you just can't get close enough to your subject, either because you are at a sports venue such as a Grand Prix or football match, or because your subject is shy or dangerous, as with much wildlife.

▲ *A wideangle shot makes a striking photograph.*

Luckily, by changing the arrangement of lens elements within the lens, optical scientists have created wideangle lenses (which make things look further away) and telephotos (which appear to bring them closer) and most cameras nowadays come with a zoom lens that is slightly wideangle at one end and telephoto at the other. These lenses, by dint of where they make you stand, produce

Digital Camera Handbook

an optical side effect that can be put to good compositional effect.

Shooting from close with a wideangle lens creates the illusion of exaggerated perspective so that subjects up close to the camera appear much larger than those further away. By being close to a foreground area you can give this much greater prominence in the image. This works very well with low angles. Want to add a strong leading line cutting diagonally through the image? Use a wideangle and get closer to it to make it really jump out at you.

Being close to a portrait subject or candid street scene provides a sense of immediacy to the viewer. Photojournalists often favour wideangles for the sense of drama they can give to a scene. The wider the angle of the lens (ie. the shorter its focal length in mm), the more exaggerated the effect. However, if a lens has too wide an angle the field of view begins to distort. Straight lines begin to turn into curves until, at their logical conclusion, wideangles become fisheye and everything (including the shape of the image itself) becomes circular. These lenses can be good fun but should be used sparingly – their useful applications are quite limited.

▶ Wideangle lenses are great for capturing large structures, giving them greater prominence.

TAKING GREAT PICTURES

COMPOSITION: TELEPHOTO PERSPECTIVE

▲ *Telephoto lenses are great for candid shots.*

Telephotos have the opposite effect to wideangles. When used from afar they compress perspective, making objects which are in reality quite far apart appear to be almost on top of one another. Distant hills or other elements in a landscape are apparently 'brought closer' and made more prominent in the image.

Cars on a racetrack seem inches apart when viewed head on (not side by side) when in reality they may be some distance apart. The telephoto trick is used in movies to good effect. In a scene where someone may be running down a railway track towards the camera with a train coming up behind them, the use of a long telephoto lens will imply that the person is about to be run over when in reality there may be more than 50 metres (164 feet) between them.

▶ *Where zoom lenses bring the viewer into the scene, telephotos provide a more detached view.*

▲ *Natural patterns can appear emphasised.*

With telephoto lenses perspective is flattened and appears more two dimensional, which also helps to emphasise natural patterns and tonal contrasts within a scene. Portraits and street scenes take on a different tone. Far from getting a sense of being in the middle of the scene, as the viewer is made to feel with wideangle lenses, the viewer now becomes a voyeur, distant and more detached from the emotion of the moment. This is not necessarily a bad thing. It all depends on what you are trying to convey. Telephotos are also good for getting natural candid shots of your children, since you can observe them in their own little world without intruding into it, disturbing them and ruining any chance for a spontaneous and unselfconscious moment.

One side effect of telephotos is their reduced depth of field. The zone of sharp focus seems narrower so your focusing needs to be more precise with a telephoto than with wideangles. With telephotos, you cannot get away with manually setting the lens to a point such as 2 metres (6 ½ feet), stopping the lens down to f/8 and leaving

it there, in the knowledge that everything in the frame will be in focus. However, the narrow focus effect of telephotos can be helpful, especially with portraits, because it makes it easier to throw any distracting background detail out of focus and really concentrate the attention on the face of your subject.

▲ *Make sure your focusing is precise.*

COMPOSITION: USE OF COLOUR

So far we have concentrated on using shapes, lines and perspective as composition aids, but one image component that has a huge impact on the viewer is the colour contained within a scene. The very best colour

▲ *Vivid colours result in striking images.*

photographs are those which use colour not simply incidentally, but are composed around the colours themselves. They are an essay in colour. Therefore it is worth taking time to understand how colour applies to photography.

▼ *Capturing a single colour is very effective.*

The colour palette is divided into three primary colours: red, green and blue. By varying the proportions of these three colours every other colour in the spectrum can be produced. Most digital camera sensors are composed entirely of blocks of red, green and blue-filtered pixels. Each primary colour has a secondary or complementary colour, made up by combining the other two primaries. The complementary of red, therefore, is cyan (a type of turquoise) as it's made up of green and blue. Green's complementary colour is magenta (bright pink) made from red and blue, and blue's complement is yellow, which is what you get

▲ *Colour combines with patterns to great effect.*

when you mix red and green light. Images that cleverly use a primary colour with its secondary colour often look good. But as with all ideas, don't over-use this concept. In general scenes that contain all the primaries may clash, but there will be occasions where they look good together – such as in a stained glass window. It all depends on the context in which they are being used. It is the photographer's job to make sense of colours and, by careful use of composition, create something interesting out of them. This could take the form of a repeating pattern or random abstract.

One technique that often works well is to isolate a single colour, such as red or yellow, so that this is the only strong colour in the scene. Think of a frame-filling detail from a red London bus, or perhaps a field of vivid yellow rapeseed, which looks good not only against a blue sky (its complementary colour) but with the sky cropped out, and perhaps a lone figure walking through it. Landscapes are often essays in different shades of green. With some thought it is possible to build a collection of photographs on a single colour theme, and when you put them all together they make a great looking set.

One final point to consider is the colour of light. An object can appear to change colour according to the hue of the light falling upon it. A banana will not look yellow if it is lit entirely by red light. Brightly coloured lights are extremely photogenic – think of dusk and night photos of cities, with their neon and other multi-coloured lights.

▼ *Careful composition will highlight intense colours.*

COMPOSITION: SEEING IN BLACK & WHITE

▲ Black and white is ideal for capturing textures.

Once upon a time all photography was black and white. Early films could only record the intensity of light, not its colour. Colour photography was invented early in the twentieth century but it took another 50 years for colour to be good enough and cheap enough to gain mass popularity.

▼ Patterns, light and shadow work together here.

Digital has been colour from the outset, but despite all the advances in colour technology (for example developments of new colour dyes and pigments for printers, and improvements in the way colour is reproduced in cameras and on PC monitors), black and white photography will not go away. There is something special about black and white photography – also known as 'monochrome', 'mono' or just plain 'b&w'. It has the ability to get to the heart and soul of a subject without the distraction of colour. It isn't superior to colour, but neither is it inferior. Whether you choose colour or black and white depends on what suits the subject and what you are trying to say.

Digital Camera Handbook

▲ *Unusual subjects are brought to life in this medium.*

Although you can shoot in colour and convert your pictures to mono later you may wish to set the camera to its black and white mode, especially if you don't have a PC or you wish to print directly from your camera.

Either way, to achieve successful black and white images you must first learn to see the world in a different way. You need to visualise a scene without its colour in order to assess how it may look as a black and white print. For example, scenes that rely on colour for their impact, such as a carnival or fairground, are unlikely to succeed in mono. Some colours that look different in the real world may reproduce as the same tone in black and white. For example, the three primary colours (red, green and blue) may all reproduce in black and white as the same shade of grey.

Subjects that work best in mono are those that explore shapes, tones and textures, and the interplay of light and shadow. Portraiture also works very well in mono, and can be more flattering than colour, because blotchy skin, spots and ruddy cheeks can be made less obvious or even made to disappear.

▼ *The moody feel of this shot would be lost in colour.*

Black and white film users have traditionally used colour filters over the lens to control the relative tones of the colours on the film. For example, a red or orange filter darkens a blue sky. This is unnecessary in digital because the individual colour channels (see page 286) can be independently adjusted later, on the PC.

Section One: Camera Basics

FOCUSING: MODES

Probably the worst technical mistake you can make is for your picture to be out of focus – which is why modern digital cameras are stacked with technology to help to ensure that this doesn't happen. Most of the time it works, but occasionally it doesn't. With a little knowledge, the failure rate can be reduced to almost zero.

▲ *The closest object is usually assumed to be the main subject.*

These days we take automatic focusing (AF) for granted but the technology is quite recent. There are two types of AF. Simple budget cameras use 'active AF' in which an infrared beam is fired at the subject to measure the distance and then the camera sets the lens to focus at that distance. Simple cameras can only focus on a limited number of distance zones, and the camera sets the one closest to the measured distance. Sophisticated cameras have more zones, or can focus on any point from about 30 cm (12 inches) or closer to infinity. These also tend to use 'passive AF' to achieve focus, wherein the camera examines subject edges within the image and adjusts the lens to make them as sharply defined as possible.

In both cases the camera has to guess which of the many elements in your picture constitutes your main subject. It generally assumes that it is the closest and most central object in the frame and focuses on that, and nine times out of ten it is correct. Simple cameras measure distance from the centre of the frame, so if your subject is off-centre the camera my look past it and focus on some more distant

Digital Camera Handbook

▲ *Today's cameras can shoot even distant subjects in perfect focus.*

object. One way to avoid this is to use the focus lock, which almost all cameras have. This involves pointing the central point at your subject, pressing halfway down on the shutter button and holding it there, then repositioning the camera before taking a picture.

Some more advanced cameras avoid the need for this by employing several focus points dotted around the frame – in fact several dozen, in the case of some single lens reflex cameras (SLRs). These measure the distances of all the elements in the frame, and complex algorithms then work out which one is the subject. It is also usually possible to manually select between the various focus points if you feel the camera needs some help. If an off-centre subject has much higher contrast than a central one, the system may be fooled.

All cameras use, by default, a 'single shot' focus method, where once the camera has locked on to the subject, and focused, it will stay at that point until you either take the shot or let go of the shutter button. This is fine for static subjects but for moving subjects most cameras offer a 'continuous AF' mode, whereby the camera keeps refocusing as long as your finger is half-depressing the shutter, and you

can fire at any time, whether the subject is in focus or not. Some sophisticated cameras feature a predictive focus mode, in which the camera measures the rate and direction of subject movement and focuses just ahead of the action, ready to fire as the subject snaps into focus.

▶ *Moving subjects can be shot in focus in 'continuous AF' mode.*

Section One: Camera Basics

DEPTH OF FIELD TECHNIQUES

To exert maximum creative control over the visual appearance of your picture, it is essential that it is you who is telling the camera what to focus on, not the camera telling you. This may mean using the focus lock, or changing the focus mode, or perhaps leaving the comfort zone of AF altogether in favour of manual focusing. This is more difficult with compacts, but some models enlarge the central portion of the LCD to aid accuracy. With SLRs of course, manual focusing is simple and straightforward – just a bit slower than AF.

However, creative control is not just about the point of focus, it is also about the depth of the zone of focus. In other words, how much of the scene in front of and behind the main subject do you wish to be sharp? The answer may well be 'all of it', especially in the case of landscapes, where you may want everything, from the foreground flower to the horizon crisply sharp. But with a portrait, for example, do you really want to see the background sharp enough to distract from the main subject?

This zone of focus is known as the depth of field, and deciding how much you want is one of the most important creative decisions you will make. A shallow depth of field is ideal for making your subject stand out from its surroundings, such as for drawing attention to a single flower in a field, or a single face in a crowd.

The depth of field is controlled by the size of the lens aperture. The smaller the aperture (i.e. the higher the number) the more depth of field you will get. The wider

Digital Camera Handbook

the aperture, the shallower your depth of field will be. Depth of field extends both in front of and beyond the point focused on, in the ratio of one third in front and two thirds behind for distant subjects and half and half when you are very close to a subject. The exact amount of depth of field you will achieve depends on several variables in addition to the relative size of the aperture. Larger image magnifications reduce the depth of field, while smaller image magnifications increase the depth of field. So longer focal length lenses (i.e. telephotos) provide less depth of field at a given aperture, while wideangles provide much more. Equally, the closer you are to your subject the less your depth of field will be, so at a given aperture your depth of field will be much shallower at 15 cm (6 in) than 2 m (6 ft). Therefore a wideangle lens at a small aperture focused far away gives you maximum depth of field, while using a telephoto at a wide aperture close-up will provide the shallowest.

▲ *Both the foreground and the horizon are in focus using a small aperture.*

▲ *A shallow depth of field allows you to focus on the foreground...*

▲ *...or you can focus on the middle distance.*

METERING: HOW EXPOSURE METERS WORK

Just like film, digital sensors need the right amount of light to produce a good picture. Too little, and the picture will be too dark. The shadow areas will disappear into a black abyss, and even the light areas will look grey and muddy. Too much light and the picture will be washed out – all the light parts of the picture will disappear into a paper-white void.

▲ The shadowed area below the building is slightly lost here.

Digital sensors are especially vulnerable to overexposure (too much light). Once detail is lost from the brightest areas (the highlights) it cannot be retrieved even with a computer. So the trick is to select an exposure that gives an image that is not so dark that the detail in shadows fills-in (ie. goes black) and disappears, nor gives an image so light that the highlights burn out (ie. go a completely featureless white). This gives the photographer a fairly narrow window to work within.

Digital Camera Handbook

That is why cameras come equipped with complex light measuring aids. The exposure meters on even basic digital cameras take sophisticated measurements from several parts of the frame and calculate what's important. At their most basic, meters work on the principle that most scenes contain a fairly equal measure of light and dark areas, and that if you could mix all these tones together you would get a perfect mid-grey. This works in most situations. For example, a landscape containing grass, sky, some trees, and a cottage will contain a range of tones which, if you were to remove the colour, would all be varying shades of grey, and probably mostly mid-grey at that. Faces are lighter than mid grey, but once clothes and backgrounds are taken into consideration the scene is usually within the bounds of what the meter can handle.

▲ *A camera's light meter will often struggle to capture snow.*

There are, however, times when this theory falls down, such as when the scene is composed of almost entirely light tones (such as snow or beach scenes) or when the picture is mostly dark (such as a spot-lit performer on a stage). In these situations the meter often gets it wrong. It tries to turn the snow into grey, and does so by reducing the exposure (causing underexposure). It tries to turn dark backgrounds into mid-grey too, resulting in overexposure. The meter does not, after all, recognise the subject, only how light or dark it is, and how much light is falling upon it.

You need to keep an eye on what your meter is doing, and learn to recognize the situations when problems are likely to arise, in order to avoid disaster.

METERING FOR LIGHT OR DARK SUBJECTS

▲ *A light subject on a dark background can pose problems.*

Most cameras offer a variety of exposure measuring options to suit not only the variety of situations you will encounter, but also a photographer's preferred way of working.

The most basic type of meter is a straight centre weighted type. This takes a basic reading (or several readings) from a large area of the scene, but biased towards the centre area, and averages it out to achieve mid grey. In situations where the photographer thinks the meter may be wrong, they can either switch to manual, or use the exposure compensation feature to override the meter in increments up to a couple of stops either way.

▼ *A light meter will struggle with a mostly dark subject.*

The multi-segment meter is more sophisticated – the frame is divided into a number of segments, from five to 45. Readings are taken from each of these segments and then compared with a database of thousands of subjects to look for patterns that help the camera to know when to override its averaging instincts. For

Digital Camera Handbook

▲ Balancing the foreground and background needs precise exposure measurement.

example, the camera may recognize when it is looking at a person backlit by the sun and compensate accordingly. This system increases the camera's hit rate, and reduces the instances of incorrect exposure, but the drawback is that, because the camera is doing its own thing it is very difficult to predict when it may still be wrong, and compensate accordingly. At least with instant review in digital cameras you can tell when a meter has really got it wrong.

For those who trust only their own eyes, spot-metering may be the most useful mode. Spot-metering takes a reading from a tiny area of between one and five per cent of the frame. The photographer looks for a tonal area that will give a good result (usually mid-grey) and points the spot-metering zone directly at it, for a very precise measurement. Alternatively the photographer can take readings from the darkest and lightest parts of the scene and find the average.

▲ Spot-metering may be the answer when shooting dark scenes.

Bear in mind that what you can see on the LCD is only a guide. It is usually too small and too low in resolution to indicate your exposure accurately. Some cameras offer a histogram display (which shows the distribution of tones in a picture as a graph) or an overexposure warning (in which areas of burned out highlights flash on and off), but there is no point finding out after you have taken the shot that the meter got it wrong, if the moment has gone and it is too late to re-shoot.

Section One: Camera Basics

EXPOSURE MODES

Left to their own devices, cameras measure the light and set the exposure without any intervention from the photographer. All but the most basic models offer a variety of exposure modes, each of which employs different criteria in deciding which of the various settings to select. Some are fully automatic, others require some input from the photographer. Here is a brief rundown of the main modes:

▼ *Many cameras have a pre-set 'beach' mode.*

Auto Mode In the auto mode (usually marked in green) the camera takes care of everything. Not only are you not required to make any decisions, in most cases you are prevented from doing so. This is an ideal mode for novices, and most of the time the results will be fine.

Program Mode The camera still does everything, but it does offer you some degree of override. For example, it is usually possible to apply exposure compensation (subtly increasing or decreasing the exposure an image receives), alter the shutter speed/aperture combination using program shift (which still keeps the overall value the same) or switch the flash on and off.

Digital Camera Handbook

Shutter Priority This is a semi-automatic mode, in which you have to choose which shutter speed to use, and the camera then matches it with the corresponding aperture that will provide the right exposure in the prevailing conditions. This mode is ideal when photographing moving subjects. You can choose a fast shutter speed to freeze the movement, or a slow one to blur it. Please note that you need to check that the selected shutter speed is able to deliver a correct exposure with the available aperture range.

Aperture Priority In this mode you select the desired aperture, and the camera sets the necessary shutter speed. So, if you want a shallow depth of field, pick a wide aperture, and the camera will set a fast shutter speed. As you stop down the aperture to get more depth of field, the shutter speed will automatically increase in duration to compensate. Please note that you need to ensure that the camera can set a shutter speed within its range given the aperture you have selected.

Manual Mode In this mode you set both the aperture and shutter speed, based on information provided by the exposure meter. This mode is useful for shooting panoramas, when you want every exposure in a sequence to be the same, and do not wish any frames to be influenced by any dark or light bits in the scene. Studio photography is another situation where manual is best. The meter will still show its recommendation; you need to decide whether to ignore it or not.

Scene Modes Sometimes called subject modes, these are a selection of pre-set modes covering a variety of types of subject. Common examples are landscape, portrait, sport and night modes, but you can also get special modes for beaches, skiing, parties, text, etc. In each mode the parameters are optimized for the subject. This may include things such as the ISO and white balance, as well as the shutter speed and aperture.

▶ *A landscape mode would be ideal here.*

PHOTOGRAPHING MOTION

▲ Experimenting with the aperture and shutter speed can produce exciting results.

The aperture controls the intensity of the light reaching the sensor, and the shutter speed determines the duration of the exposure.

In fact, it does more than that, because, just as the aperture affects depth of field, so the choice of shutter speed can have a profound effect not only upon how the subject is recorded, especially if that subject is moving, but also on whether the movement of the photographer results in the image being ruined by the effects of camera shake (see pages 70–71).

Most SLR shutters are of the focal plane type, which means that they are comprised of two vertical or horizontal blinds. The first one opens to expose the sensor, then the second one closes behind it to end the exposure. The time delay between these curtains determines the shutter speed. At high speeds, the second curtain must

Digital Camera Handbook

▼ A fast shutter speed freezes a moving object.

actually start to close before the first one has completed its journey, creating a moving slit which travels across the frame, and the faster the speed, the narrower the slit. This has an effect when using flash (see pages 72–77).

With moving subjects, the longer the shutter is open, the more the subject will have moved across the frame during the exposure, creating a blur as it does so. At fast speeds, the narrow slit moves so quickly that only a fast moving subject will have time to move across the width of that slit before it is moved on to expose the next band of the scene.

Therefore, if you want to record a moving subject in sharp focus, you need to set a fast shutter speed – and the faster the motion, the faster the shutter speed needs to be. However, you may not always want to 'freeze' the motion. With some subjects, such as racing cars, the target can look stationary rather than 'frozen in time' thereby destroying any sense of motion and dynamism. Sometimes it is best to deliberately allow the moving subject to record as a blur, by a controlled amount, to show that it was moving. In these situations a slower speed will be required. There is a third option – by using a slower speed, but moving the camera in time with the subject so it stays at the same point in the frame, the subject will remain relatively sharp but the background will be blurred by a streaking motion. This technique is known as panning.

Its difficult to suggest specific shutter speeds for specific moving subjects because there are so many variables, including the speed and direction of travel, distance from the lens, and of course the degree of blur or sharpness required. The big advantage of digital is the ability to experiment and see the results

▲ Animals in flight can be captured cleanly.

immediately, so it won't take long to ascertain the optimum speed in a given situation, simply by trying a few of them out and reviewing the results.

▲ *Shadows and bright light can combine to great effect.*

LIGHT

The word photography comes from two Greek words, and means drawing with light. It is the perfect name for the medium, because photography is all about light. Without it there would be no photographs, but it is not enough for there merely to be a sufficient quantity of light to take a picture. Photographers talk about the quality of light, and this is much more important than the quantity, since you can always make up for lack of light by using a longer exposure or higher ISO, but bad light quality is much more difficult to fix.

The quality of light is a combination of the size, distance, direction and colour of the light. These various qualities guarantee an almost infinite combination of lighting effects which, in the case of natural light, are constantly changing. The human eye barely notices these effects, but the skilled photographer must learn to understand and manipulate them.

▲ *Soft, afternoon light can make a beautiful photo.*

Digital Camera Handbook

HARD AND SOFT LIGHT

The size of a light source has perhaps the strongest influence on the quality of illumination. The smaller the source, the 'harder' or higher contrast the light falling on the subject will be – it becomes an intense, brightly lit area surrounded by very deep shadows. An anglepoise lamp is an example of a small light source, but so is the sun on a clear, cloudless day – because although in reality the sun is vast, it is so far away that it appears small. The distance is another determining factor. As a light source moves further away it becomes smaller, and therefore harder in quality. In a home studio situation photographers can use this to their advantage when arranging the lights.

One way to make the light source larger is to diffuse it. Outdoors this is achieved by clouds. On an overcast day the sun is hidden by cloud, so the

▲ *'Harder' light can also result in an impressive picture.*

entire sky becomes one big, soft light source. The illumination it creates is virtually shadow-less. In the studio photographers use all sorts of devices to modify their lights to achieve a similar effect, such as softboxes (light translucent tents fitted over the lights through which the light is fired) or umbrellas (white or silver to bounce the light back onto the subject).

LIGHT DIRECTION

As well as the size and hardness of the light photographers must pay attention to its direction. For even, frontal illumination there's a rule that says photographers should keep the light source (sun or otherwise) behind them, so it lights the part of the subject that is facing the camera. While there is nothing wrong with that, the result can look a little boring creatively, and sometimes it is more interesting (yet also more challenging) when it is coming from elsewhere.

For example, turning 180 degrees so the light is directly behind the subject will produce an entirely different result. No light falls on the camera-facing side, so it will be in shadow and, depending on how you choose to expose, could render as a silhouette (if you take your exposure reading from the light, not the subject). You will also get a halo of light around the subject's edges, emphasising its outline, which can look very attractive. Moving the light to the side will light one half more brightly than the other, leaving the non-facing side in shadow. Sidelighting is great for revealing the texture of a surface, as the light glances across the surface casting highlights and shadows on every tiny bump or crease.

COLOUR TEMPERATURE

The final factor that determines light quality is its colour (technically known as its colour temperature, as it is defined in degrees Kelvin with relation to the light emitted by a notional perfectly black body heated to that temperature). Daylight is constantly changing in colour, though we rarely notice it. First thing in the morning, and again at dusk, it is at its warmest (ie. its most yellow-orange). At midday it is bluest. Atmospheric conditions affect things

▲ Daylight is often 'cooler' in temperature during winter.

too – a cloudless blue sky produces a bluer light on the ground, for example, than direct sun. The time of year, and your location in the world, all have a bearing on the colour of light, with some countries, at some times of year, having warmer light than others.

Artificial light is a completely different colour. Traditional tungsten filament light bulbs produce a very orange light compared with daylight, and fluorescent tubes can often add a greenish tinge which is rarely attractive.

Digital cameras control this light colour with a function called the 'white balance', and with most cameras it adjusts automatically (just as our eyes do). Most cameras also offer a range of manual presets for when the auto setting is wrong, or for when you wish to override the camera's choice.

THE RIGHT LIGHT

There is no right or wrong type of light – only what is right or wrong for a given subject. Some types of photography cry out for a soft, diffuse light, others look better with a harder, more characterful light. Some look good in a warm light, others a cooler, more neutral one. Landscapes, for example, are often at their most alluring when the light is low, hard and from the side, or you are shooting into it. The long shadows this creates add shape and contour to the land. Beauty portraits are almost always lit by soft, shadowless light, as harder light will emphasise any wrinkles or blemishes in the skin.

The photographer's job is to match the light to the subject – either by rearranging it (if indoors) or, in natural light, moving to a different shooting position or waiting for the light to change (which may well be on a different day).

▲ *Sunrise and sunset produce a very warm, soft light, perfect for atmospheric pictures.*

▲ *The harder, brighter light of direct, undiffused sunlight can also result in a great photograph.*

TAKING GREAT PICTURES

ISO SENSITIVITY

Photographers often talk about there being enough light to take a picture. This means sufficient brightness to take a picture without the risk of camera shake – that blurring of the image caused by our natural and unavoidable body movement during the exposure.

▼ *A blurred effect in low light can sometimes make for a great picture.*

At higher shutter speeds this movement is not noticeable in the picture, though the threshold depends on many factors, including the steadiness of the individual and the choice of lens – the greater the zoom magnification the higher the speed needs to be to avoid shake. Generally, with a lens at the standard (non-zoomed) position the minimum safe shutter speed is around 1/60 sec, but this rises significantly as you zoom. Some people are also more prone to shaking than others, and it's worth doing some tests to see what your safe shutter speed is.

That works when there is enough light for the camera to set that speed (and with program modes it will always try to) but what happens when the light fails? Or what if you need to use an even faster shutter speed to capture a moving subject, or a small aperture (for greater depth of field), which pushes the shutter speed below that threshold?

Automatic cameras will turn on the flash, which you may not want, and which doesn't work with distant subjects anyway. Another option is the tripod. The last option is to increase the ISO rating.

In the days of film the ISO (formerly called ASA) was a measurement of the sensitivity of film (i.e. how much light was required to record an image). Film came in different sensitivities, but the faster (more sensitive) the film, the more grainy it was. The sensors of digital cameras work in a similar way. In most cameras, the default sensitivity is ISO 100. You can raise the sensitivity of the sensor to at least ISO 400 and often ISO 1600. As with film, each doubling of the number doubles the sensitivity, but digital offers the advantage of being able to do this for individual pictures, rather than the entire roll of film – you can shoot one picture at ISO 100 and the next at ISO 400.

However, the higher the ISO, the more the image quality suffers. This is because, in order to raise the sensitivity the camera amplifies the electrical signals from the sensor, and also therefore amplifies the 'noise' (non-signal impulses). The lower the light levels, the greater the proportion of noise in an image and the result is analogous to increased graininess in fast films.

Noise can take many forms, but often shows up as a blizzard of tiny, multi-coloured dots, most visible in dark areas and areas of continuous tone. It is intrusive and unattractive, destroys fine image detail and lowers contrast, so it is always best to use the lowest ISO setting that conditions will allow – even if that means using a tripod.

▲ *Use a high ISO setting to capture sharp images in low light.*

FLASH

BUILT-IN FLASH

When the light level drops to a point where it is no longer safe to take a picture without risking camera shake, most cameras automatically switch on the flash. This is fine for emergencies, but unfortunately flash is not always the best solution – and the result is often disappointing photos. At least with digital you'll find this out immediately, rather than when you get your prints back.

Flash spreads out over distance, and only has a very limited effective range. Double the distance, and the intensity of the light hitting a given point drops by a factor of four. If not enough light reaches the subject, the resultant image will be underexposed. Built-in flashguns are usually very small, so you have only got a very small intensity to start with. The maximum range is 3-4 m (10–13 ft). Beyond this, flash is largely a waste of battery power. Increasing the ISO also increases the usable flash range – double the ISO setting and the flash range increases by a factor of 1.4. Switch from ISO 100 to ISO 400 and you double the range.

Within its specified range using a flash will give you a picture, but it may not be a very flattering one. Direct flash is harsh and, when the background is dark, can lead to very washed out faces. It can also cause 'red eye'. In low light, our pupils open wide to let in as much light as possible, and flash entering the eye from the camera position illuminates the blood vessels on the retina and reflects back through the lens. Anti-red eye settings can reduce this problem, but it should be remembered they are red eye reduction, not red eye elimination, functions.

Cameras provide a selection of flash modes for the optimum result:

Auto The camera does all the thinking. Fine for party pictures (except for the red eye), indoor gatherings etc.

▲ Flash is useless for subjects beyond about 4 metres.

Auto with red eye reduction This can reduce red eye, but the delay it causes between pressing the button and the picture taking often results in unnatural expressions and is generally more trouble than it is worth.

Slow sync flash In auto flash mode the camera sets a shutter speed of 1/60sec or faster, which reduces the dim available light to a sea of blackness. If you want to show something of the environment in which you are shooting, slow sync flash combines the flash with a slow shutter speed to record the ambient light – though you will need to rest the camera on a stable surface and ask people to keep still to avoid blurring.

Flash off Sometimes flash is prohibited (such as in museums and public places) so you should set this mode to override the camera's natural instinct to turn it on. In this mode the camera sets a longer shutter speed, so you will need to find something stable to support it.

Flash on Fires the flash even though the camera does not think it is necessary (see page 77 for more on this).

▶ Flash can be prohibited in some places. If shooting with flash off, you will need a steady hand.

▼ *Accessory flashguns are a good investment.*

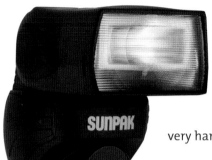

EXTERNAL FLASH

Some photographers invest in a separate flashgun for more power. Most built-in flash units are very small and low in power, and suitable only for close-range record shots. Being small, the light is also very harsh, and cannot easily be modified.

Accessory flashguns are usually much more powerful than a built-in flash, and offer a greater usable range, as well as having other advantages. Firstly, because the flash head is further away from the camera (usually sitting on top of the camera, in the hotshoe) the risk of red eye is greatly reduced. This is because the angle at which the flash enters the lens is always the same at which the reflection exits (just like a mirror). So, for example, if a flash is 30 cm (12 in) to the left of the lens, the red reflection of the illuminated blood vessels will bounce not into the lens but 30 cm (12 in) to the right of it.

The flash head is larger so the light tends to be less harsh, but on many flashguns it can be softened even further by tilting or rotating the head so that it points sideways onto a wall, or upwards to the ceiling. Bouncing the light off a white surface in this way creates a much softer, more natural and flattering light on the subject. Make sure that the surface is neutral though, as it will reflect any colour onto your subject's face. Most flashguns can also accept a variety of flash modifiers, such as mini softboxes and reflectors, which fit over the head and diffuse the flash to make it softer.

▶ *External flashguns are much more versatile than built-in flash.*

74

Taking Great Pictures

Flashguns also offer the ability to trigger the flash at the end of the exposure rather than the beginning (called second, or rear curtain sync) for more natural flash shots with moving subjects, the option for strobe flash (a burst of several flashes in quick succession) and high speed flash at fast shutter speeds (for very fast action work).

Zoom flashguns feature a fresnel lens in the head which adjusts to compensate for the focal length of the lens in use – sometimes automatically. Not only does this mean that the flash can spread out to cover the extended field of a wideangle, but when narrowing the angle by using a telephoto lens,

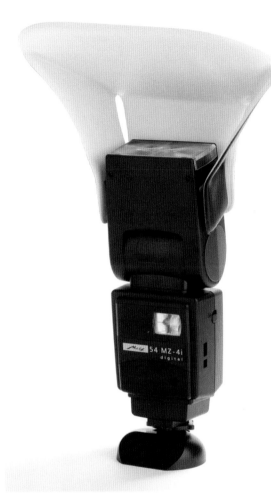

▲ *A mini softbox or reflector will diffuse the flash and soften the light.*

none of the flash is wasted lighting parts of the scene that are not in shot, resulting in more light on the subject or greater range at the same aperture. If, however, as is often the case, the aperture of your camera's lens is smaller at the telephoto setting than at the wideangle setting, the increased concentration of light may be cancelled out by the smaller hole in the lens letting the light hit the sensor. Finally, flash uses a colossal amount of battery power, and by using a separate flashgun you are preserving your camera's valuable battery power for picture taking.

OFF-CAMERA FLASH

Flashguns don't have to be used on the camera. They can be taken off and fired in synchronisation with the shutter either via a sync lead attached to the camera, or via a slave cell, which detects the burst of a small flash attached to the camera to trigger the main one in sync. Off camera flash enables an infinite variety of creative lighting effects to be achieved, and you can use several units for multi-flash effects.

Professional studio photographers use mains powered studio flash units, which not only boast much greater power and range, but the ability to accept a large variety of modifiers, such as umbrellas, reflectors of various shapes, and softboxes up to a couple of metres across (to simulate the effect of natural windowlight). They also come with built-in tungsten modelling lamps, so that you can see easily the effect that the light is having on the subject as you move and modify it. Many enthusiasts also use affordable studio flash units, especially if they specialize in indoor studio based still life or portraiture.

▼ Fill-in flash is perfect for reducing shadow on sunny days

FILL-IN FLASH

So far we have only talked about flash in the context of low-light photography, but ironically, flash is often more useful in bright light than low light. On sunny days, when faces are covered with unsightly shadows (especially in the eye sockets and under the noses and chins) flash can 'fill in' these shadows to

▼ Fill-in flash throws a more even light on the subject.

provide a more even light. Few cameras will work this out for themselves unless the subject is backlit and in silhouette, when some of the more sophisticated multi-pattern metering systems will suggest the use of flash to light the front of the subject. Usually it is up to the photographer to observe how the light is falling on the subject, look at the shadows and, if necessary, switch the flash on manually. In program mode most cameras will then calculate how much flash is needed to balance it with the ambient light. Generally, it should be one or two stops less bright than the natural light at the subject plane. With a separate flashgun you can usually adjust the flash output independently of the camera exposure, via manual control or flash exposure compensation. A few sophisticated digital cameras also offer the ability to adjust built-in flash output in this way.

USEFUL FILTERS

Film camera photographers often use filters to influence the appearance of their pictures in a number of ways – to change the colour, to darken selected areas, to create special effects. With digital photography many of these alterations can be done afterwards on the computer, sometimes with more control, so filters have fallen out of favour somewhat.

▲ Filters can change colours without a PC.

However, photographers are now beginning to turn back to certain filters because they offer several advantages over PC-based alterations. The first is that not everyone wants to spend hours in front of a PC correcting their pictures, and would prefer to get it right in the camera. This is especially the case with those who prefer to print directly from their cameras, via a Pictbridge enabled printer or one with media card slots.

It is also the case that, while colour correction and enhancement filters are less necessary now due to white balance control, and superior colour balance options in editing software, some filters just cannot be replaced by the computer. These, ironically, are the most useful:

▲ A polarizer has darkened the sky here.

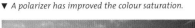

▼ *The foliage looks a little lifeless here.*   ▼ *A polarizer has improved the colour saturation.*

UV/Skylight The technical reason for using one of these, virtually colourless filters is to reduce haze and ultraviolet radiation which lowers contrast and causes bluish colour casts, but with modern lens coatings and sensor technologies this is less of an issue. The main reason now is to protect the lens element from scratches, fingermarks and other damage. It is cheaper to replace a filter than a lens, or indeed a camera with a damaged lens.

Polariser This highly useful filter reduces reflections from non-metallic shiny surfaces such as water, glass and even foliage. The effect varies according to the angle of the sun, and how far the photographer rotates the filter on the lens, but at its optimum point the result is a drastic increase in colour saturation. Skies become bluer, foliage greener, every colour becomes more vivid. This effect is simply impossible to duplicate on the computer. Polarisers do cut down the light by 2–3 stops (i.e. from needing 1/125sec shutter speed to needing a 1/30sec) but, in the right conditions, the sacrifice is worth it.

Neutral density For some effects, where long shutter speeds are required (such as photographing moving water as a soft blur) or wide apertures (for minimal depth of field) the light level may be too high to get the required exposure combination. Neutral Density (ND) filters are colourless, neutral grey filters that cut down the light entering the lens without affecting its hue.

Graduated (grad) ND filters: Digital cameras struggle with overexposure. Areas of a scene that are significantly brighter than the rest may end up washed out and lose all detail – which cannot be recovered later. This is a particular problem with bright skies. Grad ND filters are grey on one half, fading to clear, and are designed to reduce the brightness of the sky to balance it with the ground below. They can also be used upside down to reduce the harsh reflections on the surface of water.

MAKING GREAT PICTURES

Section One: Camera Basics

PC PRINCIPLES

PIXELS & RESOLUTION

Digital photographs are made up of small squares of colour called pixels, and the number of these in an image is the resolution. These pixels translate to your computer monitor.

CAMERA RESOLUTION & MONITOR RESOLUTION

Camera resolution is decided by the number of pixels on the sensor. A typical 2 million pixel picture will be made up of 1,600 x 1,200 pixels – in other words,

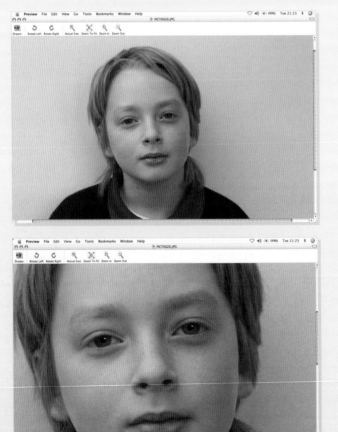

1,600 pixels across and 1,200 pixels down. If this is then shown on a monitor with a similar resolution at 100 per cent view, the image will match the display pixel for pixel and fill the entire screen. A larger resolution image of 4 million pixels (2,304 x 1,712 pixels) will be too big for the screen, so only part of the image will be shown. It is generally recommended to set your monitor at the highest resolution to maximise image detail and sharpness.

◄ *An image at 2 million pixels (top) fills the screen, whereas only part of the image is seen at 4 million pixels.*

Digital Camera Handbook

A confusing addition to the resolution issue is that most computer monitors display images at 72 ppi, or pixels per inch. This further refines the screen size, by indicating exactly how many pixels are in a single inch of the computer screen. Using this knowledge we can then work out how big an image will appear on screen. If 72 pixels equal 1 inch, and an image size is 1,600 x 1,200 pixels, then the screen size of the image will be 1,600 divided by 72 and 1,200 divided by 72. Thus the image will be 22.2 inches long by 16.7 inches wide.

This is an important aspect to remember, especially if you are preparing images for websites or any other screen-based viewing. A 22 x 16 inch image will not fit on most computer screens, so the image will need to be altered to a viewing size that will display well on the majority of monitors.

DPI OR PPI

Printing images can cause confusion. Rather than pixels, printers use dots of ink, and the print resolution is referred to as dpi, or dots per inch. The simple rule to remember is ppi for screen, dpi for print. The same rule is used for estimating the final print size, but this time divide the number of pixels by 300, so our 1,600 x 1,200 pixel image becomes a 5 x 4 print. You divide by 300 because the best results are usually obtained at 300 ppi, although the human eye can rarely see beyond 200 ppi.

▼ A close-up of the dots of ink used by a printer.

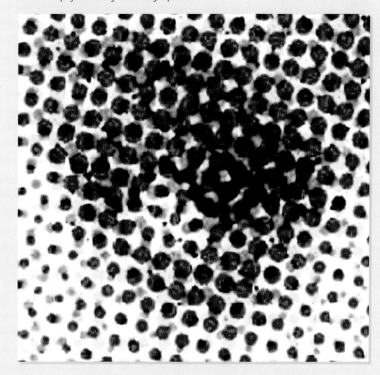

Section Two: Computer Basics

DIGITAL COLOUR

▲ *It can be hard to reproduce colours in a printed image.*

Colour is one of the biggest issues in digital imaging. From replicating the colours of a scene with your camera to displaying the colour on a computer monitor and printing your images, colour can be complicated. It is now easier than ever, though, thanks to digital technology.

CAMERA COLOUR

The pixels on a camera sensor are covered by colour filters in a red, green and blue array. Each colour has 256 tonal variations from lightest to darkest, resulting in up to 16.7 million (256 x 256 x 256) colours.

Most digital cameras do not accurately reflect real world colours. Research shows that consumers prefer more vivid colours in their images, with more saturation. This is partly due to memory – we remember colours more vividly than they really are – and also because we prefer to see deep blue skies, healthy skin and bright, bold colours, which may not be a true representation of reality. Cameras have been developed to cater for this.

COLOUR PROFILES

Colour profiles are standards that allow different devices to match a particular colour. Each colour in a single pixel is recorded as binary data, described by a string of up to 24 numbers. Every device that uses that image, be it a camera, PC or printer, needs to be able to understand those numbers and replicate it accurately. So a standard colour space (the extent and limit of the colours that can be represented) is used that all devices understand. There are two common colour spaces used in digital imaging.

SRGB

sRGB is the most common and simple profile to use, and most compact cameras will only offer this option. It can reproduce most colours, but by no means all that are displayed on a monitor. Use sRGB for images that will be viewed unretouched. While using a restricted colour space may seem like throwing a lot of useful data away, printers cannot always display those colours captured and manipulated in other colour spaces. In effect, sRGB saves you from throwing away data at a later stage.

ADOBERGB

This is a second option in more sophisticated digital colours. It has a wider range of colours than sRGB, which means a broader range of colours can be recorded and also gives more scope when you are manipulating the exposure and colour of an image. Professional printers use AdobeRGB and it is the preferred choice for images that need to be retouched on a computer.

COLOUR MATCHING

▼ *The technology needed to reproduce colour accurately is improving all the time.*

Printed pictures can often look very different from what is seen on a monitor. This is due to the different nature of the two mediums. Monitors output in transmissive light – the light comes from behind the image into the eye. Images therefore tend to look brighter and more colourful. Prints are viewed via reflective light – the light is bounced from the print to the eye, so they look darker unless you view them under a very bright light. In addition, the inks used may not replicate the brighter colours of a monitor, although modern printers and inks are developing all the time.

FILE FORMATS

Cameras take images in a number of file formats. For a compact camera this may be the commonly used JPEG, while for more sophisticated cameras other formats such as RAW and TIFF are options.

image.JPG
2,048 x 1,536

JPEG

By far the most common and popular format, JPEGs are processed images that are compressed into smaller saved files. When opened, the file returns to its original size. Because of their small size JPEGs can be stored quickly, meaning that your camera is faster to operate, and more images can be stored on your memory card and hard drive. However, the compression system can sometimes cause defects in your images. Compression means using less storage space, which means less image data. Consequently JPEG is known as a 'lossy' format as it throws away some of the image information (see page 86).

RAW

The RAW file is essentially a digital negative, the data that comes immediately from the camera, bypassing the camera's processor (which adds its own parameters and algorithms to the file) and retaining all the original information. Many photographers prefer to add these processing changes themselves for maximum artistic or technical effect. RAW files vary between different makes and models of camera, and special software is needed to open and use the files before saving.

RAW

Digital Camera Handbook

TIFF

image.tiff
441 x 229

Once the most popular format, a TIFF file is processed by the camera but not usually compressed, often resulting in very large files. This makes the camera slow to work with because of the amount of data that needs to be processed, and memory will be limited. TIFF is a popular format in which to save images on a computer, however, particularly if you choose the uncompressed option. This means that all the data left by the software is present and the image quality will not be reduced. However the large file size does mean that fewer images can be stored on your hard drive or CD.

DNG

DNG is a fairly new format developed by Adobe, to overcome the archival problems of RAW files and the danger that files from older cameras will be unsupported by future software packages. The DNG file is converted from the original file, with no loss of information, but Adobe has promised to continue supporting the file type indefinitely.

PSD

If you use Photoshop and make adjustments to the images using layers or other means, you should save any work in progress as a PSD. This saves the state of the file and layers, allowing you to go back to the image and make corrections and changes without destroying the original image.

Section Two: Computer Basics

COMPRESSION

Picture files can be very large, so it is often necessary to compress the file to make it smaller. This involves a selective discarding of 'unnecessary' image information. This will increase the speed of saving and loading the image, as well as allowing more space on your memory card and hard drive.

Image files are either stored as compressed or uncompressed. JPEGs are compressed files that are smaller when stored than they are when opened. For example, a 3 megapixel camera will produce a maximum file size of 9 megabytes (MB) of binary data. This means that when you open your picture on the computer it uses 9 MB of memory. If you look at the size of the unopened file in your pictures folder though, it will probably be about 1 MB. That is because the file is compressed. An uncompressed file will show a file size of 9 MB both when opened and when closed.

LOSSY COMPRESSION

JPEG compression is referred to as a 'lossy' compression. This means that during the compression process, some information is removed from the original file in order for the file to be saved at a smaller size. The data removed is often areas of flat colour, for example a flattish sky. An algorithm in the processor works out that all of the surrounding pixels in the sky are largely the same colour and discards as many of them as

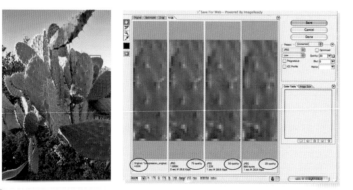

▲ *Different compression rates on a computer.*

it can (for the level of compression required), leaving a note in the file that it has done so and where. When the file is reopened the computer sees the message and replaces the missing pixels from the information that the compression algorithm left there.

While the JPEG algorithm is sophisticated, the human eye and brain combination is more so. You may notice faint blocks, obvious to the eye even though they may be only marginally different colour shades. Similarly, where large blocks of colour meet, the junction between them may look jagged. The effect of this differs depending on the compression ratio used, but it may spoil your picture.

COMPRESSION RATIOS

Most cameras offer a choice of three compression ratios. On a digital camera this is often found in the quality subheading in the main menu. Often this will be depicted as a set of stars, or by high, medium and low options. Whenever possible chose the highest quality. The lower the quality, the more your picture will be compressed, with more data discarded. This means that you can fit more pictures on your memory card, but the likelihood of picture-spoiling problems increases.

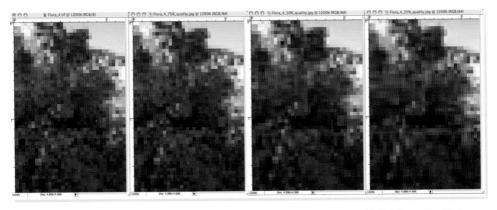

▲ *Decreasing compression rates will affect the quality of the image.*

FILE SIZES

The nature of the scene in an image to be compressed will also have a bearing on the amount of compression that can be applied. Images with lots of fine detail will not compress as well as more simple shots do.

Section Two: Computer Basics

BASIC HARDWARE NEEDS

You do not necessarily need a computer to begin digital photography, but your experience will be greatly enhanced if you have one. As a general rule, you should buy the fastest computer you can afford. With cameras getting more and more advanced, it will save a great deal of time and frustration. There are also a few extras you may like to invest in.

COMPUTER

There are two basic types of computer: Apple Macintosh or a PC (personal computer – for more on this, see page 336). Both need to run Windows, Linux or Unix software (see page 90). The important things to look for are memory, both RAM and ROM, and processing speed. The higher these are the better – you will be able to work with your photographs more quickly and have the capacity to store more images.

▲ *Good quality flat screen monitors reduce the strain on your eyes.*

MONITOR

Most computers now have flat screens, which have recently improved in quality. The bigger screen you can afford the better – it is easier on the eye and is invaluable for seeing detail in your images. It also allows more space for toolbars when using picture editing software.

PC PRINCIPLES

PRINTERS

There are a huge variety of printers available. Think about the size of image you will be making, and whether you want to print images at a larger size than A4. You may already have a printer that came with your PC – find out if it can print photographs, but remember that cheaper printers will produce lower quality images.

PHOTO PAPER

If printing your images at home, it really is worth investing in good quality photographic paper. Your images will look clearer, sharper and last much longer.

CD/DVD DRIVE

Digital photography has meant that you no longer need to have piles of photographs gathering dust as they wait to be put in albums. Instead you can store thousands of digital images on a disk. Not only does it save on space, but having back-ups of your photographs on disk provides peace of mind – if your computer broke down or was stolen, you would not lose all your images. Most computers come with a CD/DVD drive with which to view the contents of a disk, but it is also very useful to have a CD/DVD burner. This is a device that enables you to transfer data, including picture files, to a disk. Saving images to a CD or DVD will also free up space on your computer's hard drive. This is very useful, as the ease of digital photography means that you will quickly build up a huge library of images.

▲ *A CD/DVD burner is a useful accessory.*

OPERATING SOFTWARE

When you first buy a computer you need to know which operating system it uses, and this may well influence your choice. By far the most common system is Microsoft Windows, but there are other options available.

MICROSOFT WINDOWS XP

This is available in Pro or Home edition and is the current incarnation of the world's most popular operating system. If you have ever used a PC in an office, at an internet café or at school, it probably ran on Windows.

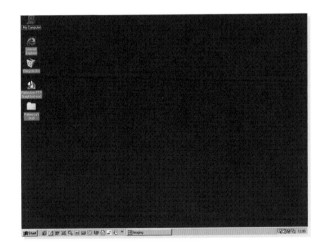

The chief advantage of Windows is its ubiquity. There is a wide range of accompanying software and good support. On the downside, Microsoft have to constantly update the system to fix bugs, security flaws and so on, which can to lead to hackers, crashes and worse. A new version, codenamed Longhorn is due in 2006.

▲ A Microsoft Windows desktop looks like this. The software icons are all ranged at the bottom of the page.

MAC OS X

Apple's latest operating system is updated yearly, with the current version known as Tiger. Mac aficionados swear by its stability and ease of use. It has long been the choice for creative users such as graphic designers, mainly due to the ease of the

▼ A typical Mac OS X desktop. Icons are ranged to the left, with the screen menu at the top.

interface, but Windows software is now catching up. It is very well supported by software developers, with many sophisticated photographic applications as well as more basic functions such as email, spreadsheets and word processing. The Mac operating system will currently only work with Apple computers, which can be more expensive, but they are also powerful and very well designed.

UNIX/LINUX

A third option, growing in popularity but still mainly suitable for advanced computer users, is a Unix-based system. Unix first started life in the 1970s at AT&T and was developed in different directions by many IT companies. Since 1995 however, there has been a single Unix Specification. Apple's OS X is a Unix variant, but there is also an open source operating system called Linux which has become increasingly popular with power users interested in looking 'under the bonnet'. Although some Unix or Linux variants are not especially user friendly, they have the advantage of being much cheaper than Windows and being open source – where a world-wide community looks for faults and suggests solutions. They are also generally stable and fast. If none of the above makes much sense to you, you should stick to Windows for a PC and OS X for a Mac.

Section Two: Computer Basics

SETTING UP YOUR COMPUTER FOR DIGITAL PHOTOGRAPHY

For people using 35 mm photography, the entire post-production process simply means sending a film to a laboratory for processing. Digital photography is different – you can manipulate, print, organize and store images in your own home using a computer.

▼ A laptop takes up less space on your desk and can be easily transported.

Once you have a digital camera you need to think about your digital darkroom setup. The digital darkroom refers to the equipment needed to process and print your photographs. The nerve centre in the darkroom is a computer – used for transferring, editing, organizing and printing. Position the computer in a place you feel comfortable working, ensuring you have plenty of light and space for your camera and any hardware such as a disk burner, printer and scanner. Each separate device connects to the computer through a USB (Universal Serial Bus) lead. If you are going to send your pictures by email or post them to the internet, you should also make sure that you are near to a phone socket or broadband connection.

Digital Camera Handbook

Many professionals use laptop computers for downloading images on location, because the fold-down screen is easily transported. If your main stipulation is convenience then this portable option is worth considering, although it is worth bearing in mind that laptops are, pound for pound, less powerful than desktop computers.

It is essential to back-up your photographs, so a CD burner is a worthwhile investment. Many new computers already have one built in, but if yours does not internal and external burners can be easily bought on the Internet or from high-street electronics shops. Internal drives are cheaper but need to be fitted, whilst external devices are slightly more expensive, yet portable. Investing in a printer to print out your photographs is another consideration and there are a wide range to choose from – although thanks the abundance of photo printing services it is not essential.

▲ *Adobe Photoshop CS2 is aimed at professional photographers.*

▼ *There is a wide range of picture editing software available.*

Depending on your interest in photo-manipulation you may need to buy some software. You can view images as thumbnails and perform very rudimentary image editing using Microsoft Paint (part of the Windows XP package), and digital cameras are supplied with basic software such as Olympus Master 1.1 or Fujifilm FinePix Viewer that can upload pictures and perform basic image-editing functions. For more intermediate editing, Adobe Photoshop Elements or Corel Paint Shop Pro offer more tools and scope for creativity for under £100, while Adobe Photoshop CS2 is aimed at professionals and costs approximately £450 plus VAT. Ensure that you have sufficient space on your hard drive before installing any programs – Photoshop CS2 requires 650 MB of hard-disc space and 320 MB of RAM.

TRANSFERRING PICTURES FROM CAMERA TO COMPUTER

Digital photographs are stored on interchangeable memory cards or in the camera's internal memory. In order to edit, manage and archive them you need to transfer the images on to a computer from the camera. This process varies slightly depending on the make and model of camera. The majority of digital cameras are supplied with a USB cable, which connects to the camera and plugs into a port on your computer. You can then transfer images by following the instructions displayed on the LCD screen.

Some digital cameras are supplied with a docking station that connects to your computer using a USB port. Once you activate the dock, the images are uploaded directly to your computer. Docking stations can stay permanently connected to your computer, making them a convenient option.

◀ *Some memory card readers are compatible with multiple card formats.*

Memory card readers are one of the most straightforward methods of transferring images from camera to computer. You connect the reader to the USB port on your computer and insert the card into the slot. A wide range of readers are available that are compatible with singular or multiple types of flash cards. The reading devices are usually small enough to stay permanently attached to your computer, and because you do not have to keep connecting and disconnecting a camera they are particularly useful in households with more then one digital camera.

Once you have transferred your photographs onto your PC you can choose to access them directly through Windows, or to use the software supplied with your digital camera. If you use Windows an icon appears on the My Computer interface entitled 'Removable disk'. Double-click it to access a folder called Digital Camera Images

▲ Cameras with docking stations can save a lot of time.

(DCIM). This contains a folder that has been given a generic name by the camera, the name varies between different manufacturers, but will include a sequence of numbers and letters, such as '100OLYMP' or '729 CANON.' Transfer the images by dragging the folder directly on to your desktop or to a specific location such as the Windows 'My Pictures' folder – a pop-up box will appear to inform you of the transfer's progress.

Newcomers to digital photography may find it easier to access their photographs using the software supplied with their camera. Connect the camera to the computer, fire up the program and follow the on-screen instructions to locate the pictures and transfer them on to your computer's hard drive (its main storage area).

USING YOUR COMPUTER

TRANSFERRING PICTURES FROM MOBILE PHONE TO COMPUTER

◄ *You can download pictures directly from your camera phone to your computer via a USB cable.*

The majority of mobile phones include digital cameras and, although at present the resolution is fairly limited, they are becoming increasingly sophisticated. While image quality cannot quite compete with a digital compact, the big advantage of using a camera phone is that modern technology enables photographs to be sent directly from a camera to a computer very quickly.

Photographs can be transferred from a mobile phone by connecting it directly to your computer and then accessing pictures in the same way you would a digital camera, or by using software supplied with the camera, such as Nokia PC Suite.

Sophisticated camera phones can also store photographs on removable memory cards – most phones include a slot for a miniSecureDigital (miniSD) or Reduced Size MultiMedia Card (RSMMC) – which are slightly smaller then those used in digital

cameras. Remove the card from the phone and you can transfer pictures to your computer using a card reader, although it is worth checking compatibility because you may need to buy an adaptor.

▲ Phone memory cards can be very small.

Another method of sending photographs to a computer is through Multimedia Messaging (MMS). Data is sent over a General Packet Radio Service (GPRS) or Global System for Mobile Communications (GSM) network directly to an email address. In order to use this you need to ensure that MMS settings are installed in your phone. You can find out the settings from your service provider by contacting them directly, or alternatively you can visit the support section on your phone manufacturer's website. By selecting the type of phone and network operator, the settings can often be sent as a text message directly to your phone.

Modern phones are increasingly equipped with Bluetooth technology. Bluetooth enables you to connect your phone to devices such as computers, phones and PDAs wirelessly without the need for any cables. You will need to turn on the Bluetooth facility on your phone, and it will then search for any devices that are within range. Once it has located

the computer it can send the photograph. In order for the connection to work, you need to be about 10 m (33 ft) away, and although the phone doesn't have to point directly at the computer, walls may hinder the transfer. Not all PC's are Bluetooth enabled, so you may need to buy a USB adaptor. Some printers are now Bluetooth enabled, enabling photographs to be sent directly from a phone to a printer.

◄ Use MMS to send picture messages directly and quickly.

HOW TO OPEN A PHOTOGRAPH

Once you have taken your pictures and transferred them on to your home computer you will want to open them. The easiest way to do this in Windows is to locate the folder containing the photographs, go to the 'View' menu and select 'Thumbnails'.

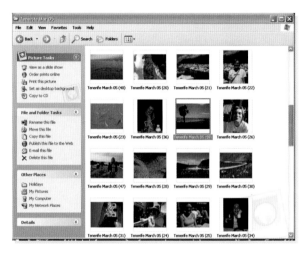

▲ The Windows XP file browser enables you to view multiple images.

Each photograph in the folder will be displayed at the same time at a greatly reduced size as a small thumbnail whilst still enabling you to see what each picture is and to differentiate between them. To display your picture in a slightly larger format, return to the View menu this time selecting 'Filmstrip.' Windows includes a Picture and Fax Viewer that you can use to view your images at an even bigger size, in a way

▲ Scroll through your images by clicking on the blue arrows.

similar to viewing a slideshow. You can scroll through the images using the controls along the bottom, enlarging them by using the magnifying glass icons, and viewing them at full size by hitting the 'Actual Size' icon. If your pictures are the wrong orientation use the green triangle icons to rotate them.

USING IMAGE-EDITING SOFTWARE

If you are intending on performing specific image-editing functions (such as cropping or adjusting the brightness and contrast) it may be better to open your photographs directly within the program you are going to use, such as Adobe Photoshop Elements or Corel Paint Shop Pro. Go to the 'File' menu and right-click 'Open' – a box will appear on screen that you can use to access the files from their current location on the computer.

One of the most effective ways of opening a photograph is to use a file browser. Found in the majority of image-editing programs and in software supplied with the camera, a file browser views the contents of a folder as thumbnails with information telling you when each picture was taken and the camera settings used. This is particularly useful to identify a specific photograph when you have numerous pictures in the same folder, and you can view them all at the same time without having to open them individually.

If you always use the same piece of software to open a specific type of file, Microsoft Windows can assign file formats to the program. File formats open the files using the specific program each time you double-click on a file, instead of using the default settings.

▼ In Photoshop CS2, the file browser is located in the Adobe Bridge section.

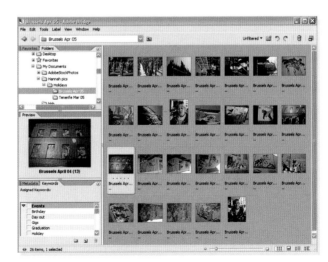

BASIC ENHANCEMENTS: CROP & ROTATE

Every photographer – from the most experienced to the novice – can improve their photographs with simple cropping and rotating.

CROPPING

The majority of image-editing programs – however basic – include a crop tool. It is very easy to use and can make a vast difference to your image. To crop is to retain only a section of an image – a crop can be large or small depending on the effect you want to create. On occasion you may want to remove a section or object from your photograph that is spoiling the overall composition, for example a person who has inadvertently walked into shot. Every image-editing program is slightly different, but typically you drag the crop tool over the section of the photo you want to retain and a virtual box appears over the photo. You can then adjust the four sides of the box to fit the area you want to crop, leaving anything you want to remove outside, before finally activating the crop.

▲ To crop, drag a box over your image and click the tick icon.

▲ Images can also be improved by rotating.

The crop tool is a good way of improving a photograph and your composition, enabling you to experiment with different compositions and to see if the overall photo would have been improved if you had left some aspects out, or zoomed in tighter on a certain area. It is also useful as not all digital cameras show 100 per cent of the image area on their LCD screens or in their viewfinders. It is worth remembering that every time you crop an image the file gets smaller, as you are literally throwing away image information. This may well affect the maximum size of your prints.

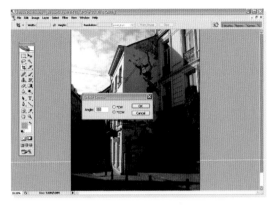

▲ To rotate, go to the Image menu and select Rotate Canvas.

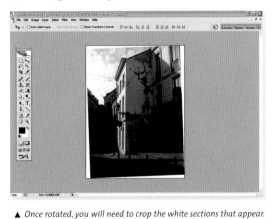

▲ Once rotated, you will need to crop the white sections that appear.

ROTATING

The rotate tool is a very useful feature. We have all seen photographs blighted by horizons that are not quite horizontal or pictures of people who seem to be veering slightly to one side. There are several ways of rotating an image – in Photoshop you can specifying the number of degrees and direction (clockwise and counter clockwise) or rotate in increments of 90 degrees. In Paint Shop Pro you can correct a horizon using the straightening tool, whereby you match up a movable line with the askew area and then determine whether you want to straighten the image vertically or horizontally.

The cropping and rotating tools work together – every time you rotate an image you will need to crop it in order to retain its rectangular format; very often you will not be able to see which area of the picture needs cropping until you have performed the rotation.

BASIC ENHANCEMENTS: COLOUR, BRIGHTNESS & CONTRAST

There are many reasons why a photograph may not look right – perhaps the day was particularly dull and overcast or perhaps the camera settings were incorrect. Photoshop Elements and Paint Shop Pro have a variety of tools to correct these problems, either automatically, where the program analyzes the image and makes a change, or manually, where you control the adjustment. If you are new to digital photography you can try automatic commands. As you become more experienced you can begin to take more control and make adjustments manually.

▲ *Overcast weather can produce a dull shot.*

▲ *Adjusting brightness and contrast can help.*

BRIGHTNESS AND CONTRAST

Increasing the brightness and adjusting the contrast between the dark and light tones can make a huge difference to a dull image. In Photoshop make adjustments by

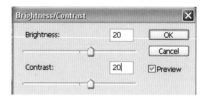

▲ *The brightness and contrast sliders are easy to use.*

Digital Camera Handbook

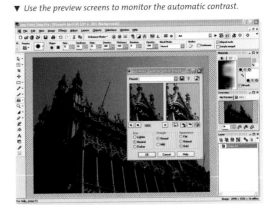

dragging sliders left down to minus 100 (to darken) or right up to plus 100 (to lighten) an image. Photoshop Elements and Paint Shop Pro both feature a tool that analyzes the photo before adjusting the contrast for you. In Photoshop the auto contrast tool is an automatic feature that works by finding the lightest and darkest point of an image and then distributing all the remaining pixels' tones between those two points on the tonal range. In Paint Shop Pro the automatic contrast enhancement offers slightly more flexibility, because you can adjust the bias/brightness (lighter, neutral and darker,) the strength of the adjustment (normal or mild) and the appearance (flat, neutral and bold).

LEVELS

The Levels command offers a greater degree of control than the brightness and contrast tool – by changing the tonal range of your photograph. It is displayed as a histogram (a vertical bar chart with hundreds of fine bars): the black lines represent the distribution of highlights, mid-tones and shadows across the image. Make adjustments to the entire picture or the individual red, green and blue channels by dragging the black, (shadow) grey (mid-tones) and white (highlights)

sliders at the bottom. Novices may find it useful to start using the Automatic Levels command found in Photoshop – this tool works by finding the lightest and darkest pixels in each colour channel, converting them to white and black and redistributing the remaining pixels between the two.

◀ *Adjust highlights, mid-tones and shadows.*

ORGANIZING YOUR IMAGES: NAMING & FILING

The immediacy of digital photography means that more people are taking photographs then ever. This is partly because you can preview your image on the LCD screen of your digital camera, deciding whether to delete or not, which is in direct contrast to film photography where you could never be quite sure of the results until the film came back from the developers.

A consequence of having so many images is that without some organization, your hard drive will soon be overrun with photographs all with impenetrable file names, so it is useful to implement a filing system. If you only use your camera occasionally – perhaps on holiday or birthdays – you can do this manually by creating a system of folders.

▲ *Generic names created by your camera can be confusing.*

RENAMING YOUR PHOTOGRAPHS

Once you have transferred your images on to your hard drive the first thing to do is replace the file extension generated by the camera – this is generally a sequence of numbers like

▲ *Select a new name and location with batch renaming.*

Digital Camera Handbook

1010080 or IMG_4309 that offers little useful information – into something comprehensible. In fact, if you reset your memory card the file numbers will revert back to the beginning, which means you could have several files with the same name.

▼ Individual names are much easier to locate.

It is labour intensive to change the names of numerous digital files individually. Photoshop Elements and Paint Shop Pro have a batch rename tool that changes the names of multiple pictures within seconds. Open the file browser in Photoshop, highlight those thumbnails you wish to rename, activate the batch rename command and enter a name – such as 'Summer Holiday 05' – and it will be allocated to each photo along with a sequential number.

FILING YOUR PICTURES

It is a good idea to have a system of folders in place to which you can transfer images once you have renamed them. The most straightforward method is to create a series of named folders for different types of photographs, including holidays, birthdays and pets. Within each genre of

▼ Make sure each folder has a logical name.

photographs you can include sub-folders that are more specific, for example 'Tenerife 2005' or 'Sarah's 14th'. Every time you upload new images it is easy to simply rename them and drag them to their new location.

CREATING A PHOTO LIBRARY

While manually organizing your photographs into folders may work for a hundred images, if your digital photographs run into the thousands it is more practical to create a photo library using specialist software. There are a wide array of programs available: Adobe Photoshop Album (which is included within Photoshop Elements) and Corel Photo Album are suitable for novices, while Extensis Portfolio and ACDSee are aimed at professional photographers and frequently offer RAW support.

▲ Use the Catalogue Files wizard to add image information to ACDSee.

Every time you transfer new photographs on to your computer open them using a management program so that it can record relevant information for each file. Extensis organizes your photographs into catalogues, which contain thumbnails of every picture with a relevant name – anything from 'Wildlife' to 'Holiday 2005'. The catalogue also retains Exchangeable Image File (EXIF) data from the camera detailing camera settings and any additional details you want to add, which could be keywords, a brief description of what the image is, copyright information and the file name. You can have as many

▼ You can organize your images with ACDSee.

or as few catalogues as you want and can keep adding to existing ones or categorize them further into separate galleries. In ACDSee thumbnails of photographs are stored in a central database, which you can organize into categories and sub-categories.

In common with many file managers, Extensis and ACDSee do not actually change where your computer stores your digital photographs (unless you specify it); rather, each catalogue acts as a portal of thumbnails to help you find a specific image, which doesn't even have to be stored on your hard drive, but could be on an archived CD. It is also much quicker to display, making it easier to find a specific image.

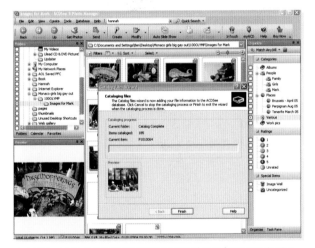

▲ *Add keywords or brief descriptions to your catalogues for easy navigation.*

When you search for an image, enter one or more keywords and the program will then scour your hard drive looking for a match and display thumbnails for each of the resulting images. Both Photoshop Album and Paint Shop Pro have this feature. Keywords can be anything from the type of occasion such as a birthday, holiday or day out, to the name of the person in the picture, or a photographic genre such as travel, nature or macro. You can usually assign several keywords to each picture.

Many image-management programs complement photo-editing software. The Extensis Portfolio Express features floating palettes that can be accessed within Photoshop without the full program being opened – this helps you to search quickly for any photograph on your hard drive.

Section Two: Computer Basics

ARCHIVING: PORTABLE STORAGE SOLUTIONS

Unfortunately computer errors do occur, and the only way to avoid this happening is to create back-up copies of your photographs by burning them on to CD or transferring them onto a portable storage device, which you can keep separate from your computer.

BURNING A CD

You can burn your photographs onto conventional CD-R's that can only be used once, or CD-RW's that you can use more than once. If you are backing up your digital photographs you probably want to keep them forever, so CD-Rs are probably the best small scale solution and are ideal for storing JPEGs. DVD is becoming an increasingly popular format for burning images, because it provides the advantage of 4.75 GB of storage per disk in contrast to the 700 MB offered by a CD. While DVDs will take longer to burn, they allow much more storage, particularly if you have saved images as TIFFs or kept RAW files.

▲ *External CD burners are available.*

To burn a CD use the software supplied with the burner, which is usually straightforward, or invest in a dedicated burning program. In Windows XP you can copy files without opening specific burning software simply by clicking 'copy to CD' in the picture tasks menu (if your computer has a burner). It is often a good idea to

Digital Camera Handbook

burn two copies – one for reference and one for storage, just in case something happens to one set of disks.

One alternative is to create a slideshow of your images complete with transitions, sound effects and captions. This is useful when you have a selection of images based around a theme, such as a family holiday or Christmas. There are a range of programs for this, varying in price, including Magix CD and DVD or Roxio Easy CD and DVD Creator. See page 114 for more on this.

HARD DISK DRIVES & STORAGE DEVICES

If you do not want to burn your images on to CD you can store them on an external hard drive, such as those from LaCie or SmartDisk. These connect to your PC via a USB cable and mount on your PC desktop. Simply drag and drop the files you wish to save. Alternatively, invest in a portable storage device. The Nikon Coolwalker and Elio Photojukebox are hard drives with capacities ranging

▲ *You can store up to 40 GB of images on the Epson P-2000.*

from 20 GB to 80 GB. Copy photographs on to them using a USB cable or through a memory card slot. Recently portable storage devices have also become viewing devices: the Epson P-2000 has a 40 GB hard drive and features a 9.7 cm (3.8 in) colour screen, which is a great way of sharing your digital photographs. Bear in mind, though, that if your hard drive fails you stand to lose all your photographs unless you also copy them to CD or DVD.

◀ *The Nikon Coolwalker provides 30 GB of storage space.*

LIVING WITHOUT A PC

You can tinker with your digital photographs on a computer to enhance them or create something artistic, and while many people will invest in a PC, it is a myth that you need one in order to enjoy digital photography.

TOUCHING-UP IMAGES

Recently some manufacturers have introduced technology into their cameras that can be used for rectifying common photo problems, which means some edits you perform on a PC can now be done in-camera. Most new HP cameras incorporate Real Life Technologies enabling common photo problems, such as red eye or underexposed highlights to be corrected in camera and Nikon has a similar process with D-Lighting and In-Camera Red-Eye Fix. While useful, this technology is still in its infancy and does not yet provide the flexibility of Photoshop or Paint Shop Pro.

▲ *New technology is starting to eliminate the need for PCs.*

PRINTING WITHOUT A PC

Most digital cameras and photo printers are compatible with the PictBridge universal standard, so that you can print directly from any compatible digital camera to any compatible printer without the need for a computer or additional software. Canon, manufacturer of cameras and printers has its own standard, Canon Direct Print, although its products are compatible with PictBridge as well. To print directly from your camera, connect it to the printer using a USB cable and instructions will appear on the LCD asking which photographs you want to

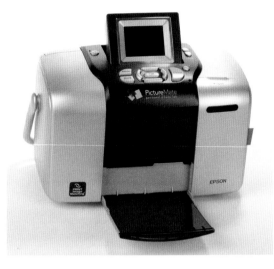

▲ Attach your camera and use the LCD screen to print your pictures.

select and how many copies you want to print.

Printer manufacturers are increasingly recognizing that not everyone wants to use a PC and many new printers include card slots compatible with a range of flash memory cards, enabling prints to come directly from a memory card.

The majority of new digital cameras support Direct Print Order Format (DPOF) so that you can select in-camera the photographs you want to print. When the camera is connected to a printer (or the memory card is put into the slot) the printer will detect automatically which images you want to print. This is a great timesaving feature and means you do not have to scroll through hundreds of pictures to find the select few.

If you do not want to print your pictures you can take your memory card to a photo developer. Specialist photographic retailers such as Jessops and even supermarkets can produce prints directly from a memory card. (See page 134 for more on using a printing laboratory.)

▶ *Some printers allow you to print directly from a memory card.*

SHARING YOUR PHOTOGRAPHS

One of the most enjoyable elements of photography is sharing your pictures, either to relive memories or to share an event with someone who missed it. Digital photography makes sharing pictures easy, because pictures are stored as computer files and you can attach them to an email or upload them to an internet photo gallery.

HOW TO VIEW YOUR PHOTOGRAPHS ON THE TV

▲ *A DigiViewer will display your images on a TV.*

The television is an ideal device on which to view digital images. Many digital cameras have a video out facility and come supplied with an Audio and Video cable (A/V) that connects to the camera at one end, and to the white and yellow audio and video point on a television at the other. Very often, modern televisions have a SCART rather then an AV connection and if this is the case you will have to invest in an adaptor. In order to see the images you will have to turn the television to the AV channel, before using the controls on the back of the camera to scroll through still images and view video clips. Some cameras have the facility to create a simple slideshow from your digital images, which you can then view on TV.

▶ *You can slot your memory card straight into this device, which will then show your pictures or movies on a television.*

Digital Camera Handbook

Photo viewers are becoming increasingly popular ways of viewing images on a television. The SanDisk Photo Viewer and the TV 6-in-One Photo Album are small, flat devices, which connect to your television (again through the AV point) and are designed to sit on top of your DVD player or TV. Display pictures by inserting a memory card into one of the slots at the front and scroll through the images using the supplied controller. Some devices also enable you to create slideshows from your images, which can be saved on to a memory card.

▲ The SanDisk Photo Viewer includes a remote with various options.

Slide shows are useful for archiving images, and also for sharing pictures. With prices dropping as low as £30, increasing numbers of households have DVD players, which makes creating a DVD slideshow of your pictures an alternative way of watching them on television. CD/DVD slideshows are more personal; you can choose exactly which photographs will appear and for how long, create captions and add fun sound effects. Operation is very straightforward – put the disc into the DVD drive and hit play.

▶ The TV 6-in-One Photo Album connects to your television through an AV point and allows you to create slideshows and view your images.

SHARING YOUR PICTURES

HOW TO MAKE A SIMPLE SLIDESHOW

In Windows XP you can make a basic slideshow by opening the folder containing your pictures and selecting 'view as a slideshow' from the picture task options. The monitor will automatically switch to full screen. Once you hit 'play' it will start scrolling through the images, or you can skip through them by clicking 'page up' and 'page down.'

There are a host of programs enabling you to create slideshows complete with transitions and effects which you can burn on to CD and watch on television. Ulead CD and DVD Picture Show is a good option for beginners. Like many slideshow creation programs it functions in a step-by-step format making it incredibly user-friendly.

Start by locating your photographs – which you can usually do using a file browsing system to find the folder containing your images – and choose which ones you want to incorporate into the

▲ *Create simple slideshows and add captions in ULead CD and DVD PictureShow.*

slideshow. In ULead CD and DVD Picture Show the selected pictures are displayed as thumbnails, which you can add to the program on their own or as a group,

▼ Most slideshow software has a range of pre-set DVD interfaces you can use as backgrounds.

before dragging them into your chosen order. It makes sense to ensure the order is logical; if the subject of your slideshow is a summer holiday, avoid beginning with a photograph taken at night or towards the end of the holiday.

You can make adjustments to the exposure of individual pictures and add captions using most slideshow creation software. If you are interested in creating more advanced slideshows, you might consider investing in Magix Photos on CD and DVD. Utilizing a timeline format similar to that found in video editing programs, software, pictures, transitions and sound effects are all positioned on different channels.

In the majority of slideshows you can specify how long each photo will appear and choose to add transitions, such as fades and wipes, pan and zoom effects or photo frames. You can also add music or use sound effects supplied with the program, which you can run on a loop so that it matches the length of your slideshow. Most slideshow creation software includes a selection of DVD templates that you can personalize. The quality of the templates varies – they are often organized into themes, including birthdays and holidays and may not be to everyone's taste. When you have completed your slideshow you can burn it on to CD or DVD and share it with family and friends.

▶ *In Magix Photos you can display frames, wipes and music on different channels.*

HOW TO SEND PICTURES BY EMAIL

Email is increasingly used as a method of communication because it is virtually instantaneous and enables vast quantities of files – including digital photographs – to be sent quickly. Three types of email are commonly used: a home Internet Service Provider (ISP,) email through work or school or a free service from an online search engine.

For a monthly fee internet service providers such as Tesco or AOL give you a selection of email addresses when you sign up. The actual process of attaching a digital photograph depends on the program – you can send it as an attachment or embed it into the file. In AOL click 'Attach File' and a pop-up box appears that you can use to locate the folder containing your pictures, before selecting the ones you want to add, then clicking 'Open'.

▲ *Make sure your photos do not exceed the provider's file size limit.*

With the majority of work-based communication taking place through email, it is inevitable that some people will email photographs from work. Whether this is allowed or not depends on the policy of the individual employer, but many actively

▲ To sign up for web-based email, you will need to choose a username.

discourage it, so it is worth checking your contract before sending personal photographs this way.

The advantage of using online websites such as Hotmail, Yahoo and Google is that they can be accessed from anywhere in the world, which is very useful if you are travelling and want to email your photographs home. With Hotmail you can send files up to 10 MB and utilize around 250 MB of storage, while Yahoo has 1 GB of storage. To obtain an email address you will have to sign up for an account by entering basic information and choosing a name.

FILE SIZE ISSUES

Before emailing your photographs you need to ensure that they are the right size, especially if manipulation has been performed in Photoshop and you have saved the file as a TIFF. JPEG is the preferred format for emailing digital photographs. The file size is much smaller than TIFF files, so you can email several files at once. Remember the more compression you apply to an

▲ Make your name unusual, as common ones will have been taken.

image, the more the quality will diminish. If your photograph is too large the upload may be very slow – especially if you do not have broadband and are trying to transfer numerous files. Many providers limit the file size of each email you can send – AOL sets a maximum of 16 MB to sent files, while others have a 1 MB limit on files you can receive. If you are in doubt, check with your provider and the person to whom you are sending the images.

HOW TO TAKE PICTURES WITH A MOBILE PHONE

Increasingly camera phones have built-in digital cameras, and while image quality is not up to the standard of proper digital cameras, they are a useful alternative on those occasions when you do not have a camera. In fact it is often easier taking a photograph with a mobile phone rather than a camera, because there are fewer features and controls to worry about.

▲ Taking a photo with a camera phone is easy, but be aware that the zoom is typically digital rather than optical, which reduces picture quality.

Every mobile phone has slightly different controls and functions in a slightly different way. You will need to select the camera function from the main menu, or press the dedicated camera button, if you have one. You then need to choose the picture size and quality, which will vary depending on the number of pixels in the camera – a 1.3 MP phone such as the SagemX8 can take photos from 320 x 240 up to 1280 x 960 pixels in size. The smaller the photo, the less space it will use in the phone memory, and the smaller it will print. You can also choose the quality, usually between high, normal and MMS – the better the quality the larger then file size will be.

▼ *For optimum quality, choose the largest file size.*

▼ *Generic file names can be confusing, so rename your shots.*

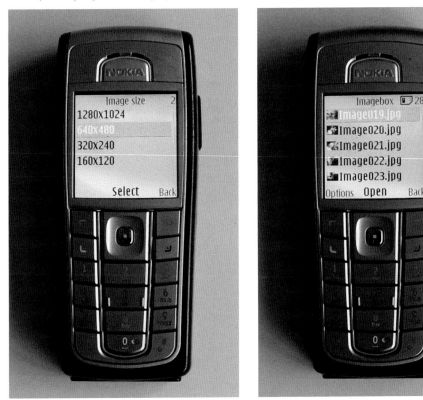

When you are ready to take a photograph the LCD display will change to show you what is in front of the lens – point the picture at your subject and press the shutter. The shutter button varies between models, so check your camera phone manual to find out where it is.

Once you have taken your photograph you are usually asked whether you want to save or delete it. Saved photos are usually stored in the multimedia section of your phone, where it is a good idea to change the name to something specific as opposed to a number.

Depending on the type of phone, you can make a selection of adjustments in camera. This could include adding colour effects, such as emboss, greyscale and negative, and adjusting the contrast and sharpening. While fun, results are less effective then Photoshop and offer less control.

Section Two: Computer Basics

HOW TO USE AN ONLINE SHARING WEBSITE

There are many online photography websites where you can display your images for free and meet like-minded photographers.

You can upload one photograph a day to www.ephotozine.com and the photos appear in a gallery of reader pictures and are stored in an individual portfolio. As well as offering a print service, you can upload your pictures into a gallery with 200 MB storage on www.photobox.com. By entering the email address of friends or relative you can share your gallery with others.

Many photo sharing websites include message boards, which you can access by registering, so that you can comment on other people's images, as well as inviting criticism of your own and getting shooting tips – a great way of improving your photography and generating healthy debate. Many people enjoy being

▼ *There are a variety of ways to upload to PhotoBox.*

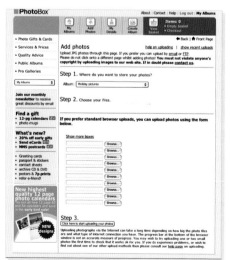

▼ *Uploaded images are displayed as thumbnails.*

part of an online community and these sites are well known to photography fans, often with thousands of members. Search engines such as Yahoo also provide online storing space, although there is less emphasis on photographic technique.

To join an online sharing website you will need to sign up. On ephotozine this involves choosing a username and entering basic information including your email address and password. Before uploading your pictures, you will need to ensure they are saved at the correct file size, which will vary depending on the site – ephotozine specifies that each picture is 500 pixels in size, less than 600 K and are in JPEG format.

▲ Invite comments from others at websites such as ephotozine.

LEGAL ISSUES

As an amateur photographer you own the copyright of every picture you take, but once your pictures go on to the Internet they are in the public domain and could be copied by other photographers. There is no way of preventing this, although Photoshop can add a watermark to your image – such as the date and name – and embeds it into the file so that it cannot be removed. You will need to register with the Digimarc cooperation (www.digimarc.com) first. It is also worth adding a caption containing your name and the year to the bottom of your photograph.

Be aware of issues regarding content. Whether it is right or wrong to upload photographs of children has provoked heated debate and while the majority of photographs are innocent, if you want to upload images of a child's birthday party to your website it is best to obtain permission from the parents first. Airport check-in desks, army bases and banks are other potentially problematic subjects. Sexism, racism and political discontent are also contentious.

HOW TO USE A TEMPLATE TO MAKE A WEB PHOTO GALLERY

A web gallery is a very effective way to share your digital photographs, and is made up of thumbnails of pictures that others can click on and view. A gallery can be viewed from anywhere in the world and by anyone, making it a great way of sharing images with friends. You could also use your gallery to sell photographs commercially.

There are companies that will create websites for you, but the development of modern software means it is easy to build your own web gallery relatively quickly – Photoshop even has a Web Photo Gallery feature that does the hard work for you. Many people will want to select the domain name of their website. You can choose anything, although if you are planning on using it to sell pictures, select something that sounds professional – a simple solution is to just use your name. There are a range of places you can buy a domain names for an annual charge, including www.123domainnames.co.uk and www.pickaweb.co.uk. It is possible to obtain a domain name for free, although if you opt for one of these you will not be in complete control of the site.

The next step is to find a web host who, for a monthly fee, will provide you with space online and email addresses. There are many Internet Service Providers (ISPs) available offering packages to suit different budgets, so shop around. It is worth finding out the hours and cost of telephone support in case you have any problems.

If you don't want to create your own website from scratch, many service providers give you free online space when you sign up. BT Yahoo Internet and Tesco Internet Access offer you 15 MB of Internet space and include software to help you create a website.

You will need to prepare your images, source them from the hard drive or CD and deposit them into a folder before you upload them. Avoid working on your original files, and instead make copies – Photoshop automatically does this, but some programs may not. It is important to choose the order of your photographs carefully – a photo diary of a day out should start at the beginning of the day, not halfway through. You will need to rename yours files individually or by using a batch renaming feature.

STEP-BY-STEP
Using Photoshop to Create a Web Gallery

Step 1

Collate the files you want to include in the web gallery and put them into a folder (see page 110 for how to do this.) In Photoshop head into the File Menu and select Automate, then scroll down the list and select 'Web Photo Gallery.'

Step 2

Click on the drop-down menu next to Styles and choose a suitable style for your gallery – the thumbnail displays different styles. Hit the 'Browse' button to locate your folder and use the Destination button to choose where to put them.

Step 3

Personalize your gallery with the Drop-Down Menu. Select 'Banner' to enter a title and author. Choose how big each photograph and thumbnail is with 'Large Images,' and 'Thumbnail' menus. You can add text over each picture using 'Security'.

Step 4

Photoshop will automatic-ally resize all the images and put them in a folder along with thumb nail images, HTML pages and a preview screen of the website which you can view in your browser.

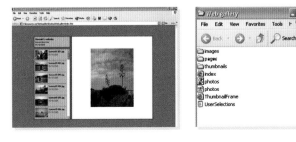

PRINTING AT HOME: WHY BOTHER?

With film photography, most consumers hand the roll of film to a chemist and return an hour later to collect their prints. Digital photography is different – you can choose exactly what to print and you have the option to print it yourself.

▲ *Print directly from your camera or using a home computer.*

WHY PRINT AT HOME?

A digital photograph is a chain of events that begins when you look at the scene, choose the right camera settings, press the shutter and preview the shot in the viewfinder. Then you take part in the post-production process by uploading your picture on to the computer and making tonal adjustments so that it looks exactly the way you want. The final link in the chain is printing.

One of the major advantages of printing at home is convenience – you don't have to trudge to a shop and then return to pick up prints, or wait for them to be delivered. You can turn on your PC and start printing – and it can be very rewarding to print your own pictures.

Home printing may initially seem daunting: colour management, size and resolution are just some of the areas you need to understand and we will look at them in detail later. However, printer manufacturers are realizing that more people want to print at home and are producing user-friendly devices such as the Kodak Printer Dock and Epson Picture Mate. Once you get used to your printer and understand how it works you will be able to print quickly, and – crucially – be able to control exactly what you print.

▲ *Kodak printer docks enable you to print directly from the camera.*

While the cost of ink and paper can be pricey and home printing cannot match some of the deals on the high street, it is increasingly affordable. Many households already have document printers, which may be able to produce photo-quality prints by using different paper or ink. The price of new printers is dropping – an adequate inkjet printer can cost less than £100.

▶ *The Epson Picture Mate features a carrying handle, allowing you to print on the go.*

Section Two: Computer Basics

HOW TO MAKE A PRINT: SIZING & RESOLUTION

Before you start printing it is important to check that your camera is capable of producing good-quality prints at the size you desire. The number of pixels in your camera determines the size you can print – the greater the number of megapixels there are, the larger the prints you can produce.

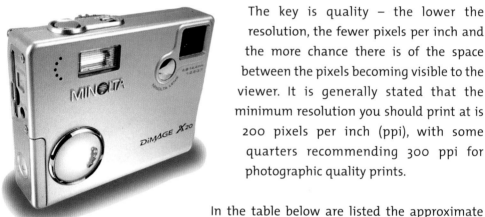

▲ *A 2 MP camera.*

The key is quality – the lower the resolution, the fewer pixels per inch and the more chance there is of the space between the pixels becoming visible to the viewer. It is generally stated that the minimum resolution you should print at is 200 pixels per inch (ppi), with some quarters recommending 300 ppi for photographic quality prints.

In the table below are listed the approximate print sizes for typical digital cameras. If you use an image resolution of 200 ppi the maximum image size a 2 MP camera is capable of producing for optimum quality is 20 x 15 cm (8 x 6 in), whereas a 9 MP camera can produce prints as large as 44 x 33 cm (17 x 13 in) at 200 ppi. It is possible to produce A4 prints from a 2 MP camera at a resolution of 120 ppi, but the quality may not be particularly high. This is not an exact calculation as printers do not print the image out as square pixels. Rather they convert the image into one made up of round dots through a process known as dithering. A good inkjet printer may have a printing resolution (the number of dots used) of 2400 x 4800 dots per inch. This dithering process means that it is worth experimenting by

Digital Camera Handbook

printing at a range of different resolutions to see what you can safely print as the dots blur the individual pixels. If a photograph is framed on a wall the pixels may not be visible to the naked eye owing to the increased viewing distance, whereas in a photo album they may be more obvious.

CHANGING THE IMAGE SIZE

You can change the image size and resolution in Photoshop through the Image Size options (or Resize options in Paint Shop Pro). Before you make any adjustments to the image size make sure that Resampling is turned off, and check the Constrain Proportions box to make sure that you don't accidentally adjust the scope of the image. Using either 'cm' or 'inches' (depending on your preference) enter the desired width you want to print in the Document Size box. You will see the Resolution change – if it falls under 200 ppi the print size is too large and for good quality prints it is advisable to enter a smaller print size. Once you are happy with your image size, tick the Resample Image box and enter your desired resolution. If you are reducing the size of the picture you will see the

▲ 9 MP compacts can produce 44 x 33 cm (17 x 13 inch) prints at 200 dpi.

Pixel Dimensions change and the image size decrease. This is because by resampling you are adjusting the pixel make-up of the entire image and as you reduce the file size pixels are deleted. Be careful if you are resampling to create a larger image size, the quality can be greatly reduced.

▶ To enlarge or reduce the size of your image, make sure the Resample Image box is ticked.

Image Size

Pixel Dimensions: 4.21M
Width: 1400 pixels
Height: 1050 pixels

Document Size:
Width: 17.78 cm
Height: 13.34 cm
Resolution: 200 pixels/inch

☑ Scale Styles
☑ Constrain Proportions
☑ Resample Image: Bicubic

OK
Cancel
Auto...

UNDERSTANDING THE PRINT OPTIONS

The easiest way to check how your print looks on the page is to preview it. With this useful tool you can see the position and size of your photo on the page before it is printed, ensuring you can make any necessary adjustments before you commit to print.

In Photoshop select 'Print with Preview' from the main menu and your photo will be displayed in a white box on the left of the page. By default the box 'Center Image' is ticked, which aligns your photo to the centre. To change its position uncheck the box and drag the photo to its new location.

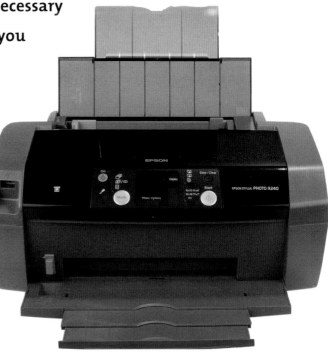

▲ *To avoid wasting paper, check in which direction it should be inserted.*

Your preview will let you know if the page orientation is incorrect – if you print a landscape photograph in portrait format you will lose half your image and waste paper. This is adjustable in most image editors through the page setup command or in Photoshop by clicking the Page Setup button.

Printers can produce prints at a range of different sizes – 15 x 10 cm (6 x 4 in) and 18 x 13 cm (7 x 5 in) are fairly standard, but you can also print up to A4 and produce panoramas. Photoshop retains previous printer settings, so if you are printing out on a different paper size, ensure the Scale is set to 100 per cent, remembering to later select a new paper size before printing. If you want the print to fill the page tick 'Scale to Fit Media.'

If you haven't chosen a print size in Photoshop you can change the size of your print when you are previewing it by adjusting the Scale, Height and Width percentages in the Scaled Print Size box. However, any adjustments you make may impact upon filter effects and because the preview screen is very small, it is more accurate to make the adjustments to the size of the picture in Photoshop before previewing.

Before you begin to print, check the paper is positioned correctly – you may need to refer to the manual to see whether it should be face up or face down. To the eye gloss and matt sides of paper can look very similar and it is easy to print on the wrong size.

Check the status of ink in your printer, otherwise your print may lack colour tones (a warning usually appears on the LCD screen of your printer). However, after the warning appears you should be able to keep printing, depending on the model of printer.

▼ Use the print preview function in Photoshop to check the position of your photo on the page.

COLOUR MANAGEMENT BASICS

Very often what you see when you take a photograph looks completely different on your monitor, bearing even less resemblance to the final print. This is where colour management is so important,

▲ *Attach the Spyder Pro to your monitor to calibrate it.*

enabling you to create a benchmark between the colours you see on the monitor and those produced by the printer.

You will be using your monitor to make judgements on the colour values in your image, so the first step is to ensure it is calibrated properly. There are two methods of doing this – through the internal settings or by using an external device. It is important to calibrate your monitor on a regular basis (at least once a month) and for accurate results make sure you use a light source similar to the conditions you normally work in.

Calibrating internally will be adequate for the majority of users. Macintosh computers will find calibration commands under System Preferences, while in Windows you can find them by selecting Adobe Gamma from the control panel and following instructions on-screen.

Start by putting the contrast of the screen to its highest level, uncheck 'View Single Gamma Only' and adjust the brightness to change the visibility of three boxes. Set the gamma (the relationship between the screen brightness and the pixels) to 2.2

and choose a white point of 5000 K for print work. The computer will create a profile, which you can then name before saving.

Spyder2 and Spyder2PRO from Colour Confidence are external devices for monitor calibration that attach to your LCD screen to measure the red, green and blue values before working with supplied software to create a colour profile.

Once you have calibrated your monitor you need to set the correct colour management options in your image-editing program – in Photoshop they are accessible in the 'Print with Preview' menu. Tick the 'Show more options' box and make sure 'Document' is checked in the Source Space options, which will

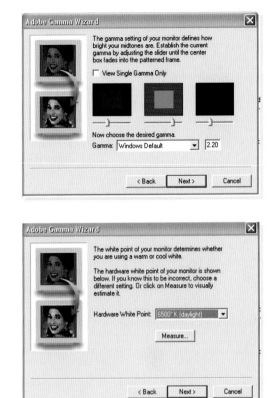

▲ Use the sliders to adjust the brightness (top), then choose a white point from the drop-down list (bottom).

guarantee that the printer uses colour information contained in the photo. Select 'Printer Colour Management' from the drop-down list next to the Print Space menu.

Alternatively, you can scroll through the list and choose a profile that matches your printer, or select 'Same as Source' which uses the colours in the photo. Finally before hitting print, choose 'Perceptual' from the drop-down (rendering) Intent list, which is designed for use when printing photographs.

◄ Tick the 'Show More Options' box to access advanced print options and set the print space.

TYPES OF MEDIA

▼ *Experiment with different photo papers to find one that suits your photography.*

It is important to choose the right paper for your prints so that you can show them at their best. It can be difficult knowing what to choose with so many different paper types and brands on the market, and the paper you choose will vary depending on what you are using your prints for.

You need to consider the type of surface you want your paper to have, from matt to satin (which is slightly shinier), or semi and high gloss finishes. The majority of processing labs use gloss, although a matt printing is often an option. The glossier the finish the more reflective it is. Bright colours benefit from shinier, glossy paper, while for more subtle photos a flatter matt surface is effective.

Digital Camera Handbook

The weight of the paper is important – the more grams per square meter (gsm), the heavier – and more expensive – the paper. For text documents, 80gsm is suitable, while photographic prints need a minimum weight of 230gsm.

Photo paper is not just white; it comes in a selection of shades – such as pearl and oyster – each of which produces different results. The whiter the paper, the brighter the colour results.

Dye-sublimation printers require special types of paper and inkjet printers may not be able to print on all types of glossy paper, so it is important that you check your printer manual or the company website to see what paper is compatible, otherwise it could cause print problems and any serious error may invalidate the guarantee. Major printer manufacturers, such as Canon, HP and Epson, recommend printing on own-brand paper because the ink and paper are designed together to produce optimum results on the page. However the photo paper market is increasingly competitive and brands such as Tetenal, Ilford and Perma Jet are well-respected – once again check to see what paper your printer is compatible with (normally shown on a leaflet inside paper packets or online at the paper manufacturer's website) before investing.

▲ *Some printers enable you to print directly onto a range of print media, including CDs and stickers.*

If you are unsure about what paper to use, many paper manufactures produce sample packs containing a selection of different paper types, which is an advisable investment. You can also print on to stickers, postcards and CD covers, as well as canvas or fine-art paper, but these can be expensive so try to avoid wasting paper with errors, and always produce a test print first.

GET IT DONE ELSEWHERE: USING A LAB

If you don't have the time or inclination to print, and you do not want to spend money on a printer, you can send your photographs to a third party to print them. Increasingly, it isn't just the traditional photographic retailers such as Jessops and Boots that offer digital printing services – major supermarkets such as Asda and Tesco also offer this service. This can be very convenient.

TYPES OF PRINTING

High-street printing is straightforward, although it varies from store to store. Self-service kiosks are becoming increasing popular with major printing manufacturers pairing up with retailers – Jessops has Fujifilm kiosks and Boots have Kodak kiosks. You use these by inserting your memory card into a slot, and selecting the photos you want to print and the desired quantity by pressing icons on the screen. It is a very simple process and

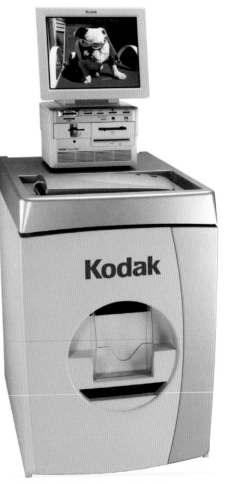

▲ *Kodak print kiosks allow you to insert your memory card and select your prints.*

you can always ask a shop assistant for help. Once completed, the machine will give you a receipt that you can take to the cashier, or you can give your memory card to the shop assistant and they will process the order for you.

The price of printing on the high street changes all the time, with the supermarkets edging out photographic stores in terms of value, but both are cheaper than home printing. In common with online photo labs the more prints you buy the cheaper the price per print tends to be. You can also reduce costs even further if you chose a longer printing time, such as next day instead of an hour.

▲ *Print kiosks are designed to be user-friendly – just follow the on-screen instructions.*

Many high street stores can print on a range of products such as mugs, t-shirts and cards, and will also burn your photographs on to CD, providing a useful back-up if you don't have a CD burner.

One of the major disadvantages of using an external printing service is that you never know what the results will be, so the standard of prints may vary.

GET IT DONE ELSEWHERE: UPLOADING TO ONLINE LABS

You can buy almost anything on the Internet and digital prints are no exception. Over the last few years there has been a huge rise in the number of online print companies. Traditional providers such as Kodak, Boots and Jessops sit alongside new web-based companies such as Photobox and SnapFish.

The advantage of buying online is that you can order prints at home and they will delivered directly to you – or the address of a friend or relative. Delivery times can range from a day to a week – most companies offer standard delivery, which can be free or cost up to £5. Alternatively, you can pay extra to have your prints delivered more quickly.

Print prices are generally cheaper online because the overheads of the online companies are low. You can also save money by buying print credits, which are stored in your account enabling you to return to the site and order prints as you desire. Shop around to find the best deal because many retailers offer introductory free prints for registering and more for referring a friend.

To save time before you upload your images you should save your photographs as JPEGs (this is the commonly accepted file

▲ To use this online printing service, you need to download software.

format because TIFF files take too long to upload) and place them all into one folder.

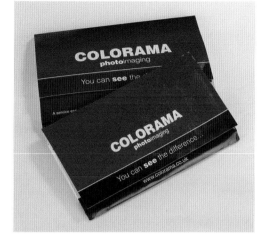

You will need to register at the website and provide your email for correspondence and your postal address for delivery. There are two methods of uploading images. Sites such as Jessops and Bonusprint need you to download a small piece of software, which you can use to transfer your pictures on to the site, whereas Photobox requires you to upload the photos directly to the site.

Ordering prints is designed to be easy and is usually a step-by-step process. You choose the number of prints, size and finish, and at the final stage you enter your credit or debit card details. Confirmation is then sent to your email address.

Some websites provide you with free memory storage for your pictures (which is often unlimited) enabling you to return and order more prints without having to upload the images again.

▼ *PhotoBox will print your pictures, and stores them in a gallery.*   ▼ *SnapFish, like many online printers, uploads files one by one.*

PRINTING YOUR PICTURES

SCANNING AT HOME: WHY?

You can convert photographs and negatives into digital files using a scanner, which is why many digital photographers choose to include a scanner in their digital darkroom set-up. Whether it is restoring prints or functioning as a camera, scanners have a multitude of uses.

The majority of households across the country will have boxes of photographs collected over the years, waiting for someone to sort them and put them in an

▼ *A scanner and a computer are all you need for a digital darkroom.*

album. A flood or a fire could destroy hundreds of pictures representing precious memories that have been collected over the years.

One way to avoid this is to invest in a scanner – a device that converts your prints or negatives to digital files through a process called digitizing. This process converts information about different light values from the picture or transparency into pixels on your computer.

▼ *Create back-ups of your old photos by scanning them.*

There are two types of scanners, and the device you need depends on what you intend to scan. Film scanners scan transparencies, including negatives and slides, and flatbed scanners scan photographs and sometimes transparencies (with an adaptor). Once a photo or negative has been digitized you can apply the same editing techniques that you would use on a digital photograph; correcting uneven horizons, repairing colour casts, cloning out unwanted elements and removing red eye. You can also use scanners to restore black and white photographs, particularly those that have been damaged and scratched.

Scanning old photographs makes it easy to share your pictures, by attaching the file to an email or incorporating them into montages and pictures books for friends and relatives. Crucially you can save the files on to a CD or portable storage device to create a back up and preserve it for future generations.

There are companies that will scan photographs for you, but it is easier (and cheaper) to do it yourself. Scanning at home is very convenient, you can set up the device next to your computer and printer and with some practice you will be creating scans in minutes.

Section Two: Computer Basics
Section Two: Computer Basics

139

FILM SCANNING

If you want to digitize transparencies, including negatives, filmstrips and slides, a film scanner is the best option. Major manufacturers including Konica Minolta, Microtek, and Nikon produce a range of devices to suit all budgets and capabilities – from a basic model that can scan 35 mm film strips to more advanced units with the capability to scan multiple slides, 35 mm strips and medium format film.

Professional photographers use drum scanners, where the picture is positioned on a drum which is then rotated very quickly as a laser passes over it, but these can cost as much as £30,000.

▲ A film scanner to suit advanced users.

MAKING A SCAN

In a film scanner light is beamed through a transparency and is picked up by a sensor. The scanning must take place in a self-contained environment, because any dust on the transparency will be picked up by the scan and will ruin the image.

The film is held in a plastic frame, which then slots in to the scanner. You will need to ensure the slide is positioned the right way around otherwise the picture will be scanned in reverse. Check the handbook supplied with your scanner if you are unsure.

SCANNING CONSIDERATIONS

There are many scanners on the market, so whether you are investing in a film or flatbed device it is important to know exactly what to look for.

- The speed of your scan depends on the connection between the computer and scanner. If you are scanning numerous files at the same time, opt for Firewire or USB 2.0, which provide fast transfer speeds. Standard USB connection is much slower, offering transfer speeds of 1.5 Mb per second, but this will be adequate if you are only planning on the occasional scan.

- When scanning a transparency (slide) you will be increasing its size, so choose a film scanner (or flatbed scanner with a transparency unit) with a minimum resolution of 2,400 pixels per inch (ppi.) If you are scanning prints look for a device with a resolution of 1,200 ppi or higher.

- Look for a scanner with a minimum bit-depth of 24-bits, 8-bits each for the red, green and blue channels. Some scanners offer higher colour depths of 36-bit and 48-bit. The higher the bit depth, the more gradation of subtle tones can be saved and the more naturalistic your images will look.

- If you have lots of slides to scan at the same resolution, it is worth investing in a scanner that can scan frames in a batch; that way you can set it up and leave it to scan.

- Ensure that the scanner and supplied driver software are compatible with your operating system.

FLATBED SCANNING

Flatbed scanners are used primarily for scanning photographs, but many include a transparency adaptor so that you can scan negatives, slides and photos. These hybrid devices have become increasingly superior over the last few years, making them a good option for anyone who

▲ Lift the lid and position the photo on the glass bed.

wants to scan transparencies and photographs. Flatbed scanners tend to be more affordable than their film counterparts – it is possible to get a rudimentary A4 scanner for under £50, which will be adequate for occasional use.

▼ The Canon Canoscan 9950F is aimed at slightly more advanced users.

The leading manufacturers of flatbed scanners – Canon, Epson, HP, Umax and Microtek – produce devices in a range of sizes.

A4 is probably the most common, although A3 scanners are becoming more widely available. There is a big difference in price between the two sizes, making A4 the most affordable option for the home user. HP has introduced a 6 x 4 inch scanner, specifically for scanning enprint photographs, which is powered by batteries so that it can be used whilst on the move.

MAKING A SCAN

Flatbed scanners work by shining light on to the surface of the photo, where it is reflected and caught by the sensor (CCD, or charge coupled device). Before you begin to make a scan, turn the device on for a few minutes to allow it to warm up. Care needs to be taken to ensure the photo is dust-free and that the glass plate is clean, otherwise particles of dirt may be visible in the scan.

▲ *This flatbed can scan photos and 35 mm negatives, and is a good choice for those on a budget.*

Open the plastic hood and position the photo on the glass plate. Make sure it is aligned carefully, or you may have to rotate the photo using your scanning software which can lead to a reduction in picture quality. Photographs are scanned on one side, which means it doesn't matter if you perform the scan with the lid open. The easiest way to make a scan is to hit the 'Quick Scan' button (located on the front of many new scanners) although for a greater degree of control you can perform the scan using the software on your computer. You will hear a whirring noise as a sensor positioned inside moves up and down making the scan.

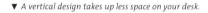
▼ *A vertical design takes up less space on your desk.*

SCANNING ENHANCEMENTS

A negative or slide contains lots of information about the picture – such as shadows and highlights – that is not evident when you print. By using a scanner you obtain access to this information and can make adjustments as you wish.

Decent scanning software enables you to adjust effects like the hue and saturation and levels and highlights. You can choose to do this automatically, or manually which offers you more control.

When you scan a transparency or photograph you can choose the output size and resolution – the larger the resolution you use to make a scan (of a picture or negative) the larger the file size will be and the longer the scan will take. To save space – and time -

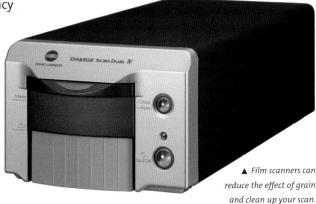

▲ *Film scanners can reduce the effect of grain and clean up your scan.*

scan using the lowest resolution and size you need, this may mean experimenting with several scans to find out what is suitable.

When you make a scan you can choose to crop and enlarge a specific area. By cropping selectively and enlarging one particular section many times, it is possible to highlight a specific aspect of the photo and get a completely different picture to the one you started with.

Digital Camera Handbook

▼ The preview screen of the Microtek ScanMaker 8700.

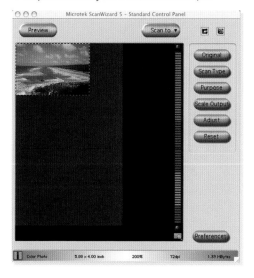

When you scan a photo or film you initially make a preview (or pre-scan) that you can use to gauge any effects. At this point you can choose to crop the picture or make any tonal adjustments. In some scanners though, the preview screen does not offer an accurate representation, so you can only use it as a guide. When you have completed your scan, it is important to check the sharpness and rescan it if necessary.

The majority of advanced film and flatbed scanners are supplied with dust and scratch removal software. Programs such as Canon Film Automatic Retouching Enhancement (FARE) Level 3 and Epson Digital ICE are designed to recognize and remove flaws – such as dust – from a scan. Utilizing scratch removal software will slow down the speed of the scan. Combine scratch-removal software with features found in your picture-editing software, such as the Photoshop clone-stamp tool, healing brush and patch tool and you will easily be able to scan and restore old or damaged pictures to their former glory.

You can also scan 3-D objects with some flatbed scanners, such as feathers and rocks, by positioning them on the glass bed. Only scanners with CCD sensors can do this. Some scanners and AIOs (all-in-ones, which are printer/scanner/fax combinations also known as MDFs, or multi-functional devices) have a different kind of sensor with a much lower depth of focus. However, whichever scanner you have, you need to be careful not to scratch the glass surface, ensure the objects are dry and whatever you do, don't force the lid if the object is bulky.

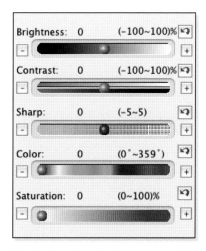

▲ Adjustments can be made when you scan a photo.

Section Two: Computer Basics

SHOOTING PROJECTS
LANDSCAPES

The rural landscape remains the greatest inspiration for hobbyist photographers. Luckily good subjects are all around us, and few of us live far from an area of natural beauty – whether farmland, woodland, lakes, mountains, deserts or coast.

▲ *Rural landscapes work particularly well.*

Most landscape photographers aim to capture an idealized view, free from cars, people, pylons, and other examples of modern life. This is one reason why they rise before dawn to be at their location when it is at its most undisturbed. This is also usually when the light is at its best, and good light is the most important ingredient of a successful landscape photograph.

Landscapes can be photographed at any time of day though, as long as the light is good, and this does not necessarily mean sunshine. Fog, mist, rain and stormy skies are often more photogenic than bland summer sun. Obtaining the best light means studying it and waiting – minutes, hours, maybe even weeks or months – for that magic, fleeting moment.

Composition is crucial. A distant view from a hilltop may look great when you are there, but pictures where all the points of interest are at the horizon rarely succeed. The best

▲ *Holidays offer a great opportunity for capturing unusual landscapes.*

Digital Camera Handbook

▲ *Clouds and natural features can be used to frame a landscape.*

landscapes usually contain detail from foreground to horizon. Look for features such as gates, dry stone walls or flora to fill the void at the front of your picture.

With few exceptions, everything in the picture should be sharp, which means using a small aperture and focusing on a point in the middle distance to ensure crisp focus from foreground to horizon. In practice, this will probably mean using a tripod, for stability at the slow shutter speeds.

Landscape photographers often favour wideangle lenses – more of the scene is in shot, the foreground has greater emphasis (for a better sense of perspective) and there is greater apparent depth of field. However, good landscape photographers are also able to see and home in on interesting details within a scene, either close up or in the distance, perhaps using a telephoto lens to isolate them from their surroundings.

▼ *Bustling city scenes offer plenty of interesting detail and contrast well with rural scenes.*

TOP 5 TIPS

1 Wait for great light and, if possible, arrive at your destination very early.
2 Frame the subject to include points of interest from foreground to background.
3 Use a tripod and set the lens to a small aperture for maximum depth of field.
4 Use wideangles for a more dramatic perspective, telephotos to isolate details.
5 Revisit locations at different times of year to record the changes.

SUNRISE & SUNSET

▲ *A stunning sunset shot is well worth the wait.*

Despite the cliché status of sunrises and sunsets, we never seem to get tired of them. They are nature at its most majestic, most magnificent. Taking good photographs of them, though, is not always so easy. This is partly because the automatic exposure and white balance functions of digital cameras conspire to eliminate just those qualities that make them so appealing in the first place, and partly because we are often so wrapped up in how lovely the sky looks that we fail to pay sufficient attention to what is going on in the foreground.

Clean, simple, uncluttered foregrounds work best. The most successful examples are those where the foreground makes an interesting and instantly recognisable silhouette. Bare winter trees, for example, or people can make very interesting foreground silhouettes. One of the best types of foreground is water: lakes, rivers, the sea – even a big puddle – because it reflects the beauty of the sky.

Sunrise and sunset prop up either end of the day like bookends. It does not matter which you shoot – both can produce spectacular results. Sunrise has the advantage of being quieter, with fewer people and cars to spoil things, but you have to get up very early to catch it.

Whichever you choose you should be at your selected spot well in advance. Use a tripod for stability. Your auto white balance will try to neutralise the colour, remove the orange hue, so turn off the auto and set it to daylight for maximum saturation – or for more control, shoot RAW files and sort out the colour balance later. You may find that auto-exposure produces unsatisfactory results too, as it tries to lighten your sky. Either take a manual reading from a bright part of the sky (but not the sun), or use exposure compensation of minus 1–2 stops. Once the sky reaches maximum saturation keep shooting until well after it has gone, especially at sunset when you can get some wonderful effects from the afterglow. Finally, bear in mind that the further north you go, the longer you have to shoot your sunset. The nearer the equator you are, the faster the sun goes down.

▼ *Silhouetted buildings look very dramatic.*

TOP 5 TIPS

1 Choose an interesting foreground, such as water, or a recognisable silhouette.
2 Get there early, and use a tripod.
3 Set the white balance to daylight – not auto.
4 Meter from the sky and check your exposures. Underexposure increases saturation.
5 Take lots of pictures, and keep shooting until well after the sun has risen or set.

SHOOTING PROJECTS

▼ *Capturing movement can result in dramatic shots.*

SPORT & ACTION

We've all got pictures of half a car or part of a person just leaving the frame as we tried to photograph them but were a split second too late pressing the shutter. It doesn't help that digital cameras in particular have a reputation for being slow to react to fast-moving situations. While this issue has now been largely solved on the newer cameras, even the swiftest cameras will let you down with fast action unless you adopt a few useful techniques.

There are two ways to shoot action: freeze the motion or introduce deliberate blur to convey the sense of speed. For family action shots the former is generally preferred so you will need to select a fairly fast shutter speed, either via shutter priority mode, manual or sports mode. If you have selected a speed too fast for the prevailing conditions your camera should warn you, but review your efforts on the LCD to be sure. To introduce an element of

▲ *The hustle and bustle of busy commuters is caught in this shot.*

Digital Camera Handbook
Digital Camera Handbook

TOP 5 TIPS

1 Set a fast shutter speed to freeze action.
2 Set a slower speed to add creative blur to convey movement.
3 Set the camera to manual focus and pre-focus on where the action will occur.
4 Select continuous drive mode and, if no manual focus, continuous AF.
5 Position yourself so that fast moving subjects are coming towards you.

deliberate blur you will need a slower speed (1/30sec or below, depending on the type of action) and either allow the subject to blur itself as it moves, or follow the subject's motion with the camera to create a streaked background.

Whichever approach you prefer you still need the camera to fire at the right moment, and there are ways to maximise its responsiveness. Turn off the autofocus and pre-focus on a spot where you know the action will take place. If you can't turn it off, use the focus lock. Failing all that, at least set the camera to continuous AF mode, which lets you take a picture without having to lock focus first. Set the drive to continuous too, so that the camera will keep shooting as long as your finger is on the shutter.

Pressing the shutter as you pan will minimise the risk of the subject leaving the frame before the shutter goes off. Alternatively, practise pressing the shutter just before the subject comes into the frame. If you position yourself so the motion is coming towards you rather than across

▼ A slower shutter speed blurs movement for an artistic effect.

your path, the illusion of speed is minimised, improving your chances of getting it both correctly framed and in focus. This technique is especially useful for motorsport photography. Remember that objects moving across the frame need a much faster shutter speed to freeze them than objects coming towards you.

Section   Two: Computer   Basics

CHILDREN

Making a record of your children's lives as they are growing up is something that both you and they will treasure when you are all much older.

With digital cameras there is no excuse for not being trigger happy, because it doesn't cost anything and you can delete the failures later. But don't just record the key events – the big family get-togethers – nor make them

▲ Try to record as much as you can of your children's lives.

grimace into the camera with fake smiles. Instead, make an effort to capture those smaller, more intimate moments when they are playing in the garden, or riding their bikes, or they are indoors doing arts and crafts. These are the moments you will remember and treasure. You can set up fun activities for the children with picture taking in mind.

▼ Children make great unselfconscious subjects.

In general, unposed shots with natural expressions that capture the children's personalities are far superior, and will bring back much more poignant memories, than posed shots. But there is nothing wrong with getting them to look into the camera if you can get genuine expressions – smiles or

▼ *Be ready to capture spontaneous moments.*

otherwise – out of them. Even the odd tantrum or sulking shot will raise a smile when viewed in later years.

Your best strategy when photographing children is to be always ready and react quickly to events. Close range shooting with a wideangle lens will provide impact and a sense of intimacy. Pre-setting a camera to manual focus, a mid-range aperture and focal point of about 3 m (10 ft) will cut down the shutter lag and make picture taking almost instantaneous. In low light set a high ISO rather than flash, which will remind them of your presence. When photographing children at close range it is generally best to get down to their level. This creates a more intimate image and gives the viewer a sense of entering the child's world, rather than being an outsider looking at the tops of their heads. That said, sometimes a shot looking directly down, with children looking up, can add humour or a sense of pathos to a situation.

With SLR cameras, or models with good zooms, an alternative strategy is to step well back with a long lens so they forget you're there, and observe, with your finger hovering on the shutter. Don't just go for full length shots showing what they are doing – zoom right in and get some frame filling head shots too.

▲ *Get down to your child's level for the best shots.*

TOP 5 TIPS

1 Take lots of pictures, all the time, and not just at special occasions.
2 Go for natural expressions, not forced smiles. Get some sad and grumpy shots too.
3 Pre-focus or set manual focus to cut the shutter delay and be always ready.
4 At close range stoop down to their level rather than looking down at them
5 Try standing some distance away and shooting candids with a telephoto lens.

WEDDINGS

Few things are as intimidating to a photographer as being asked to photograph a wedding. The responsibility of capturing what is, to your clients, the most important day of their lives, can be overwhelming. Careful planning and organization will make it run smoothly.

Firstly, talk to the couple to ascertain their needs. Find out the location, the number of guests, timings and the logistics of the day. Many young couples now prefer an informal fly-on-the-wall approach to the traditional posed shots, but a good wedding shoot should be a mix of both styles. Older guests will expect a few group shots, and these are the only opportunities to make sure that you have a decent shot of everyone who was there, because it is easy to miss people when using the reportage approach. It is also advisable to have a few posed shots of the couple, but don't keep guests hanging around while you take them – keep it brief. Be loud, clear and decisive in your instructions so people know when they are needed..

▲ *Interesting shots of the venue will break up the photos.*

Scout the venues beforehand to seek out potential locations for the posed shots, either outside the wedding venue or the reception. Go for places out of direct sun and with plain, undistracting (but not ugly) backgrounds. Make a list of the shots

Digital Camera Handbook

▼ *Be ready to capture spontaneous moments.*

otherwise – out of them. Even the odd tantrum or sulking shot will raise a smile when viewed in later years.

Your best strategy when photographing children is to be always ready and react quickly to events. Close range shooting with a wideangle lens will provide impact and a sense of intimacy. Pre-setting a camera to manual focus, a mid-range aperture and focal point of about 3 m (10 ft) will cut down the shutter lag and make picture taking almost instantaneous. In low light set a high ISO rather than flash, which will remind them of your presence. When photographing children at close range it is generally best to get down to their level. This creates a more intimate image and gives the viewer a sense of entering the child's world, rather than being an outsider looking at the tops of their heads. That said, sometimes a shot looking directly down, with children looking up, can add humour or a sense of pathos to a situation.

With SLR cameras, or models with good zooms, an alternative strategy is to step well back with a long lens so they forget you're there, and observe, with your finger hovering on the shutter. Don't just go for full length shots showing what they are doing – zoom right in and get some frame filling head shots too.

▲ *Get down to your child's level for the best shots.*

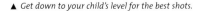

TOP 5 TIPS

1 Take lots of pictures, all the time, and not just at special occasions.
2 Go for natural expressions, not forced smiles. Get some sad and grumpy shots too.
3 Pre-focus or set manual focus to cut the shutter delay and be always ready.
4 At close range stoop down to their level rather than looking down at them
5 Try standing some distance away and shooting candids with a telephoto lens.

Section Two: Computer Basics

WEDDINGS

Few things are as intimidating to a photographer as being asked to photograph a wedding. The responsibility of capturing what is, to your clients, the most important day of their lives, can be overwhelming. Careful planning and organization will make it run smoothly.

Firstly, talk to the couple to ascertain their needs. Find out the location, the number of guests, timings and the logistics of the day. Many young couples now prefer an informal fly-on-the-wall approach to the traditional posed shots, but a good wedding shoot should be a mix of both styles. Older guests will expect a few group shots, and these are the only opportunities to make sure that you have a decent shot of everyone who was there, because it is easy to miss people when using the reportage approach. It is also advisable to have a few posed shots of the couple, but don't keep guests hanging around while you take them – keep it brief. Be loud, clear and decisive in your instructions so people know when they are needed..

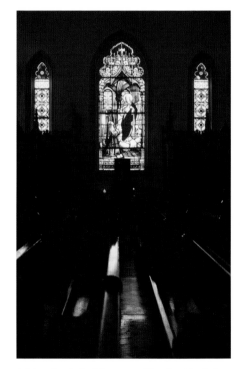

▲ *Interesting shots of the venue will break up the photos.*

Scout the venues beforehand to seek out potential locations for the posed shots, either outside the wedding venue or the reception. Go for places out of direct sun and with plain, undistracting (but not ugly) backgrounds. Make a list of the shots

Digital Camera Handbook

you need to get: exchanging the rings, cutting the cake etc. and refer to it on the day. Find out if there are any restrictions on taking pictures during the ceremony. If you are allowed to shoot, be discreet, and don't use flash. Natural light looks better and is less obtrusive.

▲ Look for interesting angles for the standard shots.

Check your equipment before the day and make sure you have a spare camera and batteries. You can never have too many spare memory cards or batteries. Check all your settings before shooting, and refer to the histogram to ensure the exposures are good. Be careful with white dresses in sunshine, which can burn out and lose detail, especially when the groom is wearing a dark suit.

▼ Try to keep the posed shots as natural as possible.

Afterwards back-up the pictures immediately, for safety. Finally, if you are not the official photographer and are just taking some behind the scenes shots, try not to get in the way of the professional.

TOP 5 TIPS

1 Talk to the couple beforehand to discuss their needs.
2 Scout the venues beforehand to look for suitable locations for posed shots.
3 Take a mix of posed groups and single shots plus natural candids.
4 Work quickly and decisively. Don't delay people for too long.
5 Take a spare camera. Check settings and results regularly. Back-up immediately.

▼ Even a market stall can make an exotic photograph.

TRAVEL

Few genres are as rich in subject matter as other people's countries. There is something about visiting foreign, unfamiliar places that fires up the creative juices and lets us see potential pictures in things that locals may have long since failed to notice.

When we think of travel photography we usually picture images of the Eiffel Tower or the Taj Mahal. But, while it is unthinkable that we should not photograph these

▲ The most ordinary subjects can make fascinating, unusual images.

familiar clichés when we visit them, try to see them with fresh eyes, and seek out viewpoints and treatments that will put a refreshing new spin on them.

Most importantly, don't limit yourself to pictures of grand views and world icons. Travel photography is all about telling the story

of the place – to convey a sense of the essence of the culture for those who have not been there. Try to capture little vignettes that encapsulate the spirit of the place you are visiting. Perhaps the unusual foods displayed on a market stall, or a sign over a shop door. Look for the small details as well as the wide shots. Use the full range of your lenses to capture the wide spectrum of subjects.

A country is its people as well as its geographical features. Take some portraits of interesting locals. Nice, tightly cropped head shots of colourful characters are always effective but pay them the respect of asking them first, even if only in a non-verbal way – unless of course you are shooting candids and are able to work unobserved.

There are a few practical considerations too. Choose a gadget bag that you can carry on your flight as hand luggage. Never check your cameras in the hold. Pack plenty of spare media cards and spare batteries. Take a tripod, even if only a pocket one, so that you can take sunsets and night shots of spectacular views. If you have a lot of kit pack a smaller day bag so that you can leave some of the heavy stuff at your hotel. Do not show off your gear but keep it discreetly in your bag or under a jacket when not in use.

▶ Look out for unusual architecture.

TOP 5 TIPS

1 Pack spare cards and batteries and take your gear as hand luggage.
2 Try to find new and original approaches to familiar icons.
3 Work to tell a story of the place, in pictures, and convey its spirit and culture.
4 Look for small details as well as general views.
5 Photograph the people, if they don't mind, but desist if they object.

SHOOTING PROJECTS

Section Two: Computer Basics

TRANSPORT

▲ *Shiny, metallic surfaces work best in diffused light.*

One of the most popular photographic subjects is transport. You can see a wealth of cameras at any air show, car show or steam railway. On the ground in a static situation, the techniques required for successful transport photographs are much the same as any others. Diffused, overcast light is generally best because the vehicles' shiny metallic surfaces reflect the sun and cause hot spots. A polarising filter is an essential addition to your lens, for reducing any reflections on the surface and dramatically boosting the colour saturation.

Wideangle lenses will capture the whole subject and lend a dynamic perspective which is particularly appropriate in this

▲ *You can even use a vehicle as a frame for your scene.*

genre. At the big shows you often find large crowds, so a telephoto or macro lens is ideal for zooming in on interesting details and excluding other people.

You may find the exposure compensation button is useful here, as very dark subjects (e.g. black metal) and very bright ones (shiny chrome) fool your camera's light meter.

Once your favoured subjects start moving, you will need to employ a different set of techniques. Air shows, for example, are notoriously difficult to shoot well. Not only is your subject travelling very fast but may at times be quite far away and at others right over your head. Aeroplanes also silhouette against a bright sky. You will need to use a fast shutter speed and experiment with the exposure settings. You will generally find you need to increase the exposure by one or two stops over what the meter says to render the aircraft correctly.

TOP 5 TIPS

1 If you have the choice, choose overcast days with soft light.
2 Use a polarizer to remove reflections and increase colour saturation.
3 Take a wideangle to get large machines in shot from close range.
4 Use a longer lens to capture interesting details.
5 Use a versatile zoom lens and manual metering for flying shots at airshows.

For tips on photographing moving cars and trains read the sports section (page 150). However, railway photography usually revolves around vintage engines and includes the whole culture: the stations, with their old enamel signs, the staff in their traditional old uniforms and so forth, so be sure to capture the bigger picture.

▲ *All forms of transport make interesting photos.*

DOCUMENTARY

Documentary photography (known also as photojournalism or reportage) is quite different from most other genres. It is not primarily a pictorialist subject – the aim is not to create an attractive image but to tell a story. It isn't a single image genre, but about about creating a body of work, with

each photograph forming a component. It can be on any subject, but usually revolves around people, society and culture.

Many famous photojournalists have made a name tackling the big issues – poverty, famine, war – but others have dedicated their lives to recording the changing face of their communities. In fact, a project can go on for as long as deemed necessary – a week, a year or an entire lifetime.

▲ *Travelling lends itself naturally to documentary.*

A great image should always be the aim, and every project should include a few individual shots that stand out for their pictorial qualities, but not every picture needs to be visually appealing. If you feel your story would be enhanced by including a close-up of a sign over a door, or the contents of a cupboard, don't let its lack of visual appeal get in your way.

There are no rules of documentary photography, so no specific techniques. It can even cross into other genres. A project to document a community could be comprised entirely of posed portraits, while another project illustrating environmental destruction may be all landscapes – if not the kind you would want to put on a postcard.

▲ Capturing a culture can make a great series of photos.

If taking on a long term project appeals to you, choose your project carefully. Pick something accessible. You could work it around your daily routine – perhaps a story on commuting, or a club to which you belong. It could be record of local tradespeople at work, or the construction of a new civic building, from foundations to completion.

Whatever you choose, obtain the consent of your subjects; you need them on side. You are liable to arouse hostility if you take photographs surreptitiously, and while you may be able to grab the odd candid, it is unlikely that you will be able to complete an entire project without being detected.

Once it is complete (or even beforehand), aim to share your project by having it published in a book or magazine, or exhibited at a local venue or online.

◄ Include relevant objects as well as people and scenes.

TOP 5 TIPS

1 Choose an accessible subject.
2 Tell its story in a series of images.
3 Don't aim for every shot to be great. Think of the overall story.
4 Your project can last a week or a lifetime.
5 Documentary projects cry out to be seen. Aim to exhibit or publish it at some point.

Section Two: Computer Basics

ANIMALS & PETS

Wildlife photography can be extremely challenging because of the dangerous or elusive nature of your subjects, but you may find domesticated animals just as rewarding. Cats and dogs make great subjects for pictures. Cats have their famous aloofness, dogs their intrinsic comedic value – both make natural subjects. On the farm, animals such as cows and pigs are also ideal camera fodder.

▲ *Be prepared to shoot quickly when photographing animals.*

Like children, animals are easy to photograph, but difficult to photograph well. A resting cat can seemingly hold the same expression for hours, while at the other extreme a dog in the park rarely keeps still long enough to see their expression. Patience, and a willingness to contrive pictorial situations is the key. By always keeping a camera handy you will always be ready when situations occur.

Animals tend to photograph well when captured head-on, looking directly into the camera. Zoom in tight to fill the frame for maximum impact, preferably at a wide aperture to throw the background out of focus. Don't be afraid to make a fool of yourself by clucking and making silly noises to attract the animal's attention and elicit some good expressions.

▲ *Animal shots work well head-on.*

Alternatively getting someone to assist, such as standing beside you holding a ball or a stick for a dog, or perhaps teasing a cat with a length of string, will help you get more animated shots. Food treats are also a good attention grabber. You can attempt to take some action shots by throwing a stick, but you will need to be quick. To capture a running dog, try to fill the frame and pan, using a long telephoto lens.

On the farm you will be less able to interact with your subjects, so patience is the best policy. Go for tightly cropped head shots or go wide and show them in their environment. Cows grazing in early morning mist is a classic favourite.

Exposure can be a problem with some animals, especially those with dark or light fur. Dark fur can easily underexpose because it absorbs so much light. White fur in sunshine can burn out and lose all detail. Try overexposing by a stop with dark animals and underexposing with brightly lit white ones, but check the histogram on the camera to make sure.

▼ Light fur may require some underexposure.

TOP 5 TIPS

1 Always keep a camera ready for any great pet moments at home. Be patient.
2 For portraits, fill the frame. Attract their attention with a toy or by making noises.
3 Try using a ball, toy or food treat to catch their attention and direct their gaze.
4 Visit a farm park to get good close ups or environmental shots of farm animals.
5 Increase the metered exposure for dark-furred animals, decrease it for white fur.

Section Two: Computer Basics

WILDLIFE

▼ Capturing wild animals on camera requires great patience.

Wildlife photography is a challenging genre. In addition to the obvious photographic skills, successful wildlife photographers need an encyclopedic knowledge of the subject, and lots of patience. First, rather than wandering aimlessly in the forest snapping anything that comes along, choose a subject that you wish to photograph and seek it out. It helps if it lives in an area local to you, because you can spend more time on your quest and get to know your subject better. Next, read up on the behavioural habits of your subject: where it lives, what it eats, when it comes out to feed and so forth.

Most wildlife is shy and there are two approaches to getting close to it: stalking or finding a spot and lying in wait. Learning to quietly creep up on your subject without it noticing is a skill that must be learned through practice. Equally, many wildlife photographers spend not just hours but days sitting silently in a hide – a small camouflaged den made of wood, canvas or other material in which the photographer waits, with small holes for the lens to protrude from.

▲ A zoom or telephoto lens is well worth investing in.

If all this sounds like too much commitment there are easier ways. Stick with common, accessible subjects such as squirrels or birds. You can attract wildlife to your garden by planting the right shrubs or putting out appropriate food.

If your taste is for more exotic wildlife, such as big cats, then you have two options: go on a wildlife safari (there are some tailored especially for photographers) or visit the zoo or safari park. You can get surprisingly good shots in these places, if you compose carefully to avoid including cages, cars and crowds in the shot.

TOP 5 TIPS

1 Study your subject. Find out where it lives, what it eats etc.
2 Stick with local subjects to start with – they are more accessible.
3 Try attracting wildlife to your garden, and shooting from the house.
4 Practice in zoos and wildlife parks. Crop tightly to exclude giveaway details.
5 Make sure you have at least one decent zoom/telephoto in the 200–400 mm range.

▲ A wildlife safari will ensure you get some great photos.

Whichever approach you take, there are certain equipment needs common to almost all wildlife photography, the most important of which is a long telephoto lens. Some photographers prefer zooms, for their versatility, others favour fixed focal length lenses for their faster maximum apertures. Either way, whether you are shooting in your garden, at the zoo, or on the Serengeti, you are likely to need lenses of at least 200 mm (equivalent) and maybe up to 600 mm. Shorter lenses can be used for environmental shots, where the animal is a small part of a wider view showing the setting. These shots provide context, but you will still want the close-ups. A sturdy tripod is also essential when using big lenses.

NATURE

Although wildlife and rural landscapes could be considered nature subjects, the term usually

▼ Look for bright colours and interesting shapes.

refs to the photography of plants, flowers, trees and the butterflies, bees and small scale creatures that live off them.

Nature photography is generally conducted in situ, and with an ethic that involves leaving your subjects the way you found them – undisturbed and unmolested. In some situations subjects can be removed with a clear conscience and taken to a studio environment (fallen leaves, for example).

▲ Insect close-ups can make stunning photographs.

The ideal light for most close range nature photography is soft, overcast light, which creates virtually shadowless illumination. Bright sun can cast harsh and distracting shadows on the subject, which makes it difficult to see fine detail, and reduces colour saturation. In some situations a strong sidelight or backlight can add an element of atmosphere, creating (in the case of backlighting, for example) an attractive halo around the subject.

▼ *Quick responses are required when photographing natural subjects.*

When photographing subjects such as flowers close up, use a tripod for stability, and make sure the background is blurred so as not to cause a distraction. You may find it easier to get further back and zoom in using a longer telephoto lens to achieve this. If you are at or near ground level a small beanbag may be easier to use than a tripod.

To enhance the light you can use creased foil or white paper as small reflectors. Occasionally, fill-in flash can be useful, in small doses. Commercially made reflectors fold up very small but can open up to provide useful fill light as well as a shield to stop the wind blowing your subject around – and therefore in and out of focus. Another trick is to use a thin piece of stiff wire behind the stem (out of camera shot) as a splint, to help keep the plant steady.

▼ *Catching the right light can make all the difference.*

TOP 5 TIPS

1　Soft overcast light is generally most flattering.
2　Low side or backlight can help to create a sense of atmosphere.
3　Use a tripod or beanbag for stability.
4　Set a wide aperture – perhaps combined with a long lens – to blur the background.
5　Use reflectors (bought or homemade) to modify the light and create a windbreak.

CLOSE-UPS

▲ *Wildlife close-ups can make stunning photos.*

There is a whole world of beauty and wonder, pattern, shape and colour just waiting to be photographed if only you can get close enough. Luckily almost all digital cameras come equipped with a macro mode that lets you get within a finger's length of your subject, and often even closer, though with digital SLRs you may need to use a macro lens or attach a supplementary close-up accessory to your existing lens.

There are two ways to choose a close-up subject. You can go out into the world and home in on leaves and plants, vehicle details etc., or you can create your own subjects at home – slice a kiwi fruit in half, or raid the children's toy cupboard. By careful use of composition it is easy to create images that show an unexpected, perhaps even unrecognisable, view of a normally familiar subject.

There are, however, some technical challenges that must be overcome. Firstly, as you get closer to your subject the depth

▲ *Unusual views of everyday subjects work well.*

▼ *Most cameras have a macro mode.*

of field diminishes, until at very close range it is reduced to a narrow plane of just a few millimetres, even at the smallest aperture. This means that accurate focusing becomes critical. A tripod is essential for macro work because a tiny movement of the camera can make the difference between a picture being in or out of focus. For small scale macro work a tabletop tripod is sufficient, though for nature close-ups in the field you will need a full size one.

This shallow depth also means that you must exercise care in your composition, manoeuvring either yourself or your subject so that the important plane of interest aligns with the plane of focus. You can, alternatively, use this rapid loss of sharpness to your compositional advantage, using it to draw the eye to a sharp focal point in a sea of blur.

Lighting can be challenging at close range. Outside close ups should be less of a problem – perhaps a small reflector to give daylight a helping hand – but indoors try experimenting with window light and artificial light such as table lamps. Does your subject look best with a soft diffused light or a hard, directional one? As always, shoot many variations and check your results on the LCD screen as you go.

TOP 5 TIPS

1 Look for subjects that are interesting or unusual at close range.

2 Set your camera to the macro mode, if you have one. (Almost all compacts do).

3 Use a tripod. Fire the shutter using the self timer to minimise vibration.

4 You'll get minimal depth of field, even at small apertures. Make the most of this.

5 Take care over your lighting. Review your efforts on the LCD to see how it looks.

▶ *You may need a tripod when shooting close-ups.*

▼ Interesting shapes and patterns are all around us.

STILL LIFE

A still life is a pictorial representation of one or more inanimate objects, arranged and lit in a visually pleasing way. It has been popular for centuries with painters and it is no less so with photographers.

There are two types of still life: the type you find and the type you create. Found still life subjects are often natural objects such as pebbles on a beach, or fallen leaves in autumn. This also includes accidental art created by weeds growing out of a rusty bucket, or bottles on a windowsill. Still life subjects are all around us if only we look

▲ The most ordinary subjects can become works of art.

Digital Camera Handbook

for them, though many need a little helping hand to maximise their potential – perhaps moving one of the elements slightly, or removing something distracting from the background.

Then there is the still life you create – on a table in the kitchen, or a studio light table. You bring all the elements together, arrange them, light them and photograph them. Any object is suitable, though if you are photographing a collection of objects it helps if there is a common theme. A still life of an apple, a razor and a toy train, for example, would not necessarily make much sense.

Both types of still life need common attributes. The most important of these is good, sympathetic lighting. Whether it be hard or soft, warm or cool, a still life will rarely inspire gasps of admiration if it is not exquisitely lit, and still life photographers spend hours adjusting the light.

If you are outdoors you can't change the light, but you can modify it with

▲ *Make sure you get the lighting right for the best effect.*

reflectors, diffusers or a blip of fill flash, or you can return another day when the light has changed. Indoors you are creating the light. Use the natural light from a window, or artificial lights, such as table lamps or professional studio lighting. Either way, use white or metallic reflectors and black card to direct and channel the light to where you want it.

With an indoor still life pay special attention to the choice of background too. Plain white is fine, but you can use textured art paper, foil, fabric, wood, sheet metal, ceramic tiles, piles of leaves or whatever you think appropriate.

TOP 5 TIPS

1 Look for natural still life subjects around you.
2 Create you own still life on a table at home.
3 With collections of objects make sure they have a common theme.
4 With a created still life, choose a sympathetic and attractive background.
5 Lighting is crucial. Spend time getting it right.

ARCHITECTURE

Architecture is photogenic. From the pyramids and Stonehenge, to the Guggenheim and the Empire State Building, we love to photograph buildings, both ancient and modern. There are some difficulties though. We may not be able to stand where we want, because other buildings are in our way. The light may be coming from the wrong angle, or there may be too many people.

▲ *Look for striking buildings wherever you go.*

The first thing to remember about buildings is that you cannot move them, so if the light is not where you want it, return at another time. Observe which façade the light strikes at a given time of day (a compass is useful here) and if you want to shoot the

Digital   Camera   Handbook

▲ *Find an interesting viewpoint.*

front, but it is west facing, you know that you will need to return in the afternoon.

Having arrived at the optimum time, the next task is to locate a viewpoint that minimizes distortion of the building. In an ideal world you would be positioned in the centre of the façade, some distance back, with a telephoto lens. Assuming you can find a central spot, you will probably be quite close and will have to use a wideangle and tilt the camera upwards to capture the top. This results in 'keystoning' or converging verticals, where the sides lean in and the building appears to be toppling over backwards. There are two solutions: try to find a higher viewpoint – such as a balcony opposite, at half the height of the building you are photographing, or get it as straight as you can and correct the perspective later on your PC.

With many buildings there are lots of opportunities for close up detail shots: gargoyles and ornate stonework on old buildings, radical angles and glass reflections in new ones. Use a telephoto lens to isolate them if necessary.

Most cities also offer a high vantage point from where you can get good shots of the entire skyline. The best time is often early or late in the day when the sun is lower in the sky and less harsh. Evenings are particularly good because the buildings are often lit up, which adds an extra visual dimension. Go for wideangle views or pick out details with a telephoto.

▲ *Even fake skylines make a striking photograph!*

TOP 5 TIPS

1. Note which way buildings face and shoot at the right time of day for the best light.
2. Shoot from a central position to minimise distortion. Avoid tilting the camera.
3. With tall buildings try to find a higher viewpoint so you can keep the camera level.
4. Look for interesting details that you can zoom in on.
5. Shoot city skylines from a high vantage point. Choose sunset or night for drama.

INTERIORS

There are so many beautiful architectural interiors in the world – in cathedrals, theatres, stately homes and other buildings, that you could photograph nothing else and never run out of subjects. But many photographers are intimidated by them, thinking that they require a great deal of specialized equipment.

There are some basic equipment needs that will make life easier, but for many locations all you need is a tripod. There are, for example, many stunning modern interiors, often with vast expanses of glass letting in a great deal of natural light. A tripod lets the photographer ensure that the camera is completely level, and allows the use of small apertures for maximum depth of field, but is not essential.

Most interiors photography, however, is of much older buildings, where light is low and a tripod is necessary – as is a decent wideangle lens, although if it is too wide you will struggle with distortion.

For general views of cavernous interiors such as cathedrals, set you camera up on the tripod at one end and make sure it is pointing straight ahead. Tilt it upwards and sides will appear to lean inwards – though in some cases, this kind of deliberate, exaggerated distortion can work well, especially to emphasize height.

▲ *Look for natural frames when shooting interiors.*

Digital Camera Handbook

▲ *Adjust white balance settings to accommodate different lighting sources.*

In low light it may be tempting to increase the ISO rating, but this will reduce image quality so do this only as a last resort (e.g. you cannot use a tripod, or exposure times extended over a minute). Many interiors feature a mixture of light sources – perhaps tungsten lamps, with daylight coming through the windows. Since it is impossible to get both right, experiment with your white balance settings. If you can, shoot in RAW mode, as this will provide more colour correction latitude later.

If you have additional lighting with you, some interiors benefit from extra flash or tungsten light to fill in badly lit shadow areas. These will have to be used off camera, and directed specifically into the areas that need it. A slave flash, which can be triggered remotely via a small blip from your on-camera flash, is perhaps the easiest to operate.

In your haste to get the wide shots, don't forget to look out for interesting details to isolate: perhaps an ornate banister, a spectacular chandelier, a painted ceiling or a stained glass window.

▼ *Bright interiors will not require flash.*

TOP 5 TIPS

1 Take a tripod, to keep the camera level and enable small apertures.
2 Use a wideangle lens, between 24 mm and 35 mm (equivalent).
3 To avoid distortion keep the camera level and avoid ultra wideangles.
4 Fit a longer lens to isolate interesting details. Look for unusual angles.
5 Keep the ISO as low as possible. Use off-camera flash if necessary to fill shadows.

▼ *Neon signs come alive in low light.*

NIGHT & LOW LIGHT

Night time can often provide some of the best photographic opportunities, especially in urban areas. The most obvious subject is architecture. Churches and grand civic buildings are often beautifully lit and can look better at night. Don't wait until it is dark – dusk is the best time to shoot, when there is still enough ambient light in the sky to fill in the unlit parts of the building, and reduce the contrast between those parts and the areas bathed in the spotlights.

A navy blue dusk sky also helps to highlight the outline of the building. Set the camera to RAW mode (if possible – if not, use daylight white balance in jpeg mode) and the lowest ISO you can, put the camera on a tripod, stop down to f/8 of f/11 and see what exposure time the meter gives

▼ *Dusky skies can intensify colours.*

you. It may be anything from 10 seconds to more than a minute. Try to avoid exposures much longer than this, as it will increase the noise levels in the image. Wait for a gap in traffic before shooting, though fast moving people will probably not record on the image during long exposures.

One of the most fun things you can do at night is shoot traffic trails, where you deliberately focus on a busy road and allow car head and tail lamps to record as streaks during an exposure anywhere between 10 and 30 seconds. Try to include the backs of cars as well as the fronts, so that you

▲ Cityscapes offer lots of inspiration for night pictures.

capture both red and white streaks. Funfairs are another occasion where moving lights make great pictures. Illuminated rides such as Ferris wheels can produce wonderful streaks of blurred colour during long exposures.

TOP 5 TIPS

1 Take a tripod.
2 Use the lowest ISO you can, select RAW mode or daylight white balance in JPEG.
3 Shoot as dusk, when there is still some colour in the sky, not when it is pitch black.
4 Stop down to f/8–f/11 and keep exposure times between 10–60 seconds if possible.
5 Try shooting traffic trails, fairgrounds and fireworks, for great motion effects.

You can also photograph fireworks displays. With a standard lens or slight wideangle fitted, set the camera up on a tripod, pointing at the sky. When the fireworks go up, open the shutter to record the burst. If you have a 'B' setting keep the shutter open, replace the lens cap, then open it again for the next burst, building up several bursts on the same exposure. Failing that, use the longest exposure time available, or take several shots and combine them into one image later.

▼ *Underwater light can be beautiful.*

UNDERWATER

The undersea world is a beautiful and fascinating place, so it is no wonder that, as more people travel to tropical climes, scuba diving and snorkelling are becoming more popular and people want to photograph the wonders beneath the surface.

Unfortunately the underwater world throws up several unique problems for photography. Firstly, the visibility in water is poorer than in air. Secondly, the water appears blue, as it filters out other wavelengths much more quickly. This in turn makes the light levels drop the deeper you go. Then there is the issue of increasing water pressure which, at even relatively modest depths, can crack and destroy the camera casing. There is also the difficulty in seeing what you are doing and accessing the controls when you are wearing a diving mask and snorkel.

▲ *If you can overcome the technical difficulties, the results can be spectacular.*

▼ *Underwater housings can improve picture quality.*

Luckily digital cameras make underwater photography easier than ever before, and most manufacturers offer a range of rigid underwater housings for their cameras, to protect against water pressure. These are sealed against water ingress and can be used to varying depths. For shallow snorkelling you can also buy watertight plastic bags relatively inexpensively. They are a bit more fiddly but perfectly usable.

The LCD screens of digital cameras make composing, shooting and reviewing pictures easier, and the ability to control the white balance helps to reduce the blue cast.

For best results underwater, get as close as possible to your subjects – the less water there is between the camera and subject the clearer and sharper your results will be.

▲ *Get close to your subject and use a wideangle lens.*

Use a wideangle lens and go within a few inches of fish and coral. The camera may not be able to focus so use the ability to prefocus manually.

TOP 5 TIPS

1 Use a dedicated waterproof housing. An Aquapac pouch is fine for snorkelling.
2 Check the seals to ensure that no water can get in to damage the camera
3 Get as close as possible to the subject to maximise quality. Use a wideangle lens.
4 Filter out the blue cast via the white balance or use flash to light the subject.
5 Use a large media card to maximise shooting time but keep an eye on your time.

Use the flash to add a full spectrum of light to the subject and reduce the blue cast. Some cameras allow the use of a more powerful accessory flash, perhaps fired remotely by the on-camera one.

The most important rule, however, is never to get so carried away taking pictures that you forget your own safety. Keep an eye on your depth and air supply – your life is more important than a few good photos.

PANORAMAS

Sometimes wideangle lenses are not wide enough to get everything in shot. This may be the case with expansive vistas from high viewpoints that stretch 180 degrees or more, so you need to shoot a panorama. While there are some specialized panoramic cameras on the market, they are expensive and mostly use film, but it is easy to produce a panorama using a normal digital camera, by taking a succession of overlapping shots.

It is important to follow the rules to avoid a disjointed panorama. Firstly, stake out in your mind the start and end points of your panorama. Set the camera to manual exposure so that the overall exposure remains consistent across the frame (in auto mode it can be influenced by light or dark elements within the scene) Keep the lens at the same zoom setting too, preferably in manual focus (having pre-focused first). Wideangle focal lengths are easier to work with than telephotos.

▼ *With a little planning and care, striking panoramas can be shot with normal digital cameras.*

When you are ready, take the first picture. Then, without moving the camera in any other plane, rotate the camera around the lens axis to the next section of your view, overlapping the scene slightly to aid joining them later. Don't rotate yourself, by turning your body, as this will make perfect alignment difficult, if not impossible.

In fact you will find this procedure much easier if you use a tripod with a pan and tilt head. By panning to the next area of the scene the camera is kept perfectly stable and moved only in the correct axis.

TOP 5 TIPS

Having rotated the camera to the next part of the scene, and ensured some overlap, take another shot. Continue this in an arc across the scene, until you reach your end point. If you like there is no reason why you can't keep going until you have shot a 360 degree view.

1 Find a suitable view with points of interest across a wide area.
2 Set the camera to manual focus and exposure and meter/focus the shot.
3 Working left to right, take the first shot, then rotate the camera to the next section.
4 Be sure not to move the camera in any other plane, and leave some frame overlap.
5 Use a tripod for best results.

Once you have joined all these shots together on your PC the result will be a long, narrow image. You can make it less narrow in height by shooting with the camera in the vertical position. Although this will give you a taller panorama, you will have to take more shots to cover the same ground.

JOINERS

Joiners share many similarities to panoramas, in that they are composed of multiple images joined together, to show a much wider area of a scene than a single shot. The difference between them is that whereas the aim of a panorama is to create a seamless, invisible join between each image, joiners revel in their fragmented nature.

▼ *Joiners are multiple images stitched together for effect.*

The term 'joiner' was coined by the artist David Hockney. Their deliberately disjointed look may seem easier to achieve than the precision of panoramas, but creating a successful joiner is rather like completing a complex jigsaw.

Before embarking on a joiner it is a good idea to plan the shot first. There is not a set way to work – you can shoot from the inside out or from left to right, it really doesn't matter. The important thing is to be methodical, so that you make sure that every section of your scene has been covered by at least one frame, and that the shots overlap in their coverage.

A good method is to draw a mental grid over the scene and make sure each square has been photographed.

One of the advantages of joiners is that you don't have to stay routed to the same spot; you can move around a bit. After all, the frames are not supposed to fit seamlessly together. They don't have to be taken at the same time either.

When joining the images together on the PC, the aim is to make the joins visible, so it helps if there are some subtle differences in exposure. You can do this on the computer, but by shooting in the auto mode there will be natural differences in density from frame to frame. It is best to avoid zooming too much, because big changes in magnification may make the result so disjointed it could be come unrecognizable – though as there are no real rules you might find this works for you.

As you bring the individual shots together on the computer to join them, align each shot roughly into the right place then move it slightly to misalign it. Alternatively you can alter the density or put a drop shadow under it to emphasise the edge.

You'll need a PC with a fair amount of RAM and a reasonably fast processor because you could have potentially dozens of images to join together, creating a massive file size.

TOP 5 TIPS

1 Joiners are an alternative to panoramas, in which the seams are celebrated.
2 Plan your shot first. Decide how many shots you want to use for your joiner.
3 Draw a mental grid over the scene. Make sure each section is covered at least once.
4 You can move around and shoot from different positions, and at different times.
5 Show the joins by misaligning frames or changing their relative exposures.

SHOWING YOUR WORK

Most photographers want others to appreciate what they do, and there are now more ways than ever to do this.

All photographers should get into the habit of making good quality A4 or A3 display prints of their best work to keep in a portfolio. Art supply shops sell a wide range of portfolio cases and clear plastic sleeves, or you can have your prints mounted on to board. However, having a portfolio does not mean that your prints will necessarily reach a wide audience.

▼ *A personal website is a great way of displaying your work to a wider audience.*

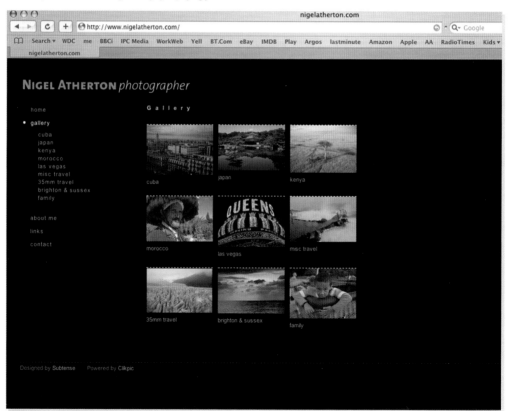

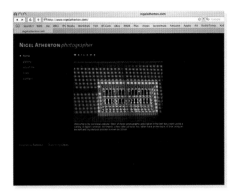

The traditional (and still the most prestigious) way is to organize an exhibition. It can be difficult to get shown in art galleries without a track record or a exceptional body of work, but many libraries, bars and cafes, and other public spaces will show exhibitions of pictures by local photographers.

Staging an exhibition is a very expensive way to show your work, with the cost of getting exhibition-standard prints, and then mounting or framing them. Another option is to self-publish your portfolio in a book. There are many publishers who will do this, for a price, but unless your work is of local or specialist interest and you can sell it locally or to outlets within your specialized market you will find this a very costly enterprise.

The cheapest vehicle to show your work is also the one that can reach the largest audience – a website. There are several options, depending on how ambitious you want to be. The simplest is to upload your pictures to a photo sharing website, where you are given some pages along with everyone else. Your webpage address will usually be the hosting site's address, forward-slash your name. The design will be basic, and the same as everyone else's pages. For something more individual some sites let you download your pick from dozens or hundreds of templates or varying style and complexity, into which you drag and drop your pictures. These companies can usually host your site too.

For something truly individual and unique you can design and build your own site. There is lots of software to help you do this (some of it is even free) or you could hire a web design company to build it for you at a price. Whichever option you choose, all that will be left to do is tell the world where to find your website.

▲ *Designing your own site is well worth the effort.*

TOP 5 TIPS

1 Get prints made of your best work to keep in a portfolio.
2 Hold an exhibition in a local café or library.
3 Self publish a book of your best work.
4 Upload your pictures to a photo sharing website.
5 Build your own website, using templates or using your own design.

SHOOTING PROJECTS

MOBILE PHONE CAMERAS

▼ Mobiles are always improving. **These days most of us are never without a camera because there is one on our mobile phones. These may not be able to compete with 'proper' cameras for quality and functionality, but it is better to have a camera on your phone than no camera at all.**

▼ Some mobile phones can capture video footage.

Camera phones are playing an increasingly important part in international news coverage, as every major disaster or incident is captured by a phone-wielding eye witness, and there are now news agencies dedicated to selling newsworthy images and video footage from our phones to news agencies worldwide.

You don't have to be witness to a catastrophe though to make use of your camera phone. Camera phones are also ideal as evidence of a crime, accident or other situation where visual proof may be useful. If, for example you are involved in a minor car accident or a parking ticket dispute, or perhaps you have injured yourself in the street as a result of a health and safety violation, a camera phone picture could be used to back

Digital Camera Handbook

▼ *Some phones have as many as 5 MP.*

up your version of events later. As a tool of crime prevention, you can record a suspicious car's number plate, or some people acting suspiciously (though any action which could put you in potential danger should be undertaken with caution, if at all).

On a lighter note, camera phones are ideal for those unexpected moments when you see a great picture but don't have your camera with you, whether an amusing incident or a funny piece of graffiti.

A more creative use of phone cameras is to set yourself a visual project, perhaps as part of your daily journey to work. You can collect pictures of car badges, or things that are yellow, or cat portraits. Once you have enough you can group them together and print them, or make a webpage gallery out of them.

There are so many potential uses of camera phones which complement, rather than replace, those of a high quality camera, that photographers should see them as a bonus rather than an alternative. And of course with the benefit of being able to send pictures instantly across the phone network to anywhere in the world, camera phones are an immensely powerful tool.

▶ *Mobile phone cameras make sending pictures to friends and family extremely easy.*

TOP 5 TIPS

1 Use them to record accidents and incidents, as evidence.
2 Use them to record suspicious activity, as crime prevention.
3 Take pictures of amusing scenes and situations.
4 Set yourself a project to 'collect' photos of certain subjects.
5 Display them on a Internet gallery or print them as a montage or mosaic.

Section Two: Computer Basics

SOFTWARE CHOICES FOR THE DIGITAL PHOTOGRAPHER

Software is the essential ingredient for turning good digital images into great pictures, whether for printing, for use in emails and web pages or for selling. There is a wide range of software solutions for image enhancement, fixing and sharing needs, both free and commercial. In this section we look at a selection of the leading digital photography-related software packages in order to discover what they are capable of and to help you make the best choices for your needs.

IMAGE EDITING SOFTWARE

Image editing and manipulation packages provide both the editing environment and associated tools for routine cropping, resizing, format conversion, as well as colour and tone adjustment. They also allow selected areas of an image to be manipulated using a wide variety of filters and other enhancement functions. Most also allow complex and cumulative layering of images and effects to enable you to create new images from your photographs.

▲ *Digital camera magazines are a great source of software reviews and application tutorials.*

IMAGE MANAGERS AND CATALOGUING SOFTWARE

With film negative strips, slide mounts and printed photos, the only way to be organized was to physically store them in an orderly manner. Digital images can be stored on your computer's hard drive or CD or DVD until you need to find them again. This may be one reason why we produce many more digital images than we ever did with film. It is easy to lose a digital image, but it is also now easy to set up a powerful database-driven storage and retrieval system using software that manages and catalogues your image files. From these you can find, distribute and share images with ease and sophistication.

OTHER USEFUL APPLICATIONS

Besides the large general purpose commercial applications you can buy, there are also many smaller utilities and specialist programs that can make a real difference to your imaging work. These include plug-in programs which become tightly integrated with the image editing applications that host them and provide either tightly focused image enhancement tools or specialized algorithms for solving challenges. They can also be specialist stand-alone programs which are tailored do a more efficient job of tackling certain tasks than more universal versatile applications.

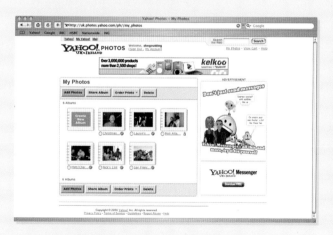

▲ *A digital image library is a useful tool.*

TRY BEFORE YOU BUY

In this broadband Internet age, most commercial imaging software packages are now available as limited time trial downloads, offering full functionality for anything from a week to a month and, sometimes, longer – with added online documentation. You can also look at photography magazines, back issues, photography web sites, etc. for software reviews and application tutorials.

IMAGE EDITING SOFTWARE

ADOBE PHOTOSHOP

▲ *Photoshop allows you to digitally alter photos.*

Photoshop is the most powerful, if not the easiest, image editing package you can buy

Adobe launched version 1.0 of Photoshop in February 1990, although it existed in various forms several years earlier, namely ImagePro, but this worked only on an Apple Mac. The Windows edition arrived in late 1992 at version 2.5. In its decade and a half of continuous development, Photoshop has become an immensely powerful software tool and established itself as both the image editing package of choice among professionals and, more recently, the top consumer-level image editing package in its cut-down form Photoshop Elements.

Very early on, Photoshop was endowed with vector drawing tools for creating paths (outlines of shapes that can be infinitely resized and later rasterized into bit map objects). Layer support, a revolutionary concept of sandwiching inter-related graphics and consequential properties to determine the overall image, was another early feature addition. Also, for a long time, Photoshop was one of the few image editing applications that offered proper colour management handling.

Adobe Photoshop has a very loyal user base, many of whom have been using earlier versions for many years. Adobe has been careful to preserve as much as possible of Photoshop's original user interface

▲ *This function allows you to adjust the tone curve.*

and working environment in order to facilitate smooth upgrades from one version to the next. A rather odd consequence is that Photoshop, which was developed initially for the Mac, is not that easy for new users to get into. In many ways, the Photoshop user interface is unintuitive and breaks many Windows application guidelines. However, that does not really matter, because nearly everyone who wants to use it is content to adapt to Photoshop's quirks in order to access its indisputably powerful features. Photoshop Elements has gone some way towards modernizing the Photoshop user interface, but there is no hint yet that the full professional version of Photoshop will follow.

PHOTOSHOP FUNDAMENTALS

There are many books that give advice on how to use Photoshop. There are also an almost infinite number of different ways of achieving a certain result. However, these are Photoshop's fundamental features and some of its most commonly used tools.

FILE BROWSING

Until recently, Photoshop's ability to browse image files on your hard drive and load them into Photoshop, was one of its weakest points, being slow and inferior to third party image management applications. That all changed with Photoshop CS2 (version 9). This version introduced the Bridge, an image browsing application shared between Photoshop and other members of the Adobe Creative Suite 2 (CS2) family. The simple browsing experience is much enhanced, with a thumbnail viewer that can be dynamically resized and rearranged, batch file renaming capability, access to extended file properties (including metadata), and the ability to search for

▼ *The Bridge is an image browsing application.*

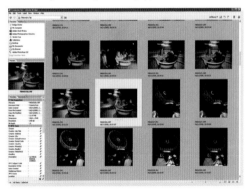

▼ *The Bridge is able to open RAW files to allow editing.*

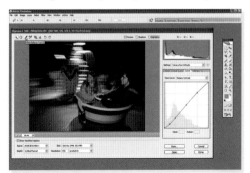

files according to metadata entries. The Bridge is also able to thumbnail preview RAW files supported by Adobe Camera RAW.

In conjunction with another new Creative Suite component, called Version Cue, you can keep tabs on projects in progress. The Bridge also lets you adjust variables that are common to other Creative Suite applications. The Bridge can't create fast, folder watched, searchable databases and portable catalogues, but these features may be included in a future release.

PATHS

A path is a shape created with a vector drawing tool. Photoshop offers a selection of these tools, including the pen tool and a variety of shape tools. Paths can be infinitely adjusted using bezier curve adjustment points along the path, so extremely fine mapping of underlying shapes and detail can be created. Paths can be used for tracing and extracting shapes and can be converted into area selections for ultra-precise masking. Extracted bitmap areas can then be vector scaled. You can also convert area selections in to paths. The possibilities for use of the paths tools are unlimited.

▲ The layers function enables you to transform the composite image in a number of different ways.

LAYERS

Imagine you are looking at your image through overlaid panes of glass, on which your image is separated. Some layers will hide all or parts of other layers beneath. By individually editing layers you can magically transform the composite image. Very fine control over how the contents of each layer influences the final image is provided. You can rearrange the order of the layers as they are stacked, delete them, insert new ones, hide them, duplicate them, alter their opacity and merge them. By using adjustment layers, you can apply tonal and colour transformations to one or a number of selected layers. Fill layers can be used to introduce solid colour or a colour gradient effect, or even a pattern. Photoshop also offers layer styles that let you add layer-based effects to images such as drop shadows.

Digital Camera Handbook

COLOUR MANAGEMENT

This is an area in which Photoshop has always excelled. Being able to calibrate and colour match your hardware is one thing, but if your software cannot make sense of colour profiles and different colour spaces, your work could be seriously limited. Photoshop is fully compatible with the commonly (and not so commonly) used colour spaces and ICC-compliant profiles. It can even show you areas of an image that exceed the colour gamut of the printer to which you are outputting. Photoshop can manage colour settings or it can let a third party application, such as a printer driver, take control.

IMAGE ADJUSTMENTS AND FILTERS

▼ The vanishing point feature adjusts the perspective.

Photoshop has an unparalleled range of tools for knocking images into shape. All the usual features are there, including levels adjustments, histogram displays, tone curve adjustment, colour selection and replacement, brightness, contrast, hue and saturation, etc. Features more closely associated with Photoshop include smart cloning tools, such as the healing brush, quick masking, perspective correction and, in the latest version of Photoshop, the new vanishing point feature, which edits detail while retaining perspective. Another very useful tool is shadow/highlight, which brings out detail in shadows without bleaching existing highlight detail. Special filters now

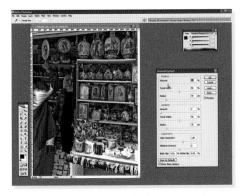

available in Photoshop include those to correct lens distortion, sharpen detail while avoiding unwanted artefacts and reduce noise without sacrificing too much detail.

Photoshop is a massive resource and even those who have used it every day for many years may only become expert with a subset of its capabilities.

▲ Use the shadow/highlight tool to bring out detail.

IMAGE EDITING SOFTWARE

ADOBE PHOTOSHOP ELEMENTS

Photoshop Elements is a simplified version of the full version of Photoshop and is aimed at non-professionals. Unlike Photoshop, Elements does not include support for CMYK colour format images, or colour separations. Some channel features have been omitted or simplified and there is no advanced tone curve adjustment option nor support for Smart Objects.

However, Photoshop Elements has a sizeable list of tricks that you don't get with the full version of Photoshop. These include its more user friendly interface, quick fix and smart fix tools, smart red eye correction, file browsing with dynamic date stamp searching, image tag assignment and searching, built in options for emailing images, burning slide shows to CD (or even DVD if you also have Adobe's Premiere Elements video editing package installed), multiple images per page arrangement and printing, easy to create calendars, posters and greetings cards, etc.

In some ways, Elements has been dumbed down, but much of Photoshop's underlying power remains, including most of the commonly used editing tools, including the healing brush in the recent releases of Elements, and Photoshop's comprehensive colour management system.

Since version three of Photoshop Elements, Adobe has integrated its Photoshop Album image management and organizer package with the main Elements image editing software. In Adobe-speak, Photoshop Elements can be broken down into three elements or workspaces. The first is the Welcome screen, which functions as a guide to the key functions of the package. Next is the Organizer, a super-enhanced image file browser. The third and final workspace is the Editor, and this is where you can make changes to an image.

▲ *Make use of the shortcuts on the Welcome screen.*

WELCOME SCREEN

It is tempting to dismiss the Welcome screen as an annoying start up splash screen, which you can delete when Elements boots up. However, new users will find that it helps to locate particular Elements resources without having to plough through complicated and unfamiliar menus and dialogue boxes. The Welcome screen has shortcuts leading to an overview of what you can do with Elements, the Organizer, the quick fix function, a more comprehensive edit and enhance mode and tools for making slide shows, greetings cards, posters, etc., plus CD burning options.

ORGANIZER

The Organizer is a development of Photoshop Album, a powerful image browser and organizer that automatically locates all images on your hard drive, imports them from your connected camera and provide you with the means to categorize or tag them under meaningful subject names. Organizer also has an intuitive graphically-aided time line

▲ *The Organizer is a powerful image browser.*

feature for finding images by date. You can also use Organizer to send colourful themed photo emails.

▲ *The image editing facilities.*

THE EDITOR

Full-edition Photoshop users might find things laid out in a slightly unfamiliar fashion, but the essential layers-based image editing and enhancement power of Photoshop is still there.

IMAGE EDITING SOFTWARE

COREL PAINTSHOP PRO

Now owned by Corel, Paint Shop Pro (PSP) was originally developed by Jasc Software. PSP has always had a good set of tools and features to accommodate all but the most demanding users and its affordable price tag has been appreciated by a loyal base of users over the years.

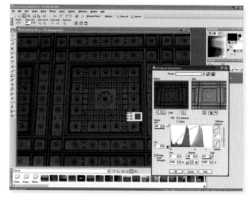

▲ *The editing tools are comprehensive.*

Like Photoshop, PSP is a sophisticated layers-based bitmap image editing package that is ideal for enhancing photos. It also includes vector drawing tools that can be used to select and extract areas with fine precision and to produce graphics that can be reshaped and scaled easily. PSP's tool bar has image editing tools for cloning, selecting, painting and masking effects. It also offers perspective correction, tone curve adjustment and one-click blemish removal tools.

▲ *The Learning Center provides extensive online help.*

One area that has improved vastly in the last three versions of PSP has been its online help. Context-sensitive help and PSP's Learning Center feature both work well to assist users in using PSP's wealth of features and options.

Where PSP lagged behind Photoshop was in the area of colour management. Only the latest version features a proper colour management, supporting ICC Profiles and alternative colour spaces, now increasingly important because digital cameras frequently offer options such as Adobe RGB. Colour management is essential for a growing number of adventurous users willing to optimize their printer output through printer profiling. RAW image file support has also been added in the latest versions.

THE PAINT SHOP PRO WORKSPACE

At its heart, PSP is a workspace. This is what you see when PSP boots up. It is comprised of the menu bar, toolbars, palettes and a status bar. Images opened for editing are contained in image windows, of which you can have several open at once, although only one can be actively edited at a time.

Palettes are very important to PSP. These are resizable and re-locatable boxes in the workspace, which contain information about particular tools and features that can affect an image being edited. Palettes can also contain controls for adjusting various settings.

The learning center is one palette that, by default, dominates the workspace. It contains shortcuts to

▲ *Workspace palettes are a major feature of PSP.*

reference material which can help you work with tools and commands. Advanced users will eventually grow out of the Learning Center and probably switch it off.

The browser palette is for previewing and locating image files you might want to edit. It shows image thumbnails, lets you navigate from one folder to another and from drive to drive and provides access to embedded information in image file metadata, including EXIF data. Other important palettes include the histogram, layers, brush variance, etc.

The PSP workspace can be saved and reloaded, so that you can reinstate a previous editing session, with images loaded and tools at the ready exactly how you left them when you last had to close down PSP.

IMAGE EDITING SOFTWARE

ULEAD PHOTOIMPACT

ULead is another image editing manufacturer and its PhotoImpact package has been developed through several generations. PhotoImpact boasts a huge selection of image editing tools and features and yet it is the lowest priced choice of the 'power' editors. It is also frequently bundled with items of hardware such as scanners and cameras.

▲ Cool 360 is a panorama stitcher.

Since version 8, not a great deal of development has been evident in PhotoImpact, but version 11 was substantially revised and given a new and more customizable look and feel. ULead has also mimicked Paint Shop Pro's workspace feature, enabling customization and saving of workspace configurations.

Most of the digital photographer must-have features are present in PhotoImpact. There is a layers-based application, extensive bitmap and vector editing tools, image adjustment features such as the histogram, tone curve adjustment and even correction of optical distortions, a feature that has been in PhotoImpact for several years. PhotoImpact is popular with web designers as it has plenty of specialized tools for creating web graphics.

PhotoImapact offers support for selected-format camera RAW image files via its Photo Explorer image management and organizer module. Another

▲ 360 degree panoramas can be viewed with special software.

interesting feature is Cool 360, a panorama stitcher that comes complete with an option to create 360 degree panoramas, which can be viewed dynamically with special viewer software. This software is also available as an Internet Explorer browser plug-in.

A relatively new feature in photo editing packages addresses dynamic range enhancement, usually to bring out shadow detail without obliterating highlight detail. PhotoImpact has had such a feature, called High Dynamic Range, for some time.

THE PHOTOIMPACT WORKSPACE

The PhotoImpact workspace is modular and can be configured to basic photo, standard photo, graphics, web, or advanced modes. Each contains sets of tools that are specific to the mode selected. You can switch between different modes by clicking on My Workspace, which you can find on the menu bar.

When PhotoImpact is booted up for the first time, a prompt requests you to choose your desired workspace mode. You are then greeted with a welcome screen that provides shortcuts to tasks that relate to the selected workspace mode.

Further customization of the workspace is provided in PhotoImpact. Toolbars and panels can float so that you can place them where you want or you can dock them. You can also reconfigure the standard tool bar to feature your choice of tool icons – it can be customized to include only icons of the tools that you commonly use. A profiles tab lets you to save, import, export and manage the user preference profiles, which is ideal if more than one person shares the use of your installation of PhotoImpact.

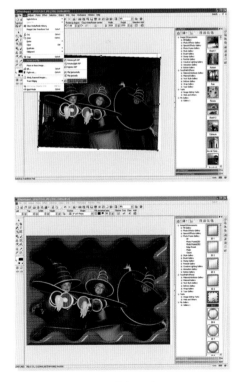

▲ *Different effects are straightforward to create.*

IMAGE EDITING SOFTWARE

ROXIO PHOTOSUITE

Roxio PhotoSuite is a photo image editing solution that is very different from the others. It is unashamedly aimed at people who are not power users and it has always been a very simple introduction to transferring photos from your camera, tidying them up and printing them. It does not use complex layers and highly technical jargon. Instead, it approaches image editing in an intuitive and friendly way using a browser-like user interface, with step-by-step wizards.

PhotoSuite is also available as part of Roxio's Easy Media Creator bundle, which includes video editing, media file management and organizing, CD and DVD burning utilities and several other multimedia tools.

If you can find your way around with a web browser, you can probably cope with PhotoSuite. The starting point is PhotoSuite's welcome page, which lists just nine iconized shortcuts, divided into two groups; edit and create, plus print and share.

Click on 'edit' and you will be presented with a file browser displaying thumbnails of recognized image files. Click on an image file and an editing window appears, with the image in-situ. At the top you will see four large and friendly icons for returning you to the welcome page, emailing the image, printing it or saving it. Along the left is a list of edit features which pinpoint specific actions, such as improving overall image quality, correcting facial flaws such as blemishes and flash red eye, adding text to an image, cutting out parts of an image and image masking, etc. Hover over any of these entries and sub-options pop up. Click on one of these and you are taken to an action-specific window with the necessary adjustments and buttons on the

Digital Camera Handbook

left panel. Where necessary, that panel can become a step-by-step wizard that holds your hand through the entire process.

Although PhotoSuite does not support layers, it is possible to create composite images by pasting in new components which can be moved around and positioned precisely. It also has image masking

▲ *PhotoSuite enables you to create projects such as calendars.*

with freehand or shape-based selection options. There is also a good range of special effects, including colour filters, transparency, and image repair tools including dust and scratch rectifiers and a cloning option.

There is also a photo-stitching option for making panoramas, a suite of projects for collages, calendars, greeting cards, etc, and a feature called Multi Photo Enhance which lets you apply a selected action or effect to more than one image at a time, including multiple file renaming, for example.

Finally, print and share choices provide easy-to-follow routes to printing one or more image at a time, with the option of printing more than one image on a sheet of paper, creating quite sophisticated photo emails and accessing online printing partner services.

Over the years PhotoSuite has become much more capable than its simple look and feel might suggest and it is a good place to start, but you will eventually want to move on to something more powerful.

▲ *Greeting cards are another fun way to use your images.*
◄ *Multi Photo Enhance is useful when dealing with many photos.*

IMAGE MANAGERS & CATALOGUING SOFTWARE

ACD SYSTEMS' ACDSEE PHOTO MANAGER

It can be difficult to keep track of all your digital images. However, the nature of the digital medium means that you can use software to manage your images easily, and do more with your photos than you might have imagined.

▲ *ACDSee is a multimedia file manager and organizer package.*

ACDSee, from the Canadian software company ACD Systems, is a long established photo image and multimedia file manager and organizer package for Windows. When ACDSee encounters new image or multimedia files, it creates a thumbnail image and saves it to its proprietary thumbnail database – fast thumbnailing is one of the features for which ACDSee is best known. The image file name and its embedded metadata, plus its location on your hard drive, are also recorded in a database.

Immediately, you can find files that ACDSee has previously seen by searching a date range, file type or key words targeting selected metadata fields. You could, for example, search for all camera images with a rated ISO speed of 200. You can also combine several different sets of search criteria to accurately target very specific files based on the information that they contain.

You can categorize and rate your images, as well as add searchable keywords. A handful of categories, such as Album, People, Places and Various, are supplied, but you can create as many of your own as you like. Categories can also be nested – for example, you could have 'Places' as the top category and 'Manchester' as a sub category. This could differentiate the place, Manchester, from a family name called Manchester which might be under the People category.

In fact, you could search for images shot using a Canon G7 at 1/125th second shutter speed, in Manchester, between the dates of 1st and 2nd April, with the keyword 'food' and a rating of at least 3 out of 5.

▲ *The ACDSee search function is particularly useful.*

Once ACDSee has found the image, it can be displayed at any magnification and simple image-tuning fixes can be applied. You can resize, crop and print images and convert image formats. Selected files can also be renamed using a batch renaming function. It is also possible to edit some metadata entries. You can create slide shows for burning onto CD as well as web-ready image galleries.

The on-screen layout is also customizable. You position windows precisely, showing the key tools you use most and hiding others.

The challenge with ACDSee and, indeed, any other image file management and organizing system is to consistently catalogue all your images. If only half your archive has been catalogued, only half your photos will be found through ACDSee's powerful search facilities. If you do not maintain the database, its usefulness will rapidly diminish.

▲ *It is vital to keep your images consistently catalogued and organized, or the search function will not be effective.*

IMAGE MANAGERS & CATALOGUING SOFTWARE

IVIEW MEDIAPRO

iView Multimedia originally developed its iView Media family of media file management and cataloguing (digital asset management ((DAM)) solutions) with the Apple Mac in mind, and the Windows versions of their software have a very Mac-feel about them.

▲ The list view option shows all your files with an icon.

iView offers two packages – iView Media and iView MediaPro, the former being targeted as a low price offering for consumers and the latter aimed specifically at users requiring more sophisticated features. The iView MediaPro includes support for more exotic file types than iViewMedia, including camera RAW files, image editing, colour management, scripting, advanced print options and automated folder and file watching to keep catalogues up to date. iView works by taking a snapshot of files from the hard drive and placing them in a catalogue. From then on you are mostly working with the contents of the catalogue rather than the original files.

The concept of a catalogue is attractive to professionals because you can restrict the contents of each catalogue so that it relates to one job or customer. A catalogue can be distributed to someone for previewing screen-sized versions of your images without having to provide the original files. It can work as a twenty-first century alternative to customer proof prints. If the recipient of the catalogue doesn't have a version of iView Media or MediaPro installed, you can provide a free iView Catalog Reader for them to use.

To create a catalogue you drag the folder that contains the images you wish to catalogue onto the iView Media application. It doesn't take long – for example, a folder and sub-folder containing 4,000 images will only take a minute to be processed. You can include many different files and folders from different parts of the hard drive and even add files from CDs, DVDs and external hard drives. You can create, load and save as many different catalogues as you like.

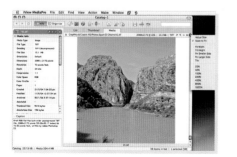

▲ *Files can also be shown in thumbnail view.*

Once this process is complete, you can view thumbnails or file icons of all the files contained in the catalogue by clicking on the 'home' button. You can switch between thumbnail, list and media views. Media view shows a resizable view of the original file and if you have MediaPro you can edit and otherwise enhance that image.

The other two key options are Organize and Info. In Organize mode you can use the Catalog Index to narrow the selection of images displayed according to specific criteria, such as date range or file type. You can also use a quick search entry at the top right of the iView window. Type in a keyword and iView will search the entire catalogue, matching that word with file metadata, file names and even the names of folders in which the original file was stored.

Info mode displays all the information associated with an individual file and also lets you add your own, including a caption, annotations and other keywords. You can then use this additional data to group images in Organize mode.

The one drawback with iView Media is that the contents of a catalogue are disconnected from the original files – if you change or delete any of those files independently, the catalogue will no longer be 100 pre cent representative. For users of iView MediaPro there is a file and folder watching option that can automatically update the catalogue when it discovers a catalogued file has been altered or deleted.

◀ *The media view option allows you to resize the image.*

IMAGE MANAGERS & CATALOGUING SOFTWARE

EXTENSIS PORTFOLIO

Portfolio, published by the graphical and imaging tools software company, Extensis, is like Adobe Photoshop in that it has been around a long time and has built up a loyal fan base, especially among imaging professionals. Portfolio is a family of software products which provide a range of power and flexibility from managing images at a personal level through to multi-user server-based provision. Since the release of Portfolio 7, there is also an interactive web-based component.

Portfolio is a catalogue-based solution rather than an extension of the computer's own file browser – it catalogues your multimedia files, either selectively or automatically, without having to change the location of each file. A catalogue can contain information about files which live in different folders across your hard drive and on CDRs, recordable DVDs, USB drives and external hard disk drives. If you are really technical, you can interface Portfolio to an industry standard relational database such as MySQL. During and after the cataloguing process you can add keywords to individual images or selections to help you locate them easily using Portfolio's powerful search facility. Portfolio 7 also has a very handy folder watch feature that automatically updates the catalogue when files are modified, added or removed.

Portfolio catalogues do not contain copies of the files referenced. Each catalogue is an index of thumbnail

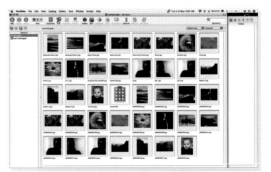

▲ *Each catalogue contains an index of thumbnail images.*

images of the original files, plus associated information, which can be edited. This information can include your own key words, plus pre-existing embedded data, such as camera EXIF parameters.

To view and search the contents of a Portfolio catalogue you need the Portfolio application, though

▲ *Limiting the images to a medium size protects them from copying.*

Extensis also provides a stand-alone Mac and Windows compatible catalogue viewer which can be distributed along with the images and the catalogue. You can also distribute catalogues without the original images, either limiting the viewer to thumbnails or medium size representations of the image, which protects your original images from unauthorized copying.

So far, much of what has been described could apply equally to iView MediaPro, although the two applications have a different layout and feel. However, what really differentiates them are the high-end collaborative working features that the more expensive Portfolio setups offer. Portfolio can act as a client for Portfolio Server, a powerful and expensive centralized image resource management system which provides convenient secure access to large libraries of images to teams of people in a workgroup.

The latest Portfolio option is NetPublish, a feature which can semi-automatically generate feature-rich stand-alone web sites, complete with site search facilities and managed image accessibility, all without having to know anything about html programming.

If you purchase the Extensis Photo Imaging Suite package, you acquire Portfolio 7 as well as some excellent additional tools such as Mask Pro, SmartScale, Intellihance and PhotoFrame, for not a great deal more than the stand-alone Portfolio price.

▲ *Portfolio catalogues your multimedia files.*

SOFTWARE IN DEPTH

IMAGE MANAGERS & CATALOGUING SOFTWARE

FOTOWARE FOTOSTATION

FotoStation, from the Norwegian Fotoware company, is a professional-class digital asset management (DAM) solution for photographers and is available in two standard forms – Classic and Pro. The Classic edition is available for both Mac and Windows users, though, at the time of writing, FotoStation Pro was only available for Windows.

▼ *FotoStation Classic is compatible with both Macs and PCs.*

The one overriding difference between these versions is that the Pro edition has a built-in image editor. This represents a modest 10 per cent difference in price, but FotoStation Classic is priced at more than $500, or more than ten times the cost of ACDSee Photo Manager, for example. So, FotoStation is not aimed at amateurs, although it has been bundled with some consumer model Nikon cameras in the past.

Like ACDSee, FotoStation works closely in conjunction with your computer's own file browser. You can browse any folder that your operating browser can see and FotoStation dynamically thumbnails any image or video files it recognizes at quite a pace. FotoStation has reasonably comprehensive RAW image file support, too – not as comprehensive as Adobe Camera RAW, but better than iPhoto, for example.

Digital Camera Handbook

To focus attention on selected media files you need to create a FotoStation archive and associate it with the contents of selected folders. FotoStation will then index those folders, adding all the usual file attributes to the database, including camera EXIF and other IPTC metadata. FotoWare provides extensive facilities for editing the indexed information, adding your own custom fields and updating metadata entries. If this aspect of DAM is particularly important to you, FotoStation is one of the leaders, though it is a complicated system to understand and configure. It is also rather odd that the default configuration is set to such a simple level that unless you go to the considerable trouble of customizing it, practically all other DAM solutions provide better search access to media file properties. Another advanced feature is a custom macro or actions builder for automating workflow.

Besides a powerful logical search engine tool, there is a quick free-text search option and you can even sort your images according to how similar they are to each other. Archives can be exported for use in other FotoStation installations – as long as they

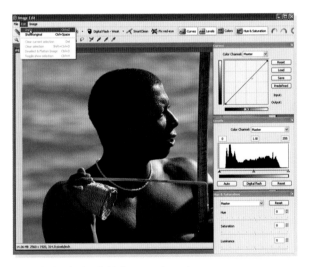

▲ FotoStation Pro is suitable for more advanced users.

share the same operating system type, but there is no portable catalogue feature as in Extensis Portfolio and iView MediaPro. However, there are comprehensive slide show and web gallery builder facilities.

FotoStation Pro also has an image editor with levels and histogram palettes, plus a tone curve adjustment tool. You also get an adjustable digital flash tool for optimizing shadow detail without sacrificing highlight information. Naturally, you get all this and a whole lot more in Photoshop CS2, but the advantage of FotoStation's built in editor is that it can be summoned up instantly as you browse your image archive. FotoStation can work with external or removable storage media and colour management is fully supported.

IMAGE MANAGERS & CATALOGUING SOFTWARE

COREL PHOTO ALBUM

Photo Album is another member of the Jasc Paint Shop Pro repertoire acquired when Corel took over Jasc in 2004. Rather than clone ACDSee or Adobe Photoshop Album, Jasc decided to produce something with a detectably different slant. Some people love Photo Album, others rate it as mediocre – and it does take some time to get used to it, especially if you have used one of the competitor products.

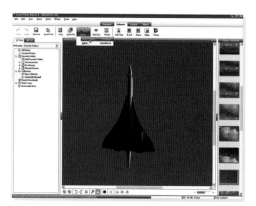

▲ Corel Photo Album works differently to other products.

The basic principle is to acquire images from various sources, such as a connected camera, memory card in a card reader or from folders that already exist on the computer, and then to provide thumbnail views of the acquired images as well as access to embedded metadata for each file. Selected images can then be grouped into collections, another word for catalogues, though, confusingly, the actual Corel Photo Album process called 'cataloging' does not directly relate to collections. The process of 'cataloging' in Corel Photo Album simply describes the basic image acquisition process that appends file information to its database. Catalogued items are only added to collections later if the user requires this.

The contents of collections can be viewed without having to create or store copies of the original files. They contain virtual reference photos that are stored in various places on your computer and which have previously been catalogued by Photo

▼ A useful feature is the exportable slideshow function.

▼ A useful feature is the exportable slideshow function.

Album. You can create collections of photos to print, place in a slide show, or show off in a book. You can also delete and rename collections, though they cannot be exported for distribution and independent viewing.

A quick and easy way of organizing your catalogued photos is to click on a little greyed out star with which all photo thumbnails are displayed. When clicked, the star turns yellow to indicate it has 'favourites' status, which means it belongs to a standardized collection called 'Favorites'. All such images can be viewed instantly by clicking on 'Favorites' in the find palette.

Corel Photo Album has quite a good keyword tagging system and it is easy to assign custom keywords to a single image or selection of images. However there is no obvious way to search using keywords in certain image metadata, such as camera EXIF information, which is a serious limitation. So you cannot search for all pictures taken with a particular make of camera or at a specific ISO setting, focal length or aperture, etc. There is also no visual tagging or rating system, apart from the favourites star toggle. However, there is support for removable media, such as CDs and DVDs, plus external storage drives.

Elsewhere there are some reasonable image tuning options, including the wonderfully titled 'thinify' option. There are also creative projects, exportable slide shows and web galleries and extensive printing options.

Corel PhotoShop Album feels as if it is more difficult to use than its competitors and yet doesn't offer as many features. It is almost as if the program was designed to be distinct from the others and yet a steep price was paid in terms of relatively limited utility.

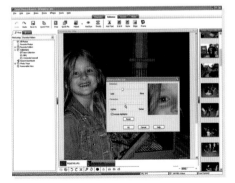

► Reducing red eye is straightforward.

IMAGE MANAGERS & CATALOGUING SOFTWARE

ADOBE PHOTOSHOP ALBUM

Adobe Photoshop Album is a stand-alone image file organizer and cataloguer, although most of its functions are also integrated within Photoshop Elements as the Elements Organizer. Photoshop Album is a powerful program with some sophisticated features, but it is primarily aimed at inexperienced users, so there is an emphasis on ease of use. A limited version of Photoshop Album, called the Standard Edition (SE) is available for free download from the Adobe website.

When you first run Photoshop Album, it automatically locates and indexes any image and video files it recognizes on your hard drive. This process is quick and unless you have several tens of thousands of image files, should only take a minute or two. Being a consumer-oriented application, Photoshop Album will not recognize RAW image files or less mainstream image file formats. (However, the version of Album integrated since Photoshop Elements 3.0 does recognize RAW images supported by the version of Adobe Camera RAW installed in those versions of Elements.) By default, if duplicate files are discovered only one instance of a file is catalogued.

You can either let Album search the entire hard drive or you can point it at selected image folders and sub-folders. Album can

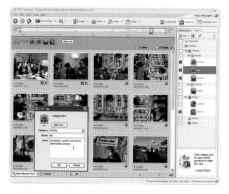

▲ *Photoshop Album's catalogue system is a powerful tool.*

also download images from a connected camera, a memory card loaded into a card reader and a scanner.

Photoshop Album creates a catalogue of image thumbnails and information for each image. If you change or delete the original image, the catalogue will not immediately reflect these changes. However, Album does try to keep its catalogue synchronized with original files by checking their state periodically. If you choose to delete a catalogue entry, you are given the option of deleting the original file at the same time.

Album's trademark feature is its visual time line search bar. Across the top of the Album workspace is a bar graph with varying sized columns arranged in date order – the most recent to the right. Each column represents a month in the calendar and the relative height of the column indicates the quantity of images available to view in that month. Just click on a column to display the images it represents in that month. Alternatively, there is a more conventional calendar view, with thumbnails inserted in each day entry.

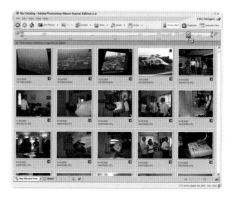

▲ The visual time line search bar is a trademark feature.

Another great feature of Photoshop Album is its visual image tagging system. You can create categories to be associated with images and assign one of a selection of icon designs to that category. Next, you can drag and drop categories into the category spaces for each image or selection of multiple images, assigning that category tag to those images without touching the keyboard.

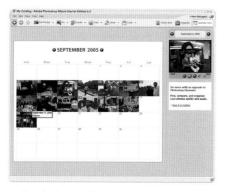

▲ The calendar view shows which photos were taken when.

As Photoshop Album doesn't catalogue the entire original file, you can only view a reduced size view of an image. For a full size view, use Album to launch an image editing application of your choice and automatically load that image. Full versions of Photoshop Album can create slide shows and web thumbnail galleries.

IMAGE MANAGERS & CATALOGUING SOFTWARE

APPLE IPHOTO

iPhoto is the free photo image organizing application supplied by Apple for Mac users. It is an easy to use application that has been tailored to fit the Mac OS environment seamlessly. It is also designed to work with a connected iPod device, so that you can transfer photos from your Mac to your iPod and keep photo albums on either side of the connection in sync. iPhoto is part of the iLife suite of applications bundled with most new Macs, but if you need the latest version of iPhoto you may need to buy the latest iLife release if you don't already have an earlier version of iLife, or if your version of iPhoto is particularly old.

▲ *All images appear in thumbnail form once imported.*

In many ways iPhoto is similar to other image management and organizer applications. It can automatically download images from your connected camera or memory card in a card reader. It displays thumbnail views of your images and these can be resized using a slider. Apple uses the metaphor of a roll of film for each image acquisition session, so each time you download some photos you are prompted to create an identity for your new roll of virtual digital film. You can also import images that are already on your Mac's hard drive.

Once imported, all images in your Photo Library can be viewed in thumbnail form, searched and located by file name, folder name, date, etc. iPhoto has a flexible free-

▲ *iPhoto can create a 'book' of your images.*

format text search box for this purpose. You can then organize your photos into albums and add keywords, comments and titles for improved searching.

Hidden away in the latest versions of iPhoto are some useful keyboard shortcuts. For example, to find photos taken on an anniversary, in other words on the same date every year, hold down the control key and click on the target date in the calendar – all the photos stamped with that date will be found and displayed.

Earlier versions of iPhoto had only basic image tweaking and editing facilities – limited to functions such as crop, rotate, remove red eye, convert to black and white, etc. Later versions have been significantly updated and include RAW file support for a small, but slowly growing band of camera models – mainly Canon – and the introduction of an Adjust palette, with histogram display, for modifying exposure, levels and some colour attributes.

One area that remains frustrating is iPhoto's export options, especially if you were hoping to use this with your RAW files. Although you can preview and adjust your RAW files to some extent, the experience is less satisfying and effective than using Photoshop with Adobe Camera RAW installed. Also, iPhoto will only natively export to JPEG from RAW format and its standard quality settings are somewhat mediocre. Luckily, you can use iPhoto to export in original format and let your RAW images be processed in an alternative RAW conversion application.

Besides image viewing and organizing, iPhoto can also turn albums into slide shows and web galleries and you can easily make photo emails. There are also various printing options, including connection to online commercial printing services.

▶ *The crop tool is one of the basic image editing functions.*

OTHER USEFUL APPLICATIONS
IMAGE STITCHING

The seamless stitching of several images together is ideal for assembling ultra wide panoramas. Another use of stitching, often overlooked, is expansion of the view vertically as well as horizontally, especially if you are lacking a suitable wideangle lens to use in portrait mode. The result may look like an normal single shot at first glance, until you see the perspective and the detail.

Although good stitching programs can cope with small variations in exposure and colour balance between images, it is better to set your camera to manual exposure and white balance settings and determine the correct and constant values for these variables by pointing the camera at the main focus of your intended panorama.

There are several stitcher programs available, each with its own particular strengths and weaknesses. One of the most comprehensive and sophisticated is Panorama Tools, which is free but difficult to master. A popular stand alone program is RealViz Stitcher Express. Photomerge, a stitching plug-in bundled with Adobe Photoshop, is another popular choice.

REALVIZ STITCHER EXPRESS

Stitcher Express, from imaging stitching specialists RealViz, can build panoramas for web sites, printing and for 3D viewing. It can create up to 360 degree panoramic images using horizontally and vertically overlapping images. Virtual camera angles with zoom,

▲ *The first step is to align your images.*

Digital Camera Handbook

▲ *Choose the stitch image option (top) before adjusting.*

pan, and roll motion are possible. Results can be rendered in planar, cylindrical or spherical projection, supporting QuickTime Cylindrical QTVR and Cubic QTVR.

The full version, aimed at professional users, is five times the price. For this you get features including QuickTime VR Hotspot Edition, the ability to convert panoramic files from one format to another, better control over image blending options, VRML and ShockWave 3D support, and automatic vignetting correction.

The advantage of Stitcher Express is that it is a simple and straightforward program, with easy to understand instructions. There are three workspace tabs: start, stitch and render. Stage one is to load the component images into Stitcher's browser pane. Then, one at a time and in the correct order, you drag and drop each image into the stitch tab workspace and press the stitch button. Once that frame is aligned you move the next one into position. Once they have all been connected up, you move to the render tab to preview your result in low resolution and export the final composite.

Besides the usual static views, you can choose to output your panorama in QuickTime movie format, so that you can rotate and tilt the scene with your mouse.

▶ *Straightening the horizon is the next step.*

▼ Render the image (top), then create.

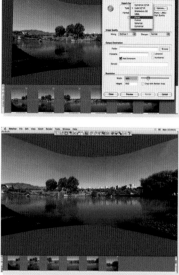

ADOBE PHOTOSHOP PHOTOMERGE

Photomerge is supplied with most recent versions of Adobe Photoshop and is therefore one of the most widely distributed of all panorama stitchers. Photomerge is much simpler to use than Stitcher Express, and although it only caters for static rendered results, it will attempt to automatically align selected donor images. It also has rendering options for both normal perspective and cylindrical views, and is very fast at assembling the initial preview.

Despite this, Photomerge is not as tolerant of poorly fitting donor images and there are fewer configuration options, such as focal length equalization. Care must be taken when photographing the segments to be stitched, as overlapping of 25–40 per cent is required. If the overlap is less, Photomerge may not be able to assemble the panorama automatically. On the other hand, each segment must not overlap excessively – more than 70 per cent can cause difficulties, and blending may not be as effective.

In the latest versions of Photoshop Elements, Photomerge is accessible via file > new menu. You can locate Photomerge in Photoshop CS and CS2 by going to file > automate menu. Instead of creating a new conventional image editing session, a file selection window will pop up. Navigate to the folder containing your images, select them and click OK. If the automatic arrangement mode is ticked, as it is by default, then the Photomerge plug-in will load each image as an individual layer and align them in order, assuming that they are within the acceptable overlap zone. You will be presented with a preview of the panorama, and may have to manually fit any segments that can't be automatically arranged. Manual fitting may result in a less successful final product.

If there are obvious changes in density or there are splits in the joins, tick the advanced blending mode. If no optimizing is necessary, you can view the panorama in perspective view, characterized by increasingly large views to either side of the central segment. If your version of Photomerge has a vanishing point position tool, use this to minimize perspective error. Tick on the cylindrical mapping option for an optically corrected view. The panorama can then be exported and any rough edges smoothed to create the final result.

If you can produce a satisfactory panorama with Photomerge, you can probably produce even better ones with a superior package such as RealViz Stitcher.

◄ The end result using RealViz Stitcher.

OTHER USEFUL APPLICATIONS

DVD BURNER SOFTWARE

When recordable CD drives were first developed, the software for transferring your files on to CDs, or CD burner software, was very simple – you selected the files for copying and pressed go. Since then, that basic functionality has been built into both Windows XP and Mac OSX. For developers of 'burner' software, the challenge has been to add value in terms of new features and options.

The advent of mainstream digital photography has coincided neatly with the rise of recordable CDs and DVDs, and most digital photographers would struggle without such a resource. Two popular CD and DVD burner packages are Roxio Easy Media Creator and ULead CD and DVD PictureShow. These packages make it easy to find and archive your photo files, set up and distribute automated slideshows and more.

▲ *DVD players are great for showing pictures.*

DVD-PLAYER COMPATIBLE SLIDE SHOWS

DVD players of the type that are plugged into your TV don't generally have the ability to read and display image files, although some can display standard JPEG

Digital Camera Handbook

images. To create a slideshow that can be viewed using a domestic DVD player, you need to create a movie that plays as a series of scenes showing your static images, perhaps separated by animated transitions. Many slideshow packages are not able to produce DVD slideshows – this is because there is uncertainty concerning the ownership and charging for commercial rights involved in the MPEG2 technology required for creating DVDs. Instead, you normally have to make do with VCD (Video CD) quality slideshows, which most DVD players are compatible with. However, the on-screen resolution of VCD is very low and if you have a good sized, sharp TV, the viewing experience will be not be particularly good.

ROXIO EASY MEDIA CREATOR

Easy Media Creator is actually a suite of 18 different applications tied together by a home page-style application launcher. It is a Windows-only package, but Roxio offers a separate suite for Mac users called 'Toast'. Easy Media Creator applications are very easy to use, but more ambitious users might find them lacking in sophisticated features.

▼ *Roxio Easy Media Creator.*

Some of Easy Media Creator applications are available separately as potentially costly stand-alone packages, such as PhotoSuite for photo image editing, VideoWave for editing videos and Backup My PC for managed PC system backups.

PhotoSuite has been covered on page 204. The other Easy Media Creator applications of use to a digital photographer include Media Manager for organizing and retrieving your media files; Disk Copier for making security backups of your disks or copies for distributing; Label Creator for creating designs that can be printed on to disk labels; and MyDVD SlideShow, for creating slideshows with animated fades between each picture and the option of an audio soundtrack. Slideshows you have built can also be recorded to CD or DVD.

ULEAD CD & DVD PICTURESHOW

ULead CD & DVD PictureShow is an easy to use and affordable slideshow builder package that turns still images and video movie clips into CD or DVD shows – the latter advisable for better on-screen quality.

ULead Photo Explorer, an album-style photo image manager and organizer package, is available by itself or bundled with CD & DVD PictureShow. This is where you will find the more utilitarian options for copying folders of images to CD or DVD for backup purposes.

The CD & DVD PictureShow workspace is divided into a three-stage building process: organize, theme and burn. The first stage is to organize the images and video clips you want to turn into slideshows. You can arrange the order and also apply simple image fixes to address colour balance, sharpness, exposure and even-out skin tones. You are presented with a selection of four different 'fixed'

▲ *With ULead PictureShow, the first step is to organize your images.*

▲ *The theme stage allows you to customize the presentation.*

versions of the image and you can select the one that looks the best. You can also decorate the images with clip art and text before selecting the destination disk format (VCD, SVCD or DVD). If you can't stretch to DVD, SVCD is better than VCD.

The theme stage adds motion menus and audio and customizes your disk menu appearance, slideshow photo frames and effects. If you are creating a slideshow from a video clip, you can trim unwanted sections from the beginning and end. At this stage with still image slideshows, you can introduce animated transitions between each image, modify the duration of an image and choose effects like a subtle pan and tilt motion as each frame is displayed.

The theme stage also gives you the opportunity to import music files to form a soundtrack for your show, although some ready-made tracks are provided for simplicity. It is also possible to fit the slideshow to the length of your soundtrack, neatly fading the sound out just as the slideshow finishes. A full preview of the show is then accessible and you can skip back to the initial organize stage any time you like.

▲ *You are now ready to burn your slideshow to a disk.*

There are two options once you are satisfied that your slideshow is ready to be burned to CD or DVD – either you can burn a disk to create a final CD or DVD, or you can create a folder on your hard drive containing the necessary files in order to burn as many copies as you like. As a final touch, you can design and print both a CD label and an index insert for the disk jewel case.

▲ Phase One is a powerful processing package.

PLUG-INS: THE BEST AROUND

RAW PROCESSING

PHASE ONE CAPTURE ONE

Danish company Phase One is probably best known for its Capture One RAW conversion package. It is arguably the most powerful RAW conversion solution and is also one of the most expensive. If you don't need the direct camera connection features of the Pro version, there is a cheaper LE version.

Capture One is laid out on-screen in three distinct areas with an image file thumbnail browser to the left, an image preview pane in the centre and an adjustments settings and status panel to the right. Click on an image on the thumbnail browser and it is instantly displayed in the large preview pane. You can choose to see burned out highlights coloured in red and it is reassuring to see these areas reduce when adjusting the exposure bias.

There are five adjustment settings tabs – capture, white balance, exposure, focus and process. The capture tab displays a histogram and information about storage resources. The white balance tab contains two magnified before and after preview panes displaying the area around your mouse pointer when it is over the image. There is fine control over colour temperature and tint, plus hue and saturation. The exposure tab also has magnified before and after previews to monitor adjustments made using tone curve and levels adjustments. The focus tab deals with sharpness, noise and banding suppression. The process tab exports processed images with batch processing.

RAWSHOOTER ESSENTIALS

Another Danish company, Pixmantec, has stirred up a lot of interest with its RAW image conversion package, RawShooter Essentials (RSE). It is a sophisticated piece of software, and it is free to download from Pixmantec's website. If you are familiar with Phase One's Capture One software, you will instantly have a feel for RSE, which isn't surprising because Pixmantec is run by former Phase One people.

▲ *RawShooter Essentials is a sophisticated package.*

RSE has a very unusual on-screen layout and user interface. Across the top you will see thumbnails of RAW images contained in a target folder. The centre of the screen displays the main preview of an image being worked on and to the right is a panel containing all the adjustment and export controls.

When optimizing images, a selection of preset adjustment profiles representing flat, indoor and outdoor views can be selected and applied one after another in real time, saving time in finding a ballpark match before fine-tuning. There are the usual colour, contrast, brightness white balance and sharpness controls, and an enhanced 'detail extraction' sharpness tool. Settings applied to each image are saved in the same folder as the original image and associated with it when that image is reloaded. Semi-automated batch conversion processes speed up the workflow.

A more fully-featured commercial professional version of RSE is being developed and this may add a tone curves tool and other more advanced correction tools for things such as chromatic aberrations and lens distortion.

ADOBE CAMERA RAW

Adobe Camera RAW (ACR) is the official raw conversion support for Adobe Photoshop. It is a plug-in which, in its version 3.x form, is compatible with Photoshop CS2 and Photoshop Elements 3.0. There is no ACR support for Elements versions 1 and 2. If you need to keep up to date with the

▲ *Adobe Camera RAW is part of Adobe Photoshop.*

latest cameras, Adobe is nearly always releasing support for new cameras before anyone else.

When you open a RAW file that is supported by ACR, a preview window opens and you are presented with tools for preparing the image to be converted and either loaded into Photoshop for further editing or for direct export to a standard format image file.

You can reset the white balance, adjust overall exposure, tone levels, saturation and fine tune shadow and highlight brightness and contrast. The overall versatility of ACR depends on which version of Photoshop you are using. If you are using Photoshop CS2, you will have four additional tabs housing advanced sharpening and noise reduction functions, lens distortion and chromatic aberration corrections, tone curve adjustment and camera profile adjustments, saved and re-usable adjustments, cropping, user preference settings, image straightening and batch processing.

ACR is a very competent RAW conversion solution, especially for Photoshop CS2 users, though if streamlined workflow is a priority, Phase One Capture One and RawShooter Essentials have the edge.

BREEZEBROWSER

Breeze System's BreezeBrowser excels in the area of image browsing and, especially browsing and managing RAW files. Its RAW conversion capabilities are comparatively basic and it has an uninspiring user interface, but it has an interesting noise reduction function and good batch processing facilities. It does have some extended features for getting the most out of Canon RAW files, and powerful and elegant RAW processing solutions for some jobs.

▲ *BreezeBrowser specializes in browsing and managing RAW files.*

▲ DxO enables you to improve the quality of your pictures.

DXO OPTICS PRO

Paris-based DxO is relatively new to the image processing software scene but has already made its mark with Optics Pro. This is a camera or camera plus lens specific solution for optimizing images using pre-researched data on the characteristics of a particular camera model's sensor and lens performance. As

the software knows what needs to be corrected from a model-specific profile, it can be more precise and adventurous with its processing functions, including correction of chromatic aberrations and geometric lens distortions, optimization of dynamic range and reduction of image noise. It will work with JPEG or TIFF images produced by supported cameras and lens combinations, but it is at its best when processing RAW files. It works extremely well but, so far, only a relatively small number of camera and lens models are currently supported.

▶ The top image has been improved using Optics Pro.

PLUG-INS: THE BEST AROUND

UPSCALING: GENUINE FRACTALS & PXL SMARTSCALE

If you want to print a tightly cropped portion of an image that is lacking in pixels, or make a huge enlargement from a normal resolution image, the image file needs to be expanded substantially. This means stretching the image data to fill many more pixels than the original. For example, a six million pixel file printed 20 inches wide at 300 ppi will need its pixel dimensions updated from 2000 x 3000 to 6000 x 9000, which is 48 million more pixels than the original file. In the resulting print, you would see individual pixel squares, especially when it was viewed close up.

By upscaling, you can avoid the aliasing effects of visible pixels. Most image editing packages will upscale using a relatively simple bicubic interpolation process. One original pixel is transformed into several new ones resulting in a smoother result, although as the image information is spread out it looks soft and some critical detail can break up or appear smeared. In some particularly bad examples, patterning can result, also obscuring detail. Sharpening will almost certainly be necessary, but this can introduce new and unwanted effects too.

Clever software can do a better job of upscaling, such as the two Photoshop plug-in solutions from onOne Software – pxl SmartScale and Genuine Fractals. Originally

Digital Camera Handbook

part of the Celartem Extensis label, both SmartScale and Genuine Fractals were sold to onOne in 2005. In fact, Genuine Fractals was developed by a company called LizardTech, and SmartScale used to be called VFZoom.

ONONE GENUINE FRACTALS

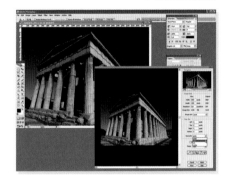

▼ Genuine Fractals.

Fractals are complex mathematically-generated objects that have recursive properties – large fractal shapes are composed of smaller and smaller versions of the same shape, making them eminently scalable. Theoretically, you can apply fractal mathematics to represent real world detail and then scale it up or down, without loss of information. In reality, Genuine Fractals can produce cleaner-looking image scale results than plain bicubic interpolation, though the image will still need sharpening. Genuine Fractals works best when there is a lot of amorphous or natural detail.

▲ OnOne Pxl SmartScale improves definition.

ONONE PXL SMARTSCALE

SmartScale uses vector analysis and transformation of the original image for upscaling. Vectors are ideal for scaling and this is why drawing programs, such as Adobe Illustrator, use vectors rather than bitmaps. SmartScale is particularly good at scaling images with plenty of sharply defined detail with discernible edges. The one vulnerability of Smartscale is a tendency to produce results that appear over-sharpened, though there is a degree of sharpening control in the software.

A word of warning about any expensive upscaling solution, such as Genuine Fractals or SmartScale – they are not a magic solutions and the benefits are limited, especially with certain images and when used in isolation.

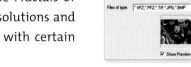

▶ The benefits of software programs such as SmartScale can be limited.

PLUG-INS: THE BEST AROUND

SHARPENING: PIXELGENIUS

PixelGenius, a company formed in 2001, have developed a range of plug-ins for Photoshop which provide photo enhancement resources designed from a photographer's perspective. The effects in PixelGenius's PhotoKit plug-ins are actually incorporated into Photoshop by Adobe, but the plug-ins enable the user to think in photographic terms to find and apply the right effect.

PhotoKit plug-ins are not designed to be used with any other applications apart from the latest Photoshop generations. Some PhotoKit effects are now also available for Photoshop Elements in a special PhotoKit EL edition.

PIXELGENIUS PHOTOKIT SHARPENER

The sharpness of an image is a subjective thing, but badly sharpened digital images can exhibit nasty side effects such as worsened noise, halos along sharp edges, an unpleasant hardening of image contrast and, oddly enough, the loss of detail information. Cameras apply a certain level of sharpening to the images they produce, and all good cameras provide adjustment of in-camera sharpening levels. If you are using RAW files, you can choose your own level of sharpening as part of the RAW conversion process, though the requirements of one image to the next might be different. It can be good idea to minimize in-camera sharpening and use a suite of specialized sharpening filters, like the PixelGenius PhotoKit Sharpener.

PhotoKit Sharpener is a series of Photoshop Automation plug-ins. Once installed, instead of being executed from the filter or action menus in Photoshop, you will find three additional tools in the Photoshop Automation menu (file > automate) – PhotoKit capture sharpener, PhotoKit creative sharpener and PhotoKit output sharpener. As their names suggest, these PhotoKit Sharpener layer sets are

Digital Camera Handbook

specifically designed for each of the three stages in image capture, creative processing and output workflow. Each presents the user with two menus – a sharpener set selection and a sharpener effect selection.

It is quite easy to use PhotoKit Sharpeners – just choose a combination of set and effect and then view the result on your image in Photoshop. As PhotoKit tools operate via layer sets, you toggle the layer visibility to compare the before and after results (click on the 'eye' button in the layers palette). You can also combine the effects of several PhotoKit Sharpener layer sets.

▼ *An unsharpened image (top) is improved.*

Here is a summary of what each layer set offers.

PHOTOKIT CAPTURE SHARPENER

This deals with images scanned from various film formats, digital capture backs and a number of base digital image categories. Effects range from super fine edge sharpen to wide edge sharpen.

PHOTOKIT CREATIVE SHARPENER

Here you have the choice of being able to apply smoothing or sharpening effects via a brush or just sharpening effects applied across the whole image.

PHOTOKIT OUTPUT SHARPENER

Four options are provided for output sharpening – continuous or halftone images, ink jet printer output and on-screen web and multimedia display. It is important to note that sharpening at this stage should be applied to the image at its final output resolution.

All these effects are delivered by layer sets – you can find their application by using the layer opacity slider.

PLUG-INS: THE BEST AROUND

ENHANCING: PIXELGENIUS PHOTOKIT COLOR

Even slight adjustments to the colour balance of an image can have a dramatic effect, but images can be completely transformed by the dramatic colour effects provided by PixelGenius PhotoKit Color.

As with the PixelGenius PhotoKit Sharpener tools described previously, PixelGenius PhotoKit Color effects are delivered via layer sets selected from the Photoshop automate menu. You can load more than one effect and overlay them, adjusting the layer opacity of each set for fine adjustment.

CROSS PROCESSING

These filters try to reproduce the unusual effects of processing C41 type colour negative film in E6 slide film process chemistry and vice versa, in a variety of strengths. A selection of lab colour effects is also included.

COLOR OVERLAY

This comprises nine different colour overlay filters – red, green, emerald, blue, cyan, violet, magenta, yellow and orange.

SPLIT TONING

Primarily designed to apply to black and white images in RGB colour mode, you can also experiment with full colour images. There are twelve split toning effects designed to mimic the effects when toning silver halide prints. Colour splits available include: blue/sepia, blue/cyan, red/green, red/sepia, green/magenta, green/yellow, cyan/sepia, yellow/blue, yellow/red, magenta/yellow and magenta/orange.

TONE ENHANCE

These adjust contrast and approximate exposure bias in fractions of a stop across the range of one stop. Options include: Plus 1/4 Stop, Plus 1/2 Stop, Plus 3/4 Stop,

Plus 1 Stop, Minus 1/4 Stop, Minus 1/2 Stop, Minus 3/4 Stop, Minus 1 Stop, Contrast Mask 1, Contrast Mask 2, Contrast Mask 3, Boost Contrast 1, Boost Contrast 2, Boost Contrast 3, Midtone Contrast 1, Midtone Contrast 2 and Midtone Contrast 3.

COLOR ENHANCE

These effects improve skies, foliage, skin tones and other common photographic subjects. The choices include: Blue Enhance, Blue Enhance + Mask, Green Enhance, Green Enhance + Mask, Red Enhance, Red Enhance + Mask, Skin Tone Enhance, Skin Tone Enhance + Mask, Blue/Amber Grad 1, Blue/Amber Grad 2, Blue/Amber Grad 3, Warm/Cool 1, Warm/Cool 2, Warm/Cool 3, Grainy Contrast 1, Grainy Contrast 2, Grainy Pastel 1 and Grainy Pastel 2.

CC CORRECTION

If you have ever used conventional colour compensation (CC) filters, these will be rather familiar. You can choose from: .075CC Yellow, .15CC Yellow, .30CC Yellow, .075CC Red, .15CC Red, .30CC Red, .075CC Magenta, .15CC Magenta, .30CC Magenta, .075CC Blue, .15CC Blue, .30CC Blue, .075CC Cyan, .15CC Cyan, .30CC Cyan, .075CC Green, .15CC Green, and .30CC Green.

CT CORRECTION

For more pronounced colour shifting requirements, there are four orange and four blue based filters: CT Orange 1/8, CT Orange 1/4, CT Orange 1/2, CT Orange 3/4, CT Orange Full, CT Blue 1/8, CT Blue 1/4, CT Blue 1/2, CT Blue and CT Blue Full.

▲ *A number of different effects can be achieved with enhancing tools.*

RSA COLOR CORRECTION

This provides a set of three automatic colour balance correctors – RSA Gray Balance Standard for general purpose grey balancing. RSA Gray Balance Fine for a slower but more accurate solution than the standard option, and RSA Neutralize for tackling more severe colour casts.

PLUG-INS: THE BEST AROUND

PIXELGENIUS PHOTOKIT EFFECTS

PixelGenius PhotoKit Effects is the 'Analog Effects Toolkit', comprising 141 effects that recreate popular and expert photo enhancements and special effects originally developed for silver halide film and the darkroom.

PhotoKit Effects are also delivered via layer sets from the Photoshop automate menu. You can load more than one effect and overlay them, adjusting the layer opacity of each set for fine adjustment. You can also optimize their accessibility by building custom Photoshop actions around them.

The 141 effects are contained in eight sets:

▲ *PixelGenius PhotoKit Effects can dramtically change the look of your photograph.*

B&W TONING SET

Nine effects are featured, covering selenium, platinum, brown and cold toning.

BURN TONE SET

This set has 20 different effects for burning in areas of an image at different strengths.

Digital Camera Handbook
Digital Camera Handbook

DODGE TONE SET

The inverse of the Burn Tone Set and has a similar range of effects.

COLOUR BALANCE SET

Of the 14 options in this set, four warm an image up, four cool and six more enhance any of the six additive and subtractive primary colours.

COLOUR TO BLACK AND WHITE SET

If you try a simple mode switch from colour to mono grey scale, you will probably discover that images do not have that 'black and white sparkle' by default. It is a complex process to extract the best results when converting from colour to mono. Different areas of colour in an image result in different brightness and contrasts of grey in the mono result. Adjusting these relationships can radically alter the mood and vibrancy of a mono image. There are 12 PhotoKit colour to mono effects, with different grey balances according to the amount of red, blue, yellow, blue, orange or green in the original colour image.

IMAGE ENHANCEMENT SET

There are 13 effects in this set, all but three of them for sharpening. The remaining three effects deal with noise reduction.

PHOTO EFFECTS SET

The largest of the eight sets, with 28 effects, the Photo Effects Set simulates film grain at different ISO levels, provides a fog lens filter for making highlights glow, creates subtle vignettes and blurs the perimeter of a scene while leaving the centre sharp.

TONE CORRECTION SET

These 25 effects correct the density of black and create the most appealing highlights. In the PhotoKit manual, the Tone Correction Set is described as the most mission critical. Controls are provided to lighten and darken shadows and highlights to apply contrast masks to bias mid-tones without affecting shadows and highlights, therefore maintaining the dynamic range of the image. There are some overall exposure fine-tuning controls that can be compared to f-stop adjustments.

Section Three: Resources

PLUG-INS: THE BEST AROUND

FREE SOFTWARE

Thanks to the generosity of some programmers and organizations such as the Open Software Foundation, there is much free software available.

Some programs are freeware – which means that you are not expected to pay for it, but you can make a donation – others are shareware and you may be given the option of paying for it, or after a modest payment you can unlock certain features or become eligible for support. Then there are programs aimed at commercial users that are licensed for free use by private individuals. Some 'light' editions of commercial programs are also distributed free of charge, with the hope that you will upgrade to the full commercial version. Finally, there are full commercial programs that you can use without restriction, but you will be repeatedly reminded to pay the registration fee.

One word of caution – freeware does introduce the mild risk of software viruses, worms and spyware. Make sure that your anti-virus software is up to date, that you use a software firewall and spyware detection and, finally, make regular backups.

IRFANVIEW (http://www.irfanview.com/)

Developed by the Austrian Irfan Skiljan, IrfanView is an excellent utility for viewing images of a very wide variety of image file formats, resizing images using enhanced algorithms, converting image formats, accessing embedded metadata, creating slide shows, rotating images losslessly, batch processing and more. It has grown steadily over the years and is highly recommended to

▲ *IrfanView is an excellent piece of software.*

install for emergencies. It is also a very simple installation that is guaranteed not to mess with the Windows registry.

▲ Microsoft RAW is a free Windows XP upgrade.

MICROSOFT RAW IMAGE THUMBNAILER AND VIEWER FOR WINDOWS XP (http://www.microsoft.com)

Until recently, it was not possible to thumbnail preview camera RAW files using the standard Windows browser. However, recognizing the rise in use of RAW files by digital photographers, Microsoft has now released a free Windows XP upgrade that provides this functionality. The RAW Image Thumbnailer and Viewer consists of two components – a lightweight 'shell extension' for Windows XP that provides thumbnail views of RAW files in Windows Explorer, and a RAW Image Viewer application with an interface similar to the standard Windows Picture and Fax Viewer. At the time of writing only selected Nikon and Canon cameras were supported and you need to have Windows XP Service Pack 2 installed.

THE GIMP (http://www.gimp.org)

▲ The GIMP is a sophisticated editing package.

'GIMP' is an acronym for GNU Image Manipulation Program. The GIMP is a sophisticated layers-based image editing and manipulation package. It is freely available for Mac, Windows and Unix computer platforms. It was conceived as a free alternative to Photoshop by students at Berkeley University in the 1990s. The GIMP was used for all the graphics preparation in the partially animated Hollywood movie, Scooby-Doo. All the basic bitmap and vector path editing resources are present and it can satisfy most of your routine imaging and manipulation needs, but Photoshop and other commercial alternatives, such as PaintShop Pro, offer more extended features and a more conventional and easier to understand user interface.

Section Three: Resources

ZERO ASSUMPTION DIGITAL IMAGE RECOVERY
(http://www.z-a-recovery.com/)

Zero Assumption Digital Image Recovery is a freeware data recovery tool, specifically designed to work with digital images. It can recover digital photos accidentally deleted from digital camera memory cards and even, in some cases, after a card has been reformatted. The program will work to recover image files on a memory card if the camera is connected via USB to your computer or if the memory card is inserted in to a connected card reader. Version 1.2 supports the following file formats: GIF, JPEG, TIFF, CRW – Canon RAW data for selected camera models, MOV – QuickTime movie clips and WAV – Microsoft Waveform audio files.

▲ *Zero Assumption, a useful data recovery tool.*

MIHOV EXIF RENAMER
(http://www.mihov.com)

Mihov EXIF Renamer is a very simple program written by Miha Psenica, from Ljubljana, Slovenia. The program examines the EXIF metadata of camera images in a selected folder and reads the time each picture was taken. It then appends this time to the file name of the image. You can also edit the time stamp in the EXIF data – maybe the wrong time zone was set. It can also be helpful when creating slideshows that order the images by date, enabling you to force your own order of display.

VISUALPHOTOCOMPARE
(http://home.planet.nl/~edejong/visualphotocompare/)

This program, from EeEeSoft.tk, compares images by visual content. It can search through folders to locate images, regardless of size, that have similar appearances. It can find duplicate images and different sized versions of the same image. It works by analyzing an 8 x 8 grid over the image and calculating the average RGB

▲ *Mihov EXIF Renamer.*

Digital Camera Handbook
Digital Camera Handbook

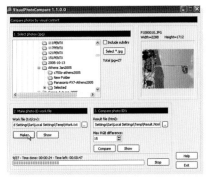

values for each cell. It can then compare the respective cell values of different images.

PICTURE-SHARK (http://www.picture-shark.com)

This rather dangerous-sounding program is actually a utility for visually watermarking your images. It has an easy to use, step-by-step wizard interface to help you to prepare your watermark image for inclusion in selected image files. You are provided control over the transparency of the watermark and its positioning and you can feather its boundary for more subtle integration with the destination image. Once set up, the program can watermark hundreds of images per minute.

MONITOR CALIBRATION WIZARD (http://www.hex2bit.com)

While a hardware-based monitor calibrator is undoubtedly the best option for ensuring your monitor is tuned correctly, software calibration by eye is a reasonable second best. Some software packages, such as Adobe Photoshop, come with such utilities for this purpose (i.e. Adobe Gamma). If you do not have such a utility, the Hex2Bit Monitor Calibration Wizard is a wizard-style calibrator that generates proprietary monitor profiles, though standard ICC/ICM profiles are recognized and can be overlaid.

KODAK EASYSHARE (http://www.kodak.com)

Kodak EasyShare is a surprisingly competent and well-presented album-based image file organizer and image fixing solution that Kodak distributes free of charge. You do not have to use Kodak

cameras or printers to use EasyShare. It will recognize and thumbnail BMP, JPEG, GIF and TIFF images and even Photoshop PSD images. It is also the only way to display and convert images in Kodak's KDC RAW format, and it can handle some of the more commonly used audio and video movie formats. Other features include photo emailing, slide show building and CD burning.

▲ *Kodak EasyShare, a file organizer and image fixing solution.*

SOFTWARE IN DEPTH

BASIC IMAGE EDITING
GETTING TO GRIPS
WITH IMAGE EDITING

Image editing is great fun and can be very simple to do, so don't let yourself be put off by the array of jargon, tools, palettes and commands. This next section will guide you through the basics of how to get the most from your digital photographs by using image-editing software on your home computer.

▲ *Use image-editing software to correct basic errors such as straightening a crooked horizon.*

Once you have taken your picture and successfully downloaded it onto your PC, you may be ready to print or share it on the Internet. However, you may wish to improve or enhance your photograph. You might not have held the camera straight and the horizon is slanted, or your subject may have red eye. Whatever your problems are, your image editing software will help you to correct them with only a few clicks of the mouse.

▲ *The workspace of Adobe Photoshop Elements is typical of most editing programs. The Toolbar sits to the left with the various palettes to the right of your screen.*

SOFTWARE PACKAGES

There are a great many editing software packages available on the market today (see previous chapter). You will sometimes find simple or cut down versions bundled with your camera, scanner or PC. They can be a good starting point for your basic editing, and over the next few chapters many of the simple techniques you will learn can generally be achieved with most of these packages.

Digital Camera Handbook

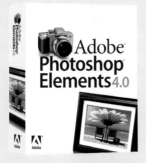

But if you are serious about creating quality and controlled results, it may be worth investing in a home package such as Adobe Photoshop Elements or Corel Paint Shop Pro. These home-editing programmes offer more sophisticated functions and tools with a complete photo-management system.

▲ *Adobe Photoshop Elements.*

▲ *Paint Shop Pro X.*

SET UP

Before you buy your software, it is a good idea to check out your PC's RAM and hard drive space. A minimum of 256 MB of RAM is normally required and 800 MB of available free hard drive space. You will also need a CD ROM drive and, for most applications, at least a Pentium III processor. The software will become more stable and run faster if you have more than the minimum requirements of processing power. You will also need a monitor that can display at least 1024 x 768 pixels on screen in 16-bit colour.

AFTER INSTALLATION

You should also spend some time assessing your work place. It is important to try to keep the monitor faced away from direct window light because the reflections may distract you. Place your PC in an internal corner with the monitor facing the wall, and try not to have an overhead light casting shadows across the screen.

Any unwanted extra light can hinder you in achieving a consistent and accurate result. Make sure you have enough desk space to move your mouse freely and that you have full access to your keyboard for any shortcuts.

▶ *Make sure your PC is set up correctly and placed in a suitable position before you start.*

WHAT IS IMAGE EDITING?

Image editing is altering the appearance of the picture from its original state – this can mean anything from small adjustments that are almost unnoticeable to extreme enhancements that dramatically change the entire image.

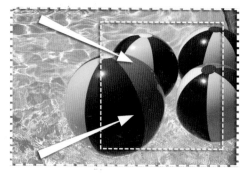

▲ *Cropping an image isolates a smaller image area and deletes the remaining pixels.*

Most of the skills in these next chapters used to be achieved in a traditional darkroom, but now you will discover how digital manipulation can be done on your PC.

By using one of the most popular and powerful home-editing software packages, Adobe Photoshop Elements, you will learn how to use tools effectively and apply commands correctly. You will learn to crop creatively, correct colours and tone and apply finishing touches such as borders and text.

THE BASICS

A digital image is made up from thousands of small squares of colour called pixels. The more pixels an image has, the higher the resolution of the image. When you edit an image on a PC, you are altering these squares of colour by changing their colour or brightness. You can copy and paste them, move them around or even delete them entirely.

▲ *Image editing can improve the appearance of your photographs.*

▲ This enlarged section of the image illustrates how its resolution is made up of small coloured squares called pixels. Screen resolution is 72 pixels per inch and home printing is best performed with at least 200 pixels per inch.

Generally you won't see these pixels as separate squares because they are too small. If an image on screen is at 100 per cent magnification, then the pixels displayed will be grouped together 72 pixels per inch (ppi) by 72 per inch. This is called screen resolution and is the default resolution for most digital cameras (some pro models will save at a printing resolution of between 200 and 300 ppi). The more megapixels your camera has, the bigger the physical size of the image will be, but its native resolution will stay at 72 ppi unless you change it. A five megapixel image may be made up of 2,592 pixels horizontally by 1,944 pixels vertically. The physical size would therefore be 2,592/72 = 36 inches (91 cm) by 1,944/72 = 27 inches (69 cm) and would obviously not all fit on your screen at once.

Resizing the image on your PC can compress more pixels into the inch (see pages 318–19 for more on resizing).

If you use the zoom tool, you can enlarge your image enough to be able to see the squares.

FINAL DESTINATION

It is a good idea to decide the final output for your image. If you try to work on a low resolution image, i.e. 4 in x 7 in image at 72 ppi, you will find that the pixels are quite noticeable, not only on screen but in the printed version. The more pixels your image has per square inch, the easier it will be to work with.

If you want to print your images from a home printer, then you must have enough pixels contained in your image to give you at least the minimum satisfactory quality. For home printers this is about 150 ppi. You can always size the image down if you want to send it by email, but it is rarely worthwhile to size it up for printing if it is not correct to start with.

TOOLS & PALETTES

In image editing software, most of the functions are displayed in little windows called floating palettes. They are movable, so they can be placed anywhere on your screen for ease of use. Everything you need to perform your chosen edit can be found on these palettes.

▲ *This is what you will see after you have launched your software.*

The first thing you will notice after launching your software is the tool bar palette on the top left hand side of your screen, the image menu bar along the top and the various palettes running down the right side. This is called the workspace and you can customize it to suit your requirements. You can close palettes which you are not using, and then reopen them using the image menu > window or the tool bar.

PALETTES

Various functions and commands can be performed from a palette. One of the most popular is the layers palette – this can build up new parts of an image, one on top of the other (for more see page 292). Special effects can be added to an image from the style palette, and technical help can be reached with the help palette.

TOOLS OF THE TRADE

The most important palette is the tool bar, which generally stays open at all times.This group of tools are

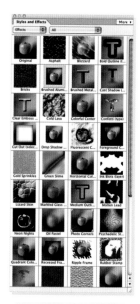

▲ *The styles and effects palette.*

Digital Camera Handbook

used directly on the surface of the image and can be accessed quickly by using keystrokes (see page 334 for more on keyboard shortcuts).

One of the most useful tools is the zoom tool, which looks like a magnifying glass. You can use this to enlarge or decrease the display of the image. If you click, hold the mouse down and drag across the image. You will notice a dotted outline appear – this is called a marquee. This dotted line tells you how much of the image to enlarge. When you have enlarged your image, you can navigate around by using the hand tool. Click and drag the hand tool to move the image around the screen.

SELECTIONS

The group of selection tools have small black triangles on their icons. If you click and hold down the mouse on these icons, a small fly-out palette will pop up offering you further options for that particular tool. The selection tools isolate areas of your image that you wish to either work on or exclude (see page 258 for more on selecting).

CROPPING & TEXT

The crop tool is accessed from the tool bar and can cut your image, removing parts that you don't need (see page 250 for more on cropping). The text tool can add words onto your image that can be re-sized and coloured (see page 268 for more on type).

PAINTING TOOLS

These tools are more for specialist enhancements that may require drawing or painting. Mainly used by designers on illustrations, these artistic tools are used sparingly by photographers because of their obvious effect.

ENHANCEMENT TOOLS

These are the photographer's favourites and are specifically designed for directly affecting the surface of an image. These tools can sharpen or blur specific areas or lighten or darken others. The clone stamp tool replicates parts of the same image area, which is essential if you want to get rid of dust, scratches, or even unwanted telegraph poles (see page 262 for more on using the clone stamp tool).

BASIC IMAGE EDITING

CROPPING

The crop tool is one of the simplest and most effective tools you can use with image editing. With this basic tool you can completely transform the composition of your picture by throwing away areas that you don't need.

With your image open so that the whole image is visible on screen, select the crop tool from the Tool Bar. Imagine you want to make your image area smaller by discarding the unwanted sections. In the upper left side of your image, click and hold down the mouse. Now drag to the right and down at the same time. You will notice a dotted line appears as you drag.

When you get close to the finish point, release the mouse. The dotted line (marquee) will stay over the image where you have just dragged.

The inside of the marquee is the area that will be retained and everything outside will be deleted.

▲ *The crop tool is found in the tool bar and is applied directly onto the image. The tinted area shows which part of the image will be deleted.*

HANDLES

At each corner of the crop marquee and in the middle of each border, you will see a small square. These squares are positioning handles, which you can use to adjust the crop area. Move your curser over the square and it will change to a double-ended arrow. Click and hold down the mouse on a handle to drag it to another position.

Before you make your crop, take some time in adjusting the marquee to make sure the area is accurate and that you are not deleting some of the image you may actually wish to keep. You might use the magnifier tool to enlarge each individual corner to aid cropping accuracy at this stage.

The outer area of the crop will be dimmed with a 75 per cent black tint. You can adjust this tint in the image menu bar by changing the opacity of the black. If you increase it up to 100 per cent, then the outer area of the selection will become completely black. To commit to your crop hit the return key on your keyboard.

FOCAL POINT

You can radically change the focus of your composition by using the crop. For instance in this example we can isolate a part of the photograph to create a more intimate result. By removing all the unwanted elements around the central subject, we now only see the main focal point.

▲ Careful use of cropping can alter an image's composition entirely. In this first example, the sky is cropped out for more emphasis on the steps, giving a sense of height. The second crop reveals more of the sky, emphasizing speed.

ROTATE THE CROP

Dragging the corner handles round can also rotate your crop. Move the curser slightly up and away from the handle and it will change to a curved double-ended arrow.

Click and pull the handle up or down to rotate.
Inside the crop marquee there is a small cross – this marks the centre of the crop area. You can move this centre position to change the axis of the rotation.

CORRECT A WONKY HORIZON

You can apply your cropping skills to correcting an uneven horizon.
Drag a crop marquee over your image making sure you have adequate space around the selection. Rotate the crop to match the horizon level. Make sure that all the crop selection is still within your image and hit the return key to apply.

CORRECTING COLOURS

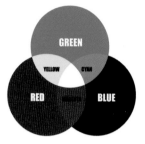

Occasionally your digital camera may interpret colours incorrectly – this could be because of problems such as not setting the white balance correctly or the natural daylight being overly yellow, like in an evening sunset. Even when you scan in a print, your scanner may reproduce colours differently to the original. With image editing software you can remove these casts and correctly enhance the existing colour that is already contained within the image.

All colours are made up from three primary colours: red, green and blue. White is created by a combination of all three colours and black is an absence of any. Where two colours overlap they create what is called a Subtractive Primary colour – you can see how these relate to each other in the colour wheel diagram below.

A cast occurs when other colours influence the whole image – for instance, the blueness of morning light or the yellow of evening sunshine. Artificial light can create problems, unless you compensate with the camera's auto white balance.

Some colour casts may be more prominent than others. You can see if your image contains a cast by looking for areas of white in the photograph. Generally it should be a clean white area where no other colours have influenced the white tone.

Most image editing software has more than one method to remove a colour cast by using auto functions.

▲ *Because the white balance was not set correctly, this image has a yellow colour cast.*

STEP ONE: AUTO COLOUR

With your image open, select enhance from the image menu bar and choose the auto colour correction command. Your cast should be removed instantly.

You can check this by examining the white areas of the image. From the image menu bar choose the window menu and select the info window. The

▲ The eye dropper tool performs auto colour correction.

small info palette will pop up. This contains the colour information illustrated by numbers. The RGB colour band is represented from black at 000 and white with all colours at 255.

Select the eye dropper tool from the tool bar. As you move the dropper over your image, you will see the numbers change value. Move the dropper to the white area of the image. The number value should be 255 or very close to it.

STEP TWO: LEVELS

If you still find there are unwanted colours within your image, then you can manually remove these by using the levels command from the image menu > enhance

drop down menu. The levels palette allows you to lighten or darken each colour

▲ Manual colour removal with the levels palette.

individually from the RGB drop down menu. Use the middle slider to increase the colour by moving it to the left or reduce it by sliding it to the right. Try not to make large adjustments, move the slider by small amounts and then re-check the white areas with the eye dropper.

▲ With fine-tuning in your image editing software you can create a much more pleasing result.

CORRECTING BRIGHTNESS & CONTRAST

▲ *Dull and flat, this image is in need of tonal correction.*

Sometimes your images may appear a little flat and lack punch. This can happen if the camera has not metered the correct exposure. Any brightness and true white may become quite grey resulting in muddy highlights and very little detail in the shadows.

You can correct this in Photoshop by adjusting the brightness and contrast of the light and dark pixels separately. It is worth remembering that too much lightening can 'blow out' any highlights and cause those image areas to look plain white, with little or no detail in them at all. With that in mind, it is easier to correct under exposed images than it is overexposed ones. You may find that your photos only need small amounts of enhancement to look much better.

METHOD ONE:
BRIGHTNESS & CONTRAST

The brightness and contrast function in most home-editing packages is a very basic tool. Found in the image menu bar, under the enhance > adjust lighting > brightness/contrast drop down menu, the palette consists of a brightness slider and a contrast slider. Drag the brightness slider to

▲ *The brightness and contrast sliders will help with tonal correction.*

Digital Camera Handbook

the right and it will increase the lightness of all the pixels in the image at once, light and dark. Drag the slider to the left and the image will darken.

The same thing happens with the contrast slider. Drag the arrow to the right and you will increase the lightness of all lighter pixels and darken all of the darker pixels in the image. This isn't the most accurate method of enhancing your image, as you will be adjusting areas that do not necessarily need it, but it can be a quick fix if you are in a hurry.

METHOD TWO: SHADOWS & HIGHLIGHTS

Auto functions are fine if you are not too worried about quality, but they leave little scope for fine-tuning.

Shadows and highlights, found in Photoshop Element's image menu bar (choose enhance > adjust lighting > shadow/highlights), gives you more control over how best to enhance certain areas.

▲ Shadows and highlights will enhance certain areas.

When you select the command, the palette appears on screen as normal, but your image is automatically enhanced at the same time. This is a good starting point so you can then use the sliders to increase or decrease the amount of enhancement. The top slider affects only the shadow pixels, the middle slider controls the highlights and the midtones are altered from the bottom slider. You can move the shadows slider back to 0 per cent to return to the original state before continuing if you wish.

▲ The enhanced image.

Once you have adjusted the sliders to enhance the shadows and highlights, the image may still look a little flat. Use the midtone slider to increase the overall contrast – this will hopefully eliminate any unwanted grey pixels.

SHARPENING YOUR PHOTOGRAPHS

Once you have downloaded your photos onto your PC you can zoom in to see the overall quality of the image. You may find that your image is slightly soft or blurred.

▲ *This image illustrates how the fur on a cat can benefit from sharpening.*

Blurring of your photos can be caused by many things, but generally it is either camera shake or a moving subject, but even a good quality camera can sometimes produce slightly soft results without any movement at all. Photoshop Elements and other image-editing packages offer a variety of choices for bringing the sharpness back to your image.

The filters sharpen, sharpen more and sharpen edges are all found in the filter drop down menu in the image menu bar and are all one-click auto functions that have no adjustable options. They are fine for a quick fix but they can leave you with disappointing results.

UNSHARP MASK

The unsharp mask palette can be accessed from the image menu – select filter > sharpen > unsharp mask. This option provides three sliders to control the amount of sharpening and a preview window so you can tell

▲ *Select the sharpen option in the filter menu.*

Digital Camera Handbook

just how the filter will affect areas of the image. You can click and drag from inside the preview window to change the view.

The top slider is called the amount and this gives the overall strength to the sharpen filter. This can be an amount from 0 per cent up to 500 per cent. Most images need only an amount of up to 50 per cent, but experiment first, making sure you change your view in the preview window to check the results.

▲ *The preview window shows how the filter will work.*

The middle slider is the radius and determines the number of pixels that will be affected around the subject's edge. The third slider is the threshold slider and is used to decide the difference between the pixels of the subject's edge and the surrounding pixels. The more you move the slider up, the further Photoshop will go past the subject's edge to look for pixels to sharpen. Play around with the sliders before you hit the OK button. Too much sharpening can result in a 'halo' effect where some of the pixels become too bright.

TOOL BAR: SHARPEN TOOL

This method is one of the most efficient ways to sharpen specific areas of an image. The sharpen tool can be found from the tool bar.

The sharpen tool is brush based and can be resized in the image menu bar. Select a suitable sized brush and keep the sharpen strength set to 50 per cent – you can adjust the intensity at any time by dragging the strength slider up or down.

Click, hold down the mouse and drag the sharpen tool over the area you wish to sharpen. The longer you keep the mouse pressed down, the more of the image you will sharpen. Like the unsharp mask, don't over apply it or it will become obvious.

▲ *Though subtle, the whiskers and fur are now sharper and more defined.*

SELECTING

Not all image enhancements are performed across the entire image. There will be many occasions where you will want to adjust only specific sections. Most software applications give you access to a variety of tools and commands that will allow you to isolate parts of your photograph relatively easily.

When making a selection, the edge of the area is usually displayed with a flashing black and white dotted line. This area is called a marquee. Everything within this line will be affected by your enhancements.

MARQUEE TOOL

The most basic of selection tools, you can choose from either a rectangular or elliptical shape.

▲ *The marquee tool can be used either as a rectangle or elliptical.*

Click in the top left corner of your image, where you want the selection to be and hold the down mouse as you drag down and to the right. The marquee dotted line then expands as you drag until you release the mouse. The dotted line then starts to flash, indicating that the selection is now active.

MAGIC WAND

The magic wand tool is probably the easiest way to select pixels in your image. Simply use the tool to click on a subject area that contains the same colour, for example a blue sky or green grass. The wand's selection will continue to determine the same tone and colour and work its way around until it gets to a different colour and then stops. The marquee will then be displayed showing you all the pixels selected. You can now perform your chosen enhancement from within the area. This is not the most efficient method of selecting but it is certainly one of the quickest. Choose select > deselect when you have finished to remove the selection.

▲ *Using the magic wand can quickly and simply select large areas of the same colour.*

LASSO TOOL

The lasso tool comes with three different options, the freeform lasso, the polygonal lasso and the magnetic lasso. These tools require you to draw your selection area and can give a much more controlled and precise result.

With the freeform lasso tool, click in your image and hold the mouse down, move the curser icon around the area you want to be selected. A thin grey line will indicate the path you have made so far. Move all the way around your area making sure that the path connects back to the starting point. Let go of the mouse and the marquee will start to flash. When drawing the path, it is very important that you don't let go – if you do, the path will join up at both ends and immediately become a selection. If this happens, choose deselect and start again.

The polygonal lasso is easier to use because the path is constructed by clicking points around your chosen area. In between clicks, the path stays connected to the end of the curser icon until you join the ends up. When you hover your curser over the end point, the icon will display a small circle, this lets you know that you are directly over the end point.

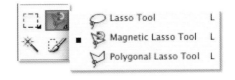

▲ *The lasso tool comes in three variations: freeform lasso, magnetic lasso and the polygon lasso.*

The magnetic lasso is a more sophisticated version of the freeform lasso as it works on the same principle of drawing, but actually works by tracing the edge of a subject. It drops down small path points as you continue around the area, right up against the edge. Again, when you get to the end point and join the path up, the curser icon will display a small circle to let you know you have completed the join.

REMOVING RED EYE

▲ *Light from the flash enters the dilated pupil, hits the blood vessels at the back and reflects directly back into the lens. Moving the flash source away from the line of sight will cause the reflection to bounce off away from the camera.*

This is probably one of the most common faults found with flash photography and can seem to ruin an otherwise great picture. With the help of your PC and software you can easily correct this, but you should also learn how to avoid it altogether.

In typical red eye conditions, the ambient light is dim, and because of that the pupil of the human eye will be fully dilated to allow in as much light as possible. The interior surface of the human eye is covered with blood vessels and these cause the red colour when the camera flash enters the eye, bouncing off the back and straight into the camera lens.

The way to avoid this is to not use the flash in the line of sight of your subject. For instance if your camera has a hot shoe, use a separate flashgun with a tilting head. This way you can bounce the light from the flash off the ceiling or walls. Or more easily, set your camera to auto red eye. This

▲ *Red eye can spoil an otherwise good picture.*

▲ *Reducing red eye is very easy with most image editing software packages.*

will send a burst of light from your camera before the main flash and force the pupils to close down before finally taking the picture. This auto function doesn't always work to perfection and you can still end up with unnatural results. So, the only way to correct red eye completely is with your computer.

Nearly all image editing software packages give you the tools to remove this annoying fault. Normally based on a soft brush shape, this useful tool can reduce the red hue found around the pupils. Remember that when using brush based tools, you must choose the size of your brush and its softness before you start, making sure that it will fit only within the eye area.

METHOD

The more popular image editing software packages such as Photoshop Elements will now give you auto tools to make erasing red eye even easier. Just select the red eye removal tool from the toolbox and click, holding the mouse down and drag a marquee over the offending eye and the redness will simply disappear.

You can adjust the size of the brush and the darkening strength from the image menu bar by moving the sliders between 0 per cent and 100 per cent. You do need to be subtle when using this tool.

▶ *Select the red eye removal tool from the toolbox and drag a marquee over the eye.*

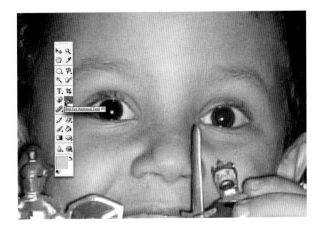

REMOVING UNWANTED DETAILS

It is very frustrating to find that your composition has been ruined by unwanted elements such as telegraph poles and wires or people walking through your shot. All these can be removed with the use of the clone stamp tool. This brilliant tool is also indispensable when scanning in your prints as it can remove dust and scratches and repair tears and rips.

The clone tool works by copying neighbouring pixels and laying them over the top of the area you wish to erase. As this is a brush based tool, it works best when you adjust the brush size continually throughout to suit the area. For fine details, it is advisable to keep the brush as small as possible to avoid obvious repetition of pixels. This is a very powerful tool and needs plenty of practice and patience, but when mastered, it can be one of the most effective tools at your disposal.

▲ This image is fine except for the telegraph poles. They can easily be removed with the clone/rubber stamp tool.

▲ See how the clone stamp tool can erase just about anything as long as you have a clear area to copy from. Just remember to avoid obvious repetition of pixels.

Take a good look at your image, decide on exactly what needs to be erased and where best to copy the new pixels. Remember that you are replicating existing areas of your image so be aware that it should match as best as you can or it will look obvious.

STEP ONE

Use the zoom tool to enlarge the working area. Now select the clone stamp tool from the toolbar. The tool is displayed on screen as either a cross, to pinpoint the area you are working on, or a circle if you press the caps key on your keyboard, to illustrate the size of the brush.

Choose a suitable brush size from the image menu bar by dragging the size slider up or down. You can also select how soft the edge of the brush is from the options area.

STEP TWO

Move the clone stamp tool over the part of the image you want to copy from. Hold down the control key (option key for Mac) on your keyboard and click in the image. By doing this you are defining exactly where to copy.

STEP THREE

Either dab or stroke over the area you want to remove. As you move over the image, you will notice another cross following you. This second cross lets you know exactly from where the new pixels are being picked up. So you can check if you are going too far over the image, as the second cross will show you if you are about to pick up unwanted pixels. Remember that if you do make a mistake, choose edit > undo clone stamp to undo the last action.

▶ Select a brush, choose where to copy from and start erasing.

ADDING BORDERS

Making a border or a frame can add a finishing touch to an image. It can enhance an otherwise average picture to create more interest or it can help draw the eye into the focal point.

▲ *Select the default colours.*

There is an almost infinite number of ways to create borders or frames with image-editing software, but in this chapter you will learn how to make a simple black border and also a more complicated graphic frame.

METHOD ONE

The first step to a simple black border is to make sure that your foreground swatch in the Tool bar is set to black. The default setting for the swatches are a black foreground and a white background. Click the small black and white boxes next to the swatches to get the default colours.

Open your image and choose select > all from the image menu bar. This will create a marquee around the entire picture. You can now select edit > stroke (outline) Selection. Enter a suitable pixel width for the size of the border – it is worth experimenting with this, as you may not like the first attempt. Make sure that black is selected in the foreground option and that the location is set to inside.

You will lose some of the image area with this option, so make sure you don't need any of the edge of the image.

▲ *The second method increases the image size.*

Digital Camera Handbook

METHOD TWO

If you want to add a border without losing any of the image area, you will have to physically increase the size of your file to make room for it. To do this, make sure the background this time is set to black. Now select image > resize > canvas size. In the dialogue box click the relative check box and enter the desired size in the width and height number boxes. Click OK and the image will increase in size making a black border exactly the size that you input in the height and width number boxes.

MAKE A FRAME

You can also make a frame for your photograph. To create a white border with a thin black line set back from the image, follow the steps to increase the canvas size as before, but this time choose white as the background colour. Select the border size as before. Now click on the little arrows above the black and white swatches in the tool bar – this will swap the foreground with the background. Select the image > resize > canvas size option again, but this time, enter a small amount in the width and height number boxes. Make sure that black is selected as the background colour and click OK.

Click on the arrows to change the black and white swatches around again in the tool bar. Now for the last time select the image > resize > canvas size option and enter a much larger number in the width and height number boxes. Make sure that white is selected as the background. You should now have a frame that starts as white then thin black and then a larger area of white.

▶ *Adding a black and white border enhances this portrait.*

ADDING VIGNETTES

A vignette is a soft edged frame that gives your image a timeless quality. It is an old technique and was used in early photographs as an upmarket way of softening the edges of studio portraits.

▲ *Create a romantic frame to an image by adding a vignette.*

Normally white and an oval shape, a vignette can be used to help draw the eye away from cluttered backgrounds and direct it to the central subject. Much of the background can be lost with this technique, so it is advisable to have a central subject with a great deal of space around it.

These steps show you how to create a white, oval vignette, but any shape or colour can be created by using layers. If you are unfamiliar with using layers, turn to page 292 for an introduction.

STEP ONE

With your image open, decide how much of the image you will need to lose when applying the vignette. If your subject is composed up to the edge or into the corners, you may lose a lot of the image. From the image menu bar, choose layer > new layer to create a new transparent layer over the top of your image.

▲ *Choose new layer from the layer menu to create a new transparent layer.*

Digital Camera Handbook

▼ *Decide what you want the oval shape to include.*

STEP TWO

Select the elliptical marquee tool from the tool bar and click in the top left corner of the new layer. Hold down the mouse and drag across the layer from top left to bottom right, making sure that you have an even oval shape and that there is enough space around the edge of the picture.

STEP THREE

Now inverse the selection, choose select > inverse from the image menu. You should now have a flashing dotted marquee running around the oval shape and around the edge of the photo. Make sure that your colour swatches on the tool bar are set to black and white. From the image menu, select edit > fill selection and make sure that white is selected. Fill the selection with the white.

▲ *Fill the background with white to create your oval image.*

STEP FOUR

You now need to soften the inside edges of the oval frame by using a blur filter. Choose filter > blur > guassian blur from the image menu bar. In the guassian blur preview window, drag the slider to about half way and watch your image as the preview takes place. Make sure, as you adjust the slider to suit, that you don't see any of the original picture's edges underneath. When you have finished, choose layer > flatten image from the image menu bar. This will merge the white vignette layer and the image together.

◄ *Soften the edges with a guassian blur.*

ADDING TEXT

There are many occasions where you may wish to have text on top of your image, for example, after making a white frame you may decide to personalize your

▲ *The text tool.*

image by putting the title of the picture and your name in the corner of the frame. Or perhaps you would like to make a gift and put a message across the image, such as 'Happy Birthday' or 'Happy Anniversary'.

TEXT TOOL

The text tool can be found in the tool bar – it looks like an uppercase T. There are four options: horizontal, vertical, horizontal mask and vertical mask. The vertical tool runs text from the top of your image to the bottom, while the mask tools can place images within the text.

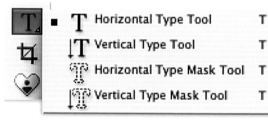

▲ *The text tool bar.*

When you have selected the horizontal type tool, click anywhere on your image and a text curser will start to blink, indicating you may now start to type. A new text layer will also appear in your layers palette and as you type, the text will be stored in this new layer.

As you start to type, you will probably want to make the text smaller or larger straight away to help you view it more clearly. Double click the text to highlight the whole line (this means a dark rectangle will cover all the words).

The text options can be found in the image menu bar. Use the 'set font size' drop down menu to select the desired size so that you can see all your text. Click at the end of the text line to deselect the highlight.

You will notice that the Text tool options are very similar to any word processing software. From here you can change the font, which is the style of the text, make it bold, italic, a different colour, etc.

▲ *There are many different fonts and styles to choose from.*

TEXT AS A GRAPHIC

When you have finished typing you will want move the text to a suitable place in the image. Select the move tool (black arrow) from the tool bar and click and drag the text to your new location. As the text is still on its own layer, you can still change the words, colour, etc.

A bounding box will appear around the type, this is for transforming the text physically by grabbing hold of the handles (which look like small squares) and drag them up, down or left and right to stretch the type.

You can now add special effects to the text. From the styles and effects palette found in the image menu > window > styles and effects, you can click on any of the pre-set text effects.

▶ *Position the text whever you like on the image.*

ADDING SOFT FOCUS

This filter effect is one of the oldest and most popular in photographic history. A soft focus filter creates a hazy, romantic blurring of the image that can be flattering to the subject. This effect is used mainly with wedding photographs or portraits.

Traditionally a piece of gauze was stretched over the camera lens to distort the light, but with the help of your PC, you can recreate this beautiful effect simply and quickly.

Although this method is used to create a 'dreamy' quality for your image, it can also be used to help reduce noise. Noise is an unwanted grainy effect normally associated with low light photography (for more on noise, see page 314).

▲ *Create a flattering soft focus effect with your image editing software.*

Not all images will benefit from this effect, so choose your photograph carefully before you begin. Having said that, half the fun of image editing is experimenting, so feel free to have a go at applying the filter to other images such as landscapes and still lifes.

STEP ONE

With your image open, duplicate the background layer (for more on layers see page 292). Choose layer > duplicate layer from the image menu bar.

STEP TWO

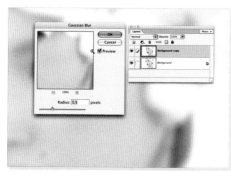

From the filter menu, choose filter > blur > guassian blur. A preview window will pop up allowing you to set the strength of blur with the slider. Choose a setting that will blur the image but still retain the basic shapes. Click OK.

STEP THREE

Click on the layer blend drop down menu from the layer palette. Choose the soft light mode from the settings.

STEP FOUR

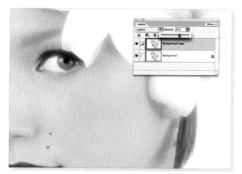

Select the opacity slider from the top of the layers palette. Drag the slider to the left to reduce the strength of the blurred layer until you happy with the blending. If you think certain areas don't need blurring, use the eraser tool to remove the unwanted sections.

◀ Work through the steps to achieve your final effect.

ADDING LOST DETAIL TO HIGHLIGHTS & SHADOWS

Sometimes when we take photographs the pictures can result in little or no detail in the shadow or highlight areas. This problem is normally associated with very sunny weather. The high contrast scene can confuse even the very best of digital cameras and the spot meter may find trouble in deciding on how best to operate.

Generally if the camera compensates for correct shadow detail, the highlights will be over-exposed. Similarly if the camera records pleasing highlights, the shadow detail may become too dark. In some extreme cases, the image may contain neither highlight or shadow details, resulting in an almost black and white picture.

Most basic image editing programs such as Photoshop Elements will struggle to give you a complete range of highlight and shadow options. More expensive professional programmes such as Photoshop CS can

▲ This photo is suffering from highlight blowouts.

▲ Add texture with the noise filter to reclaim some of the missing detail.

▲ *Add grain, or 'noise' to the image to improve the detail.*

give you a better chance of reclaiming detail with dedicated filters that perform the solution automatically.

PROBLEMS & SOLUTIONS

The trouble with over blown highlights or under exposed shadows is that any lost detail is almost impossible to retrieve because the information simply isn't there. You could try to use the burn tool to darken areas of the image or the dodge tool to brighten, but this may end up a grey murky mess, and still gain no detail. The best option in this case is to add a little grain called noise to the image. (For more on noise see page 314.)

With your image open, choose filter > noise > add noise. Set the options to a low setting – 4 or 5 may be adequate. Keep the distribution to uniform and select OK. Although this increases the grain in the overall image, it does put some texture into the white highlights and gives you something to work with.

Select the burn tool from the tool bar. In the options, select midtones from the dropdown menu. Choose a suitable sized brush for the area you want to work on and set the strength slider to low. Gradually darken the new texture of the highlights until you are happy. Take some time to experiment with this method, as it may not be right for every image.

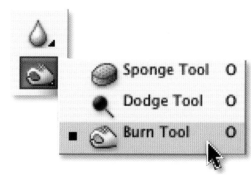

▶ *Select the burn tool to darken the highlight texture.*

USING DIGITAL FILTERS

Popular image editing programs contain lots of filters, which can transform your image into a work of art or completely destroy it with incorrect use. In Adobe Photoshop Elements the array of different filters are separated into groups, found in the image menu bar in the filter drop down menu. There are so many that you will find books dedicated entirely to the specific subject of filters.

ADJUSTMENTS

This group of filters adjust the brightness, colour and tonal value of your image. As with most filters, they work globally on the image unless areas are isolated first with a marquee.

The invert filter changes colours into their opposites, making a negative image. This is particularly useful if you want to scan in a film negative with your home scanner and want to process it into a positive.

The posterize filter determines how many levels of tone are stored in your image. This is great if you want to create a piece of 'pop art'.

ARTISTIC

These filters need to be applied with subtlety and to a suitable image. The range of artistic filters are displayed in a large preview window before the filter

▼ The styles and effects palette in Photoshop Elements contains a huge number of digital filters.

Digital Camera Handbook

is applied. Click on the palette's filter icons to select each one and use the preview to help determine the strength and options of each filter.

The coloured pencil filter attempts to replicate the use of sketching with pencils. The sliders allow you to adjust the length of each stroke, the pressure and the paper brightness. The watercolour filter works in the same way, imitating the use of a wet brush with coloured paints and adjusting the detail and intensity to suit.

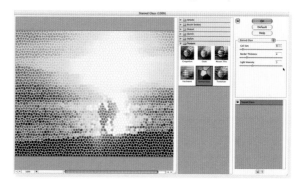

▲ Most digital filters have a large preview window and a range of options.

BLUR

As we have seen in the soft focus technique (page 270) these filters can recreate the effect of blurring the camera lens. Motion blur simulates the effect of movement, blurring the image in a straight line that can be set in the filter's preview window. Radial blur works in a similar way to motion blur, but recreates the effect of spinning or zooming.

DISTORT

This group of filters physically warp the entire image. Use the spherize filter to create a 'bubble' in the photograph. This can be a fun filter to use if you want to enlarge specific areas. The twirl filter makes your image look like it is whirling down the plughole.

▲ Just a few of the artistic filters in action.

RENDER

The render group contains one of the most widely used and popular filters, the lens flare. This adds a star burst over your image, as if light is straying directly into the camera lens. This is very useful if you want to add drama to a sunset or a bright light.

USING PLUG-INS

Most image editing software packages give you an exhaustive supply of filters and functions to use and are normally sufficient for most home users. To increase functionality even more, you can add bolt-on programs called plug-ins to your software. These little applications are made by other companies and are installed onto your PC like normal software. They sit within your editing software and can be accessed through its interface, normally through the image menu bar.

Most plug-ins work like standard filters with a preview window and option sliders. Some of the more sophisticated plug-ins act like a stand-alone programme, launching it's own window that fills your screen.

Plug-ins can be downloaded from the Internet, or can be purchased on CD from stores – some are free of charge. As with the standard image editing filters, there are a great many plug-ins available.

IMAGE RESIZE

One of the more useful plug-ins is an image resizing filter. This allows you to enlarge your photos and increase the resolution, without losing any image quality.So if you have an image that is only 5 MB in size, running it through the filter could result in an image of at least 10 MB, allowing you to print bigger enlargements.Genuine Fractals at www.ononesoftware.com has the most popular of these plug-ins.

ARTISTIC

Artistic filters are probably the most common plug-ins available and can include interesting choices such as fire, wood, chrome and glow, which are useful for making backgrounds, etc. Eye Candy at www.alienskin.com provides a fantastic array of weird and wonderful artistic filters.

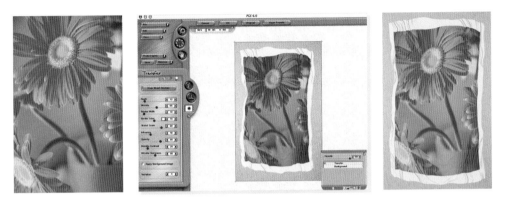

▲ Plug-ins are normally controlled through their own window. Make all your adjustments before applying the filter to your image.

▲ Artistic frames are easy to create with a dedicated plug-in.

EXTRACT

If you are feeling a little more adventurous with your image editing, you may like to try cutting out subjects from their background. This is great if you have a cluttered or ugly background that you would like to remove. There are ways to do this within your standard software (see page 278 for more on replacing a background) but it can be quite a drawn out process. Some plug-ins make this task much easier.

Launched within your software, this filter requires its own window to display the range of options. Pixels are selected to keep and others to drop – when extracted, the dropped pixels are deleted from the image.

The company Extensis provide a collection of image enhancement tools that include Mask Pro 3, one of the better extract plug-ins. Mask Pro is now only available as part of the Photo Imaging Suite of five programs. They can be found at www.extensis.com.

FUN FILTERS

There are plenty of exciting plug-ins that can manipulate images in different ways. www.thepluginsite.com is a great place to start looking for fun filters.

PROJECT: CHANGE A SKY

▲ A landscape can be completely transformed by replacing the background or sky.

You cannot control the weather when you are taking photographs, and although you may strive for a vibrant blue or storm-filled skyline, you may not have the time to wait for the perfect shot. With the help of your home image editing software, you can replace your dull sky with a more interesting one.

You will need to pick a replacement image of the sky, so take time to look at the direction of light and even the colour, for example a sunset sky may look out of place in a midday landscape. Try to choose images that will match as much as possible, making the blend more believable.

STEP ONE

Open the image of the new sky. Choose select > all from the image menu bar and then edit > copy.

STEP TWO

Now open the image with the sky that you want to replace. Select the magic wand tool and click on the sky. If the sky is a continuous tone and colour then generally the magic wand should select all the area. Make sure the marquee is up to the edge of the land.

STEP THREE

If the magic wand tool selects only part of the sky then, from the image menu bar, choose the select > modify > expand. This command expands the selection further out to take in more pixels.

STEP FOUR

If there are still isolated areas that the wand has not picked up, then hold down the shift key on your keyboard. The magic wand icon should change to include a plus sign. You can now continue to click in the extra areas until the whole sky is selected.

STEP FIVE

Choose edit > paste into selection from the image menu bar. This should now place the new sky over the old one. Use the Move tool to adjust the position of the sky to the desired area.

STEP SIX

If your sky doesn't fit into the new area of the original scene exactly, or if you want to elongate or change the shape of clouds a bit, you can use the transform tool. Choose image > transform > free transform to stretch (or shrink) your sky to its new position.

◀ *Follow the steps above to achieve some dramatic effects.*

PROJECT: CORRECT DISTORTION

▲ *Some images of tall buildings can look distorted because of perspective.*

A photograph conveys three-dimensional objects in a two dimensional form. You can see two dimensions (height and width), but the only way to see the third dimension (depth) is with perspective. If you look down a long road, the edges of the road appear to be closer together until they finally meet in the distance (the parallel lines eventually converge). Clearly the road does not get smaller, but perspective allows us to determine that distant objects appear smaller. This rule also applies in photography and is used to illustrate depth in an image.

Perspective is normally useful for photographers but sometimes it can be a hindrance. As lines converge, they can go up as well as across, so for instance a building may look distorted if you have taken the picture at ground level. A wideangle lens may increase this problem and distort the building further. One way to correct this at the shooting stage is to move away from the subject to reduce the amount of distortion, or to take a higher shooting position. If this is not possible, then you can use image editing software.

Though you will lose some of the edges of your image, you can attempt to correct the distortion with image editing software. ▲

In these next steps you will learn how to correct distortion by using the distort tool, but be aware that you will lose some of the surrounding edges of your image.

STEP ONE

With your image open, double click on the background layer in the layers palette. Click OK to accept the new layer. This converts your image from being a locked background into a layer. If an image is still a background, then it cannot be physically altered.

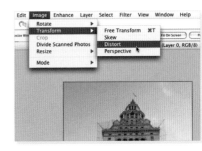

STEP TWO

Drag the bottom right corner of the image window out so that you can see plenty of grey area around the photo. As you use the distort tool, you will be working into the grey workspace, so make sure that you have enough room.

STEP THREE

From the image menu bar, choose image > transform > distort. Immediately you will see a bounding box appear. A bounding box has handles that can be clicked and dragged, distorting the image physically.

STEP FOUR

Click on the top right corner bounding box handle and drag out into the grey area. Make sure as you drag that the side of the distortion starts to become straight. Keep dragging until you are happy with the result. You may have to click and drag the bottom corner handle back into the image if your distortion still needs adjustment. When you are finished, use the crop tool to complete the process.

PROJECT: CREATE A PANORAMA

Wideangle lenses can capture more than conventional sized lenses, but when you are shooting a spectacular vista, they fall short of capturing the drama all around you. Apart from a fish eye lens, which distorts the image, there is no way you can capture that degree of width in a camera. Creating a stitched panorama on your PC is the best and most effective solution to this problem.

▲ *Your series of pictures should overlap slightly.*

As you will have learnt from page 184, creating a panorama requires some initial effort at the shooting stage. A series of pictures is required for this project, taken from the left of the subject and panning the camera as you proceed to capture your images. Make sure that your pictures overlap as this will help to give you a seamless blend at the editing stage.

The better image editing software programmes generally come with an automated panorama stitcher function that allows you to select your series of images and transform them into a panorama. The programme works within its own window and automatically places the images next to each other, looking for similar areas of pixels to overlap. It transforms any perspective distortion straight away and then merges the images together into one wide picture.

Remember at the time of shooting to make sure that the light does not change as you take your pictures, the stitching software may struggle if some images are darker or lighter than others in the series.

Digital Camera Handbook
Digital Camera Handbook

STEP ONE

In Photoshop Elements, choose file > new > photomerge panorama. Browse your folder containing only the series of images you want to merge together. Select the required images and click OK.

STEP TWO

The images will now open automatically and be transferred to the image bin, and the automated process begins. If at anytime a box appears warning that the photomerge function cannot arrange the images automatically, then you can drag each image directly from the image bin into the new window and arrange them manually.

STEP THREE

When running automatically, the photomerge preview window will open and your series of images will appear inside, overlapping each other and blending with each other at the edges.

STEP FOUR

You have the option to select the advanced blending option, which may help to smooth out any awkward joins. When the automation is complete, you can manually adjust any of the images if required. Click on OK and accept the stitched image. You will then have to save the new image as a separate file.

▲ *The completed panorama.*

PROJECT: RESTORE AN OLD PHOTO

Old photographs have a relatively short life span before they start to degrade. They can become faded, yellow, bent and torn until the image is barely recognizable. With the help of your PC and image editing software, you can save these precious photos by restoring them back to their former glory.

You can scan the old photograph, correct the overall look of the image and repair any physical damage. You will need to use the clone/rubber stamp tool, the levels command and sharpen the detail. Restoring old photos can take some time, but it is usually very rewarding.

▲ The cleaned-up image after restoration.

STEP ONE

Make sure that the old photograph and your scanner are free of dust and dirt, lay the photo down on the glass and choose your scanner settings. Choose a black and white, high-resolution setting for the scanner, to enable you to zoom right into the image as you repair it.

STEP TWO

With your scanned image ready, remember to save the file to your PC. It is wise to save a copy of this scanned image, so you can have another go at repairing it if you are unhappy with your initial results.

STEP THREE

From the image menu bar, select auto levels. This will enhance the tones of the blacks and whites and remove any greyness from the image.

STEP FOUR

First we must clean up any dust or scratches. Use the zoom tool so that you can see any problem areas more clearly. It is advisable to start in the top right corner of the image and work your way across in manageable sections.

Select the clone/rubber stamp tool from the tool bar. This tool is brush based, so you will need to choose a suitable size – for small spots select a small brush slightly larger than the dust.

STEP FIVE

Press the alt key down (option for Mac) and click next to the dust spot. By doing this, you are copying the pixels next to the dust spot. Now release the alt key and move the clone tool over the top of the dust spot. The pixels you sampled will now cover the unwanted area. As you have copied the pixels right next to the dust spot, there should be little if no difference in blending. Continue to do this over the entire image.

STEP SIX

Now you can move onto larger areas such as rips or folds. You may need to zoom out to a more comfortable magnification. At the bottom of the torn area, alt click to the side, selecting similar pixels as before. Click over the tear and brush upwards, covering the rip with the new pixels. If you get it wrong, don't worry – select undo and try again. Continue to remove all the rips and folds until you are happy.

PROJECT: CONVERT COLOUR TO BLACK & WHITE

▼ A colour photo before being converted to black and white.

You can totally transform your colour photographs and add a sense of drama by removing the colour and enhancing the black and white tones, thereby transforming a colour photograph to a black and white photo.

Not all colour images will benefit from black and white conversions, some colours, when converted, will have the same grey quality and may end up looking like one continuous tone. Take some time to look for a colour image that will be worth converting, look for contrast rather than subject. Light and dark areas in a picture are the essential qualities for a successful conversion – these will accentuate the drama and give your image 'punch'.

As with all editing projects, it is wise to save a copy of the original image first before you start.

STEP ONE

Open your colour image and look at the colours and tones. Remember that some colours will look the same when converted to grey. If you think your image needs enhancing before the conversion, use the

auto levels command to increase contrast. Choose enhance > auto levels from the image menu bar.

STEP TWO

Now select image > mode > greyscale from the image menu bar. A small dialogue window will ask you if you want to discard all colour information – click OK. The image will now be stripped of all colour information.

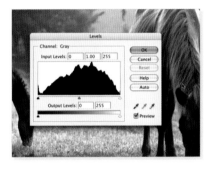

STEP THREE

Now that the image is black and white, the tone needs to be adjusted to enhance the contrast. From the image menu bar select image > adjust lighting > levels. The levels histogram will now give you the option to adjust the tone (for more on using histograms, see page 306).

STEP FOUR

To help you achieve a pure white, select the white eyedropper tool found in the bottom right corner of the window. Choose an area in the image that you think should

be bright white, click inside that area once, this sets the white point. You can also set the black point by using the black eyedropper tool and clicking in a pure black area. Click OK to accept the settings.

◀ Some colour photos can take on a whole new look by converting to black and white.

PROJECT: CREATE A DUOTONE

Another way to enhance your photographs is to put colour into your mono photo. Duotones are black and white images with two complimentary spot colours added. Some image editing programmes do not support duotones, but there are plug-ins you can buy that will allow you to access this process (Human Software at www.humansoftware.com, and for more on plug-ins, see page 276). Adobe Photoshop CS does allow you to create duotones.

You can create a sense of warmth to an image by adding yellow and brown colours, or you can create a cool look by including two shades of blue. For best results use one dark colour for the shadows and one light colour for the highlights. Use the colour palette to create your own colours – don't rely on primary colours, as they will look too stark. Remember to save a copy of your image if you want to keep the original black and white.

▶ *Add atmosphere to your black and white images by converting them to duotone.*

STEP ONE

With your black and white image open, choose image > mode > duotone. The dialogue box displayed shows duotone as default, but the drop down menu gives you the option to add more colour if you wish. Three colours are called tritones, four colours, quadtones.

STEP TWO

Each section is listed as Ink 1, Ink 2 and so on. In the Ink 1 section, click on the right square to display the colour palette window. Use the colour slider to select a colour range, click inside the main colour tone window to select the strength of your new colour. Choose a dark shade and click OK.

STEP THREE

The new colour will now appear in the small square in the Ink 1 section. Select the name input field to the left of the new colour and enter the name of your new colour. If you want to change the colour at anytime, just click on the colour square and the colour picker window will pop up again for further adjustment.

STEP FOUR

Now click on the second ink square and repeat the above steps, choosing a lighter shade of your complementary colour. As you select each new colour, you will see your image automatically update. Check your image to make sure that the new colours are working well. When you are happy, click OK to accept the duotone.

ADVANCED DIGITAL DARKROOM

Digital imaging can involve much more than quick fixes to your digital photographs. You will discover an exciting world of advanced techniques that will encourage new ways of thinking.

Traditional darkroom skills such as toning and split toning or hand colouring black and white prints can all be recreated in your image editing software – it only takes a little practise and experimenting to achieve great results.

▲ There are lots of options to be found on the layers palette. Layer blend modes, layer styles, adjustment layers and masks can all be directly accessed here.

The following chapters have been written with the most popular high-end image editing software in mind, Adobe Photoshop CS. Technically more superior than its cheaper brother, Elements, you can create and enhance your images in many ways with Photoshop CS and its earlier versions. There are many functions at your disposal, which will hopefully inspire you to get the best from your digital photographs.

Over the next few pages you will learn how layers work and why they are so helpful with complex editing. You will discover layer masks, quick masks and how they can

◄ *Channels are nested with the layers palette and display each colour separation. Masks can be stored here as an alpha channel.*

aid you in making accurate selections in your images. All these functions and tools are there to help you, so once you have grasped the fundamentals of how the palettes and commands work, you can take the time to experiment with your own images.

PREVIOUS CHAPTERS

If you have not read the previous chapters in this book then it is advisable you do so before reading this section. You will need to understand the basics of image resolution and what the software palettes and tools can do.

▲ *Advanced retouching tools are found in the tool bar. Normally brushed-based tools, they can be adjusted from the image menu bar, selecting the size, softness and strength.*

▲ *Dodging and burning are traditional darkroom techniques that can be recreated within the image editing software.*

This advanced section will inform you on the benefits of professional colour printing, how to manage your colour correctly and how to produce images ready for professional print.

By learning these advanced skills you will not only increase your working knowledge of image editing, but you may even be able, if you so desire, to sell your work to galleries, magazines and stock libraries. If you are armed with the knowledge of consistent colour and tonal control and are able to use retouching tools correctly, then you are on your way to producing satisfying results of which you can be proud.

UNDERSTANDING LAYERS

Layers are one of the fundamental elements in advanced image editing and are the separate pieces that make up a full multi-layered image.

If you have ever seen how cartoons are made, then you will know that each drawing is created on a transparent sheet. Each sheet is then placed one on top of the other over a solid background image. All the separate elements show through, resulting in one visual composite. The same principle applies to layers in a digital image. An image can be created using

▲ *Each new layer stacks up like a sheet of transparent plastic, one on top of the other.*

multiple elements, each one contained on its own transparent layer, one on top of the other. They are independent of each other and can be moved and manipulated without affecting other layers.

COMBINE IMAGES

In basic image editing programmes, many enhancements are carried out directly onto the image which means they are permanent, so making corrections or alterations is almost impossible. Layers were designed to keep the new components separate from the original image, so providing a much more controlled approach to editing.

Each layer is displayed in the layers palette – choose window > layers from the image menu bar. Thumbnails of each element are displayed in the palette and can be enlarged so that you can clearly see the contents of each. To do this, click on the small arrow in the top right corner of the palette. This displays the palette options. The bottom option can resize the thumbnails in three sizes, small, medium and large.

You can also name each layer in a text box, which is probably the most useful way to organise your layers in a document. Double click on the text field to highlight the type. When it turns blue, you can input your text. Try to keep the description short. Each layer can be displayed or hidden, turning them on or off by clicking on the small 'eye' icon on the left of the palette.

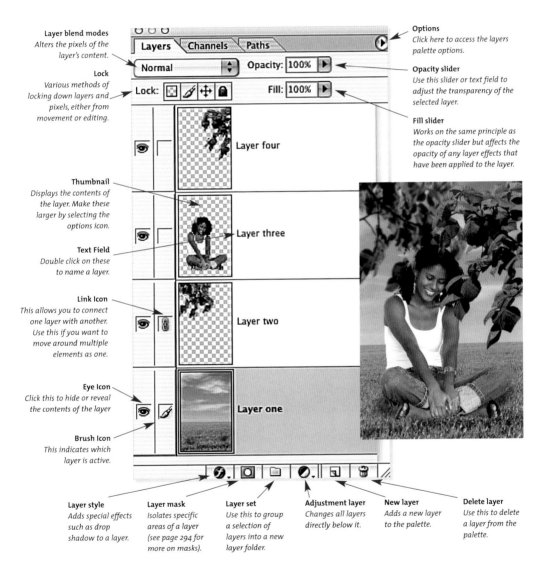

Layer blend modes
Alters the pixels of the layer's content.

Lock
Various methods of locking down layers and pixels, either from movement or editing.

Thumbnail
Displays the contents of the layer. Make these larger by selecting the options icon.

Text Field
Double click on these to name a layer.

Link Icon
This allows you to connect one layer with another. Use this if you want to move around multiple elements as one.

Eye Icon
Click this to hide or reveal the contents of the layer

Brush Icon
This indicates which layer is active.

Options
Click here to access the layers palette options.

Opacity slider
Use this slider or text field to adjust the transparency of the selected layer.

Fill slider
Works on the same principle as the opacity slider but affects the opacity of any layer effects that have been applied to the layer.

Layer style
Adds special effects such as drop shadow to a layer.

Layer mask
Isolates specific areas of a layer (see page 294 for more on masks).

Layer set
Use this to group a selection of layers into a new layer folder.

Adjustment layer
Changes all layers directly below it.

New layer
Adds a new layer to the palette.

Delete layer
Use this to delete a layer from the palette.

UNDERSTANDING MASKS

In traditional printing, when a printer wanted to hide a section of the image, he would cover the area on the printing plate with a rubber solution. This provided a mask over the image and protected the paper from the applied ink. In digital imaging, the masking process is relatively similar.

There are several ways that masks can be used in Photoshop – quick mask and layer mask are the most widely used methods. When applying a mask over an image, the colour swatches change to the default black and white, because only black can apply the mask, while the white paints back the pixels.

▲ *Selecting the quick mask mode from the tool bar allows you to paint on a transparent red mask that can be converted into a selection.*

QUICK MASK

Quick mask is accessed from the bottom area of the tool bar, directly underneath the swatches. There are two modes that you need to use: standard mode and quick mask mode.

Quick mask mode makes accurate selections with the aid of a brush. Once the mask has been applied, it will be converted to a marquee selection for isolated enhancements.

STEP ONE

Select quick mask from the tool bar and click inside your image. A red tint is applied to the image, which indicates the masked area. Adjust the brush to a suitable size and softness from the image menu. Continue to paint the red mask over your selected area. If you make a mistake, change the colour swatch from black to white, this will erase sections of the mask.

STEP TWO

As you click on 'edit in standard mode' in the tool bar, the red tint will change to a marquee. You can now apply any filter or command to the unmasked area of the image.

LAYER MASK

Layer masks temporarily hide selected pixels from a layer, even though they remain intact. Before you start, make sure you are working on a layer, as you cannot apply a mask to a background.

STEP ONE

From the image menu bar select layer > add layer mask > reveal all. You will now

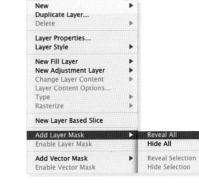

see a new blank thumbnail appear next to the image in the layers palette – this is the mask thumbnail and any masking appears here for your reference.

STEP TWO

Make sure that the colour swatches are set to black and white, with black set to the foreground. With a suitable brush size, start to paint over the area you wish to mask. Immediately the pixels will disappear leaving the checkerboard pattern

underneath (this indicates that there is no pixel information showing). To use the mask function creatively, use at least two layers with two images. As you mask off the top layer, the bottom layer will be revealed. If you want to reclaim any part of the mask, switch to white and repaint the image.

▲ *Using a layer mask temporarily hides the layer's pixels, revealing the layer or default checkerboard underneath.*

CONTROLLED SELECTIONS

As you will have read in the previous chapters, a selection is called a marquee, and looks like a flashing dotted line. The inside of the marquee is the selected area and everything outside of it is unaffected by any enhancements or adjustments.

Creating basic selections is easy when using the marquee tool, or the lasso and magic wand tools, but in this chapter, you will learn how to create controlled and precise selections with Adobe Photoshop. You will learn how to add to a selection or take parts of it away. You will even learn how to remove parts of your image effectively by using the extract tool.

You can make an accurate selection in a number of ways. One of the more precise methods is the quick mask mode (for more on masks see page 294). With this, you can paint around complex subjects, changing the size and softness of the brush to accommodate the details. Once the mask is completed it can be converted to a selection by clicking on the edit in standard mode button on the tool bar. This selection can also be saved as an alpha channel by clicking on the save selection as alpha channel icon at the bottom of the alpha channel palette.

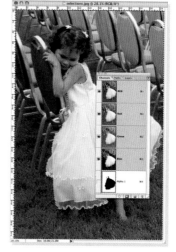

▲ *Quick mask mode can make an accurate selection that can be saved and stored as an alpha channel.*

Once stored, this alpha channel is reloaded as a selection back into the image by selecting the channel and clicking on the load channel as selection icon on the channels palette.

To add or take away a selection, use the options found in the image menu – you can use the add to, subtract and the intersect buttons. These options will help you to correct mistakes or include extra areas of the image. From the image menu bar, selections have their own drop-down menu – select. From here you can select the entire image at once or deselect an active marquee.

You can turn your selection inside out by using the inverse tool. You can also select specific pixels for a selection by using the colour range command. Follow these steps to create a colour range selection.

▲ Using colour range can enhance the preciseness of your selection. Individual colour pixels are selected with the eyedropper tool.

STEP ONE

Choose select > colour range from the image menu. In the preview window, select the image button. The black window should now display your image. Keep the drop-down menu as sampled colours.

STEP TWO

As you move over the preview window, the cursor changes to an eyedropper tool. Click inside the image in an area you would like to select. Now change the selection preview drop-down menu to white matt. Here you will see your main image update with pixels you have selected.

STEP THREE

Select the eyedropper tool with the + sign. You can now add to your selected pixels by continuing to click in the selected area. As you click, the more pixels will be revealed in your image. Use the eyedropper to remove pixels from your selection.

STEP FOUR

Use the fuzziness slider to adjust the intensity of your selection. When you are happy with your selected pixels, click on OK and a detailed marquee should run around your subject.

▼ Keep the drop-down menu as sampled colours.

ADVANCED COLOUR CONTROL

CURVES

The curve command in Photoshop is a one-stop fix for colour, tone and brightness corrections. Select the curve palette from the image menu by choosing image > adjustments > curves.

The diagonal line you see running from the lower left to the upper right corner represents the pixel's tonal range from light to dark. The black and white bars running up and across the palette are the axis of the curve palette, the horizontal represents the input levels and the vertical represents the new colour values (the output levels). From the drop-down menu, you can select either a composite of all colours or each one individually. Each colour can contain its own curve information.

To make a curve for the composite colour range, click in the middle of the diagonal line, this creates a point or handle. Once you have created the new point, you can drag it around

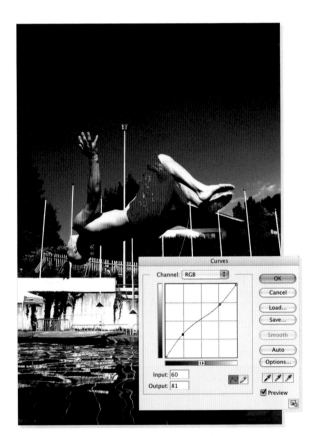

▲ *The curves tool is invaluable for correcting colour, tone and brightness.*

your graph area to alter the tonal values. In an RGB image, moving the pointer to the left or up will make the image lighter and moving to the right or down will make it

Digital Camera Handbook

darker. The steeper the curve the more contrast there will be and conversely the flatter the curve, the lower the contrast.

The point can slide up or down the diagonal line, depending on where you want establish the bow of your curve. By adjusting the composite you can correct the overall tonal brightness of all the pixels in the image at once. You can perform selective colour corrections to your image by using the same method as the composite, but you need to select the individual colour from the drop-down menu. Any curve enhancements you do will affect that colour only.

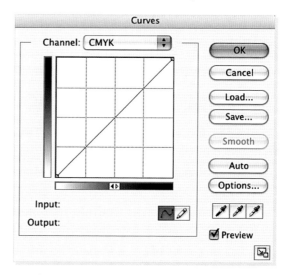

When you adjust colours in the RGB colours space, remember that as you remove the strength of one colour, another will take its place. For example, when removing red from an image by dragging the curve down you are increasing the blue, and when decreasing the blue you will be increasing the green.

Curves can be saved and reused by selecting the save button on the palette. The file is saved as an .acv file that can be stored in a folder for future use. To re-use a saved curve, click the load button on the curve palette and navigate your way through to the selected file.

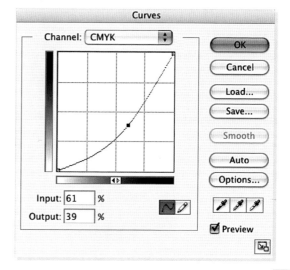

▶ A curve is created when a point is made on the diagonal line. The point is then dragged to a desired position, enhancing the colour and tone of the image. Each colour channel can be manipulated separately from the drop-down menu.

ADVANCED COLOUR CONTROL

COLOUR FOR PROFESSIONAL PRINT

▲ RGB is made from light, where as CMYK is made from ink. Black is called K so there is no confusion with the colour blue (B).

Printing at home is a relatively easy process because your images are captured in the RGB colour space and stay that way until the final print. Processing your images for professional print uses a different colour mode called CMYK. This mode is used by offset printers for books, magazines and other colour documents and is an industry standard for professional output.

RGB is a representation of the light from the monitor; all colours are made up from small dots of red, green and blue light that shine out from your screen. CMYK simulates the set of inks that a printer would use – cyan (C), magenta (M), yellow (Y) and black (K). There is a big difference between these two sets of colours, as RGB colour space is bigger than the CMYK space. These colour spaces are called gamuts.

Each device has its own colour gamut and cannot display or print past that limitation. If you encounter a colour that cannot be printed,

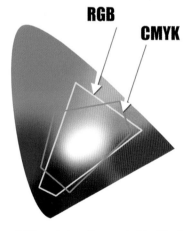

▲ This graph shows the area of achievable colour from the RGB and CMYK colour space. Notice how some colours from an RGB monitor cannot be reproduced using printing inks.

Digital Camera Handbook

you will receive an 'out of gamut' warning, which looks like a small yellow triangle with an exclamation mark.

In Photoshop you can change the colour space of your image by converting the colour mode. To do this, select image > mode > CMYK. When you change colour modes you will notice that bright hues will become a lot less vibrant because of the differences in colour gamuts. The CMYK mode is a closer representation to how your final printed image will look and as a result will not display out of gamut colours in your image window.

As well as the colour space, you must also change the resolution of your image. When capturing your images, your camera may set the resolution to 72 ppi (for more on resolution see page 80). To convert your image for professional output, you must change the resolution to a much higher rate of 300 ppi. This is because the dots of ink used by a printer are very close together and show much more image detail when printed. The printer crams more pixels into your image so that they are not visible on the printed page.

Follow these steps to convert an image for professional print.

STEP ONE

With your image open, select image > mode > CMYK.

▲ Though it is impossible to show true RGB on a printed page, these comparisons illustrate that bright vibrant colours will appear radically different between the two colour spaces.

STEP TWO

From the image menu bar select image > image size. This loads a dialogue box that allows you to select resizing options. Make sure that the resample image check box is left unticked. In the resolution section, make sure the drop-down menu is set to pixels/inch. In the resolution field, enter 300 and click OK to accept the settings.

ADVANCED TONAL CONTROL

ADVANCED RETOUCHING

These days you will find it almost impossible to open a magazine or look at promotional media for almost any product without bearing witness to the extensive use of image retouching. In fact, this is not a new phenomena – image retouching has been around almost as long as photography itself. Early Hollywood exploited the process of enhancing a film star's portrait by painting artist's inks on their prints to hide crow's feet or sagging chins.

The media continually strives to create a subjective perfection that is practically unobtainable in real life. Many models, both male and female, do not appear on the printed page without a few adjustments to their features. Adjustments may be as simple as removing a small skin blemish or as complicated as slimming down an entire body. Adobe Photoshop is the leading industry standard for image manipulation and retouching and provides an array of tools and functions that can transform almost any subject. Most of Photoshop's retouching tools employ sampling as the basis for their technique, using the image's surrounding pixels as a source material.

▲ *Before advanced retouching*

Digital Camera Handbook

The first step to successful retouching is to identify the areas that you think need to be adjusted and then decide exactly what needs to be done to obtain your chosen result. Then you need to select the correct tool for the job.

With digital retouching, it is important to remember that your work on an image should result in a subtle, almost unnoticeable finish. There really is no point in trying to cover a blemish if all you create is another, more noticeable one.

▲ With the use of specialist retouching tools, most facial blemishes such as moles, spots and wrinkles can be removed, leaving only perfect skin in their place. Powerful as these tools are, they cannot make everyone into a supermodel. Be aware that are limitations on all images, so try to keep the retouching subtle and realistic.

Do not be misled into thinking that image retouching is best suited to portraits – all types of subjects can benefit from digital enhancements. Product photography is also often subjected to manipulation – removing reflections from a car's window or adding more bubbles to a fizzy drink.

For the home user, Photoshop's retouching tools can work just as effectively on your own images, both digital and traditional prints. After scanning in a print, you may feel that there are elements that you would like to remove such as dust and hairs, etc. The clone tool is one of the quickest and easiest methods of retouching simple flaws in an image (see page 262 more more on the clone tool).

It is up to you how much retouching you decide to do, but you should always try to make it look real.

ADVANCED TONAL CONTROL
USING THE BLUR FILTERS

▼ *An dog in motion without blur.*

Using blur filters in Photoshop is not about blurring your images as a whole – it is about blurring in a controlled and effective way. For example, you can eradicate image defects such as noise (grain) or you can recreate a shallow depth of field in an image, which will give the effect of a blurred foreground or background therefore increasing the emphasis on the main focal point. (For more on creating a shallow depth of field, see page 326.) There are many different types of blurring – each one has its own way of selecting pixels and blending them into one another.

Blur filters are found under the filter menu, and come in a range of applications. The blur and blur more filters are automatic functions that soften the pixels of an image to help eliminate noise. The blur more filter is four times stronger than the blur filter.

The gaussian blur filter has a pop-up dialogue box and can manually alter the strength of the blur by adjusting the slider.

The lens blur filter creates a shallow depth of field by blurring the image in the same way as a lens. This filter displays a complicated dialogue box, which gives you the option to change the iris curve and rotation of the lens.

Motion blur is a fun way of recreating motion in an image. In the dialogue box, you can set the direction of the blur trail and the strength.

Radial blur is also a great way of recreating camera movements such as zooming your lens during an exposure to create a blur trail across the whole picture.

Follow these steps to create some basic motion blur effects.

▼ Steps one, two and three.

STEP ONE

As with most filter effects, you must be selective in choosing your image, especially if you are using motion blur – not only will it give a sense of motion, but can also be interpreted as speed. Open your image and duplicate the background by dragging it down onto the create new layer icon at the bottom of the layers palette.

STEP TWO

Select the filter > blur > motion blur from the image menu. Choose a suitable amount of strength, keeping the effect subtle. Keep the angle set to the direction of the subject. If you need to change it, click in the circle and drag the pointer around to the desired angle. Select OK. This will blur the image.

STEP THREE

Now create a layer mask by clicking on the make layer mask icon at the bottom of the palette. Select a suitably sized paintbrush and make sure that the colour swatch is set to black. Reduce the opacity of the brush to half so that some of the motion blur shows through.

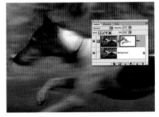

STEP FOUR

Paint the mask across the subject's focal point, revealing the detail. If you overdo it, switch to white and paint the blur back in. Adjust the size of the brush if you need to cover larger areas.

▲ The use of the motion blur filter has given the static shot of this dog an appearance of speed.

ADVANCED IMAGE MANIPULATION

ADVANCED TONAL CONTROL

USING THE DISTORTION FILTERS

Distort filters geometrically distort your image resulting in some unusual effects. They are found in the filter > distort menu and work from within their own dialogue window.

The first in the list of distortion filters is the diffuse glow filter. This filter gives pixels a soft, diffused look with a glow fading from the middle.

▼ *The filter window.*

The displace filter uses a separate file called a displacement map to determine how to distort the image. For example, if you have a circular map the image will distort in the shape of a circle. You can find ready made displacement maps in the plug-ins folder of your application.

The glass filter distorts the image to look as if it is being viewed through different types of glass. Among the glass options are frosted glass, blocks and tiny lens. The ocean ripple filter is similar to the glass filter and applies randomly spaced ripples to the image to give the impression that it is underwater.

Likewise the ripple filter creates an effect like running water over the image. The size of the ripples can be selected from the drop-down menu. The wave filter works like the ripple filter but allows for greater control. The options let you set the number of

Digital Camera Handbook

Before

Diffuse glow

Glass filter

Spherize

wave generators and length, as well as the height of the wave and wave type.

You can squash or bloat your image by using the pinch filter – simply drag the slider one way or the other. Spherize works in a similar way to the pinch filter, inflating the subject like a fish bowl. The best way to apply this filter is to create a circular marquee and apply the spherize filter from inside.

The polar coordinates filter converts the edges of the image into circular edges that bend in and meet each other. This result can be viewed through a mirrored cylinder, similar to an eighteenth century art effect.

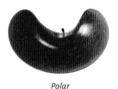

Polar

The shear filter distorts your image in a slant effect. The angle is set from the pop-up dialogue box by dragging a line across the small graph area. You can also choose to repeat pixels to fill in the extracted area or you can select wrap around, which repeats the whole image.

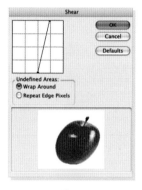

Shear

The twirl filter spins the image around into a tight point, just like a whirlpool sending water down a plughole. You can select either clockwise or anti-clockwise. Finally, the zigzag filter can make your image look like a pond ripple, starting in the middle and sending out concentric circles.

Twirl

ADVANCED TONAL CONTROL

REDUCING ARTEFACTS & NOISE

▼ Normal quality.

An artefact is the name for unwanted elements in an image and is caused by over processing or high compression. Artefacts look like little squares spread across the entire image and create an unnatural distortion. The simplest way to see what an artefact looks like is to save a low-resolution image as a JPEG file and set the compression to the lowest level of quality.

Close the image and then re-open it. You can now see that the highly compressed image has small squares or blocks all over it. This happens because the image software has to decide on how many pixels to throw away, enabling it to reduce the file size. On re-opening, the software

▲ This image has been saved at the lowest JPEG setting, meaning that the compression is very high. Small blocks called artefacts appear across the image, destroying the quality.

▲ Don't expect miracles, but the use of the median filter applied to the channels can result in an improved image quality.

automatically puts the missing pixels back in the image, but carries out this process by guessing what they look like. This effect can quite simply ruin a photograph and make it very difficult to print with any respectable quality.

Similarly, digital noise in an image also produces disappointing results. Noise looks like tiny speckles over the image, mainly in the shadow areas. Noise is caused by under exposure, setting the ISO to a high level for low light interiors or letting the camera automatically set the ISO. You can reduce artefacts or noise in Photoshop, but you cannot erase them completely.

Follow these next steps to reduce the image anomalies.

STEP ONE

With your image open, select the channels palette. Inspect each one carefully to decide which channels hold the most artefacts or noise.

STEP TWO

Select the affected channel and choose filter > noise > median from the image menu. In the median pop-up dialogue box, select a very low strength. You may want to repeat this for any other affected channel.

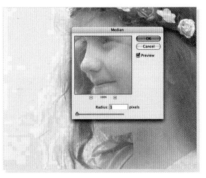

STEP THREE

Now select filter > sharpen > unsharp mask from the image menu. Select a suitable strength of sharpness that will enhance the edges of the image, but make sure that it does not increase the visibility of any remaining artefacts or noise.

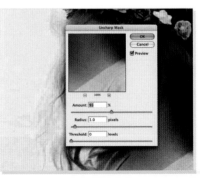

▶ *Follow the steps to reduce artefacts and noise.*

ADVANCED TONAL CONTROL

WEB-READY IMAGES

While prints may look fantastic framed and hung on a wall, there will always be a limited audience to appreciate your hard work. The Internet can widely extend your audience, but before you upload your photographs to a website, you need to optimize them. You can do this simply and quickly in Photoshop, using the save for web command. Before you do this though, you must follow these specific guidelines.

Make sure that your image is the correct size. The resolution of the web is the same as your monitor – 72 ppi. Viewing the image at 100 per cent magnification will indicate how large it will finally look. Do not make your image larger than your monitor or your audience may have to scroll across the screen. (To size your images correctly see page 318.)

▲ *Printed pictures are often never looked at.*

The colour mode should be RGB. If you have converted your images to any other colour mode, it is important to convert them back before uploading.

Save the image as a JPEG. This is the most effective format for compressing your images without losing too much of the detail.

From here you can select the save for web command from the image menu. This useful function keeps the file size as small as possible, allowing for faster download speed and quality, and keeps compression artefacts to a minimum.

Select file > save for web. The large dialogue box virtually fills the screen – the four windows display your image as four different optimization settings. Each setting shows the quality of the final image along with file size and download time. You can also select larger previews by selecting the 2 up tab or the software's favoured optimized setting. By clicking on the small arrow in the top right, you select the modem or broadband speed of the end user. As broadband is now widely available, it is probably worth selecting the 512 kbs speed.

On the right side of the dialogue box is the range of options – from here you can select the file type, compression strength and quality. You can also reduce the physical image size by selecting the image size tab and entering the exact width and height. When you are happy with the chosen setting, click on the selected preview window, which will highlight in blue. Click OK.

▼ The save for web option gives you four different optimization settings.

ADVANCED TONAL CONTROL

RESIZING YOUR IMAGES

When you take a digital photograph, most cameras will capture the image at 72 pixels per inch (ppi) – the larger the number of megapixels your camera has, the larger the physical image will be when viewed at 100 per cent on your monitor. You may have to scroll around the screen to view the image.

If you want to view the entire image at 100 per cent and make it fit on your screen, then you will have to reduce the physical size. You will need to throw away some pixels from the image. There are various ways to do this – the most controlled way is to use the image size command. The dialogue box displays the existing dimensions of the image and also the file size. You can enter the number of pixels from here if you know it. The document size option allows you to select from centimetres, inches, millimetres, percentage or other measurements from the drop-down menu. The resolution can also be set in this area, choosing pixels per inch.

◄ *The image size command shows the existing dimensions and the file size, which you can then change.*

To reduce an image using image size, follow these simple steps.

STEP ONE

Select image > image size. All three check boxes at the bottom of the dialogue box should be selected. You will now resample the image, which means that Photoshop will discard pixels from the image.

STEP TWO

If you want the image to stay screen resolution, then make sure that resolution is set at 72 ppi. Now you can choose the physical dimensions, selecting from the measurement options drop-down menu. If you know your required measurement, for example 6 x 4 in, then you can enter that figure here. Make sure that the width and height are set to inches. As an alternative method, you can select the percentage option and enter a lower figure. Click OK to accept the settings.

Increasing the size of your image is a different matter all together. When you reduce the size of an image, pixels are thrown away, but increasing the image size means that Photoshop will have to add pixels. This can have a detrimental effect on the image as the software will have to guess at the characteristics of each of the pixels and where to place them. This is called interpolation and can result in a lower quality image.

One of the best ways to enlarge your images and maintain the quality is to use a third party plug-in such as Genuine Fractals. This software sits within Photoshop and can help you to achieve a controlled enlargement by using a completely different method of adding new pixels. (For more on plug-ins see pages 228–43.)

If you don't want to buy extra software, then increasing the image size in Photoshop should be carried out in 10 per cent increments to help to avoid image deterioration. Repeat the same steps as reducing the image, but in the dimensions field, choose the per cent option. Enter 110 in both fields. Select OK to accept the settings. Keep repeating the process and continually check on the image quality as you proceed. It is not advisable to go too far with this method as it does have limitations.

ADVANCED IMAGE MANIPULATION

Section Three: Resources

ADVANCED TONAL CONTROL

PROJECT: ADVANCED BLACK & WHITE CONVERSION

It is possible to create stunning black and white pictures (with first-rate tone and contrast) from your colour originals, but it will take time and effort.

▼ *Before (top) and after (bottom).*

In previous chapters, you learnt how to make a simple black and white conversion by converting the image to greyscale. This basic technique is fine if you are a beginner because it teaches you the mechanics of how a digital image can be stripped of its colour characteristics.

However, you can achieve professional looking results by using complex techniques other than converting to greyscale. In fact greyscale is not a popular technique with most professionals because it can leave the image looking dull and lifeless and gives too few options for further modification.

The channel mixer is probably the most favoured technique for converting colour images to black and white. This process keeps all the separate colour channels intact while converting them to mono, which means that you will still be able to adjust the tone and contrast of each channel. Although the image looks black and white, the image is still RGB mode.

Digital Camera Handbook

For this project you will use an adjustment layer set to the channel mixer option. The advantage of using an adjustment layer is that the image can be closed and reopened at anytime for further modification.

STEP ONE

With your colour image open, select the layers palette. Click on the create adjustment layer icon found at the bottom of the layers palette. Select the channel mixer from the options. The new layer appears on top of the colour background layer. A small thumbnail icon of the channel mixer is displayed on the layer – double click the text field and enter the name 'mono'.

STEP TWO

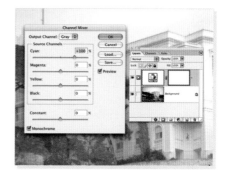

The channel mixer palette will immediately pop up. Click on the monochrome check box located at the bottom left of the palette. The colour will vanish from the image.

▲ *Step one (top) and step two (bottom).*

STEP THREE

The output channel is now only grey, but the RGB sliders will still allow you to adjust the amount of tone from each colour channel. The red channel is set at a default to +100 per cent, whereas the green and blue are set to 0 per cent. Click on each channel slider and experiment in setting the strength of each channel. Different images will produce varying results, so no two channel mixes will be the same.

STEP FOUR

It's worth creating a levels adjustment layer, so that you can fine-tune your highlights and shadows. Remember to save the image and keep it as an RGB file.

ADVANCED TONAL CONTROL

PROJECT: HAND COLOURING A BLACK & WHITE IMAGE

▲ *A black and white image.*

You can not only restore an old black and white photograph, but you can colourize it too. This project will show you how to convert a black and white image into colour by using the colour picker, brushes and the layer blend modes.

It helps if you know the original colour of clothing, hair, etc. before you start or your recipient may say, 'that wasn't the colour of the swimsuit!". The typical quality of an old image can be soft and quite grainy, so remember to take this into account when reproducing colour. You cannot add sharp vibrant hues to a soft image – it will look fake and the colours will be distracting.

▲ *After, hand coloured.*

Try to match to the original era and make the colours look consistent. As this photo was from the early 1960s, the image colours were toned down. The best way to reproduce realistic skin colour is to use another colour image as a source. Try to use an image that is similar in subject and lighting. Remember to keep the colour subtle and natural.

STEP ONE

With your black and white image open, make sure you are working in RGB colour (image > mode > RGB). Now create a new layer – layer > new > layer. Name the new layer 'main skin' tone. This will help you to navigate as the layers start to

Digital Camera Handbook

stack up. From the layer blend mode found in the top left of the layers palette, choose the colour mode.

STEP TWO

Open your colour source image. Use the eyedropper to select various skin tones by clicking in the area of even coloured skin.

STEP THREE

With a suitable soft edged brush, paint the main skin colour over the face on the new layer. You will notice when using layer blend mode set to colour, that only the hue shows through and the original tone underneath is left intact. Keep painting over the entire main subject, adjusting the size of your brush as you progress.

STEP FOUR

Zoom in and erase any overlapping colour around the edges. Next, create another new layer and name it 'darker skin'. Set the blend mode again to colour. With the eyedropper, select a darker version of the skin. Paint over the shadow areas of the subject to introduce the darker hue. Use the opacity slider to adjust the subtlety.

▼ Steps four to six.

STEP FIVE

Not everyone's skin colour is the same – here the baby girl's skin is paler than her mother's. Pick a lighter skin colour, create a new layer with a colour blend mode and paint in the new skin. Remember to do the lighter colours first. In tight areas such as fingers, adjust your brush to a more suitable size.

STEP SIX

When you are happy with the skin, continue to colour the hair, eyes, teeth and clothing, naming each layer with the corresponding item. Select a source image that has a similar subject to the background and repeat the same steps to colourize the background.

ADVANCED IMAGE MANIPULATION

Section Three: Resources

ADVANCED TONAL CONTROL

PROJECT: ADVANCED COLOUR PHOTO RESTORATION

Photographs from the 1960s and 1970s are now rapidly ageing.

Early automated photographic laboratory technology led to poor fixing and washing of prints, and emulsions don't stand the test of time particularly well when under adverse conditions, especially when kept in 'sticky' albums or hung on a wall near the sun.Over the years colours begin to fade and gradually disappear. In this project you will bring those colours back to life and repair any damage. However, do not expect an image, years old, to suddenly become sharp and detailed – you can only improve what was there originally.

SCAN THE IMAGE

First, clean your flatbed scanner, removing all dust and hairs from the glass. Scan in the image at a high enough resolution to give you enough pixel information when zooming in. It is always advisable to save a copy of the untouched image if you need to start over.

Before you begin the restoration crop the image to delete any unwanted white borders. You can always add a brand new one at the end of the project if you wish.

STEP ONE

Choose image > adjust > levels and make sure the preview option is selected. Adjust the tonal level until the details are just visible in the shadows. Don't overdo this as you may start to lose the information in the highlights.

▲ *Steps one to three.*

STEP TWO

Select curves – image > adjustments > curves – and adjust each colour channel to remove the underlying colour casts. Use the curves to enhance the skin colours to a more pleasing tone.

STEP THREE

With the clone tool, remove all the dust spots. Sample pixels as close to the offending spot as possible for a convincing repair. Also work with the healing brush when you come to important areas such as the face because this will help to retain the underlying texture.

STEP FOUR

If you come across areas of missing information, use the lasso tool to select a similar but unaffected area, make a selection and feather it by two pixels, choose select > feather and then copy and paste the selection over the missing area. Use the transform tool to rotate and resize if required. Flatten the image to blend the layers together – select layer > flatten image.

STEP FIVE

Use the pen tool to draw around individual pieces of clothing. Make the path a selection from the path options and feather it (select > feather) by two pixels to soften the edges. You can now enhance the colour inside that selection.

STEP SIX

Select image > adjustments > hue & saturation and use the sliders to enhance the existing colour. Repeat the last two steps on other sections of the image that need enhancing. Finally, increase the sharpness of the overall image by adding filter > sharpen > unsharp mask.

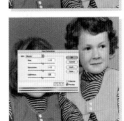

▶ *Steps four to six.*

ADVANCED TONAL CONTROL

PROJECT: CREATE A SHALLOW DEPTH OF FIELD

▲ *The image before.*

When a lens is focused on a subject at a specific distance, everything at that distance is sharp.

Depending on the aperture used, everything in front and behind the subject is out of focus and appears blurred. The area of acceptable sharpness is called the depth of field. Created in the camera at the shooting stage, a wide depth of field has a greater area of sharpness where as a shallow depth of field has a smaller area of sharpness (which results in the foreground and background being blurred). This can be effective if you want to draw the eye to certain areas of the image. Close-up photography makes extensive use of shallow depth of field, as the background is often left completely blurred, allowing more emphasis on the focal point.

▲ *The image after.*

Photoshop can recreate a shallow depth of field in your images with layer masks and the gaussian blur filter. This is a relatively simple effect to achieve but may not work on all images. Experiment with the project first to learn the skills before applying them to your images.

STEP ONE

With your image open, duplicate the background layer by selecting layer > duplicate layer from the image menu. In the duplicate layer dialogue box enter the name 'foreground' in the text field.

STEP TWO

Select the new 'foreground' layer and apply an amount of gaussian blur (select filter > blur > gaussian blur). Don't over do the strength of blur – keep it subtle.

STEP THREE

With the 'foreground' layer still active, select a new layer mask from the icon at the bottom of the layers palette. Select the gradient tool from the tool bar and select options from the image menu. Make sure the gradient is set to black and white.

STEP FOUR

Click the starting point of the gradient on the lower third area of the image and drag down to a little above the edge of the image. This will apply a layer mask that gradually reveals the depth of the image from sharpness to blur. If the blend is going the wrong way, check to see if the reverse box is ticked in the toolbar.

STEP FIVE

Now you need to blur the background to create a shallow depth of field. Hide the foreground layer by clicking on the 'eye' icon next to the layer thumbnail. Select the background layer and repeat the duplicate layer steps. Name the new layer 'background blur'. Apply the gaussian blur as before, but increase the strength.

▼ Steps four to six.

STEP SIX

With the new 'background blur' layer selected, repeat the steps to add a new layer mask as before. Select the paint brush from the tool bar and choose a suitable size and softness from the options. With black as your foreground colour, paint the mask over the middle area of the image. The top area will be left blurred while the remaining masked area will reveal the sharp area. Lastly, select the 'eye' icon for the 'foreground layer' to reveal the foreground blur.

ADVANCED IMAGE MANIPULATION

ADVANCED TONAL CONTROL

PROJECT: CREATE A MONTAGE

▲ *A montage halfway completed (left) and after (right).*

One of the advantages of digital photography is that you can take more photographs than ever before. Depending on the capacity of your memory cards, you can take hundreds of pictures of a summer holiday or perhaps a family celebration.

However, because you have so many pictures, many will never be printed. You can give some of your images a fresh look by making a picture montage. It is a great way to combine your images into one picture, is easy to do, and can make a unique and personal gift. Create a new document place each image into it in separate layers – each layer can be moved around to position each image. (For more on layers see page 292.) Then use layer masks to feather the image edges so that they blend in with each other.

STEP ONE

Take some time to go through your images and decide on which pictures you would like in your montage. Choose a theme for the montage, for instance holiday, family, pets or children.

STEP TWO

In Photoshop, create a new document for your montage. Here we will create an image of 8 x 10 in. In the image menu bar, select file > new. Enter a name for your montage in the name field and then choose 8 x 10 in from the preset drop-down menu.

Digital Camera Handbook

▼ *Step four.*

Enter a resolution of 150 in the resolution field. Make sure the colour mode is RGB and the background set to white. Click OK to accept the new document.

STEP THREE

Open your first image from the chosen collection. Choose select > all from the image menu, then image > copy. Select the new montage document and choose image > paste. The image should now appear in the new document along with a new layer containing this image.

STEP FOUR

Now make your new image a suitable size for the montage. Choose edit > free transform. A bounding box with handles will surround the new image. While holding down the shift key (to constrain proportions), click and drag a corner handle either up or down to a suitable size.

STEP FIVE

Repeat steps three and four to add more of your photographs. Try placing the images around the montage so that you form a composition. Think about how different images sit with each other and whether you want to create a focal point. Make sure that the images overlap each other by some degree.

STEP SIX

With the top image layer selected, click on the layer mask icon at the bottom of the layers palette. Select a suitable brush and softness size and start to paint around the edges. Blend the image layer with the image underneath (for more on using masks see page 294).

▲ *Step six.*

Section Three: Resources

ADVANCED IMAGE MANIPULATION

ADVANCED TONAL CONTROL

PROJECT: TONING & SPLIT TONING

Toning and split toning can enhance your black and white images by adding subtle shades of colour. You can recreate these traditional printing effects in Photoshop by using adjustment layers.

The most popular type of toning technique is sepia, which creates a warm soft shade of brown over the entire image. This effect first became popular very early on in photography and remains popular in digital photography.

Photoshop uses the colourize option found in the hue and saturation palette to add colour into a black and white image. Using the colourize option gives you the option to alter the hue and strength of the tint by dragging the sliders.

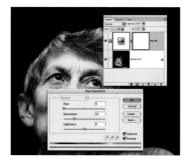

STEP ONE

Make sure your image is in RGB mode. Select image > mode > RGB. Click on the create adjustment layer icon at the bottom of the layers palette. Choose hue and saturation from the list of options.

STEP TWO

Move the hue and saturation dialogue box to the side of your image so that you can see it more clearly. In the bottom right corner of the dialogue box, click on the colourize check box. This will immediately place the image into a colour mode.

STEP THREE

Move the hue slider to create a desired tone, maybe a cool blue or a warm brown. Now drag the saturation slider to the left to reduce the strength of the tint. Finally, if you need to adjust the contrast of the image, select levels instead of adjusting brightness. (For more on using levels see page 306.)

When you have mastered the art of toning, you can move onto creating a split tone masterpiece. In this process, the shadows and the highlights will be tinted with separate colours allowing for a greater tonal range.

Photoshop uses a function called variations to produce split toning, which gives you the option to apply an amount of colour to the selected tonal range.

STEP ONE

As before, make sure that your image is in RGB mode. Select image > adjustments > variations. The large dialogue box may take up your entire screen. From the top set of options, select shadows. The added tint will only affect the shadow areas of the image.

STEP TWO

The current image thumbnail sits in the middle of the window and is surrounded by the named coloured previews. By clicking on a colour option, you add a percentage of coloured tint to the image. The more you

▲ There are many variations you can achieve when using the split toning function.

click, the stronger the tint. The new version of the image is displayed on the top section of the dialogue box along with the original version for comparison.

STEP THREE

Now select the highlights option and apply a different coloured tint. This will affect only the highlighted areas of the image. When you are happy with the desired tones, click OK.

Section Three: Resources

ADVANCED TONAL CONTROL

CREATE A SHARP MASK

▼ *An out of focus subject can be remedied with a sharp mask.*

Digital cameras have many automatic functions and most if not all have an autofocus mode (AF). This usually works well in most cases, but it can be fooled, resulting in your main subject being slightly out of focus. This may not be immediately evident when you preview the image in the camera because the screen is so small, but it will become obvious on your PC screen.

This problem can be reduced, to some extent, with your image editing software by using the sharpness filters. In Photoshop, these filters are found in the image menu and have three auto modes: sharpen, sharpen edges, sharpen more and one variable filter called unsharp mask.

You will want to limit your sharpening to selected areas of the image, because applying the filters to the whole image may be disastrous. One way to achieve this is to create a mask that will allow you to control your sharpening to only select areas. Similar to the layer mask, this will protect designated areas of the image and only apply the sharpen filter to those parts that really need it.

Follow these steps to create a sharp mask.

STEP ONE

With your image open, select the channels palette. Look at each channel individually by clicking on each one. Select the channel with the highest amount of contrast.

STEP TWO

Duplicate this layer by dragging it down to the create new channel icon at the bottom of the palette. With the duplicate channel selected, choose filter > stylize > find edges from the image menu. This will create a negative image. Then select image > adjustments > invert to convert it back.

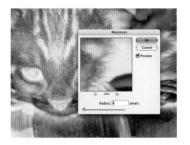

STEP THREE

Select the filter menu and choose other > maximum. Set the level to a low setting. This will increase the white area of the mask. Now select filter > noise > median and again, choose a low setting.

STEP FOUR

Now feather the edges of the mask with gaussian blur. Choose filter > blur > gaussian blur. Choose a low setting once again. Increase the contrast by adjusting the levels – choose image > adjustments > levels. Drag the highlights slider up to the left and drag the shadow slider down to the right.

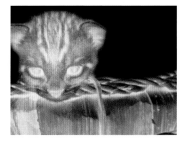

STEP FIVE

You now need to refine your mask, so select a paintbrush from the tool bar and choose black for the colour. Only white areas of the mask will affect your image, so use the paintbrush to paint over the areas that don't need sharpening.

STEP SIX

From the bottom of the channels palette, click on the 'make channel a selection' icon. This will now load your mask as a marquee selection. Select the layers palette and click on the background layer. You can now apply the sharpen filter to your selection. Choose filter > sharpen > unsharp mask.

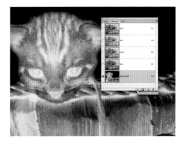

ADVANCED IMAGE MANIPULATION

GLOSSARY OF KEYBOARD SHORTCUTS

The previous chapters and projects in this digital imaging section have used the image menu bar as the route to accessing commands and functions in Photoshop.

It is always advisable to learn this method to begin with so that you become familiar with the mechanics of how the software works. Eventually, as your confidence increases, using the image menu bar may start to slow you down.

You can speed up your imaging techniques by using shortcuts to most Photoshop functions and commands. Pressing either a specific key or a combination of keys on your keyboard can automatically open a dialogue box, select a tool or perform a function without having to navigate through the menu.

Some tools are nested together in the tool bar, but have the same keyboard shortcut, for example the gradient is set together with the paint bucket and both can be accessed with the key G. To access either tool in that set, hold down the shift key and press the G keyboard shortcut. If you keep holding down shift and press G once more you can toggle between the tools. These steps can be applied to any of the other nested tools.

It is worth taking a look at this quick glossary of the most useful keyboard shortcuts, because it will help you to work faster and more effectively.

For a complete list of shortcuts, select edit > keyboard shortcuts from the image menu. From the shortcuts palette you can also customize the keyboard to make a personalized list of shortcuts that suit your imaging needs.

Digital Camera Handbook

TOOLS

Rectangle Marquee	M
Elliptical Marquee	M
Move	V
Lasso	L
Polygon Lasso	L
Magnetic Lasso	L
Magic Wand	W
Crop	C
Slice	K
Healing Brush	J
Patch	J
Colour Replacement	J
Brush	B
Pencil	B
Clone	S
Pattern Stamp	S
History Brush	Y
Eraser	E
Background Eraser	E
Magic Eraser	E
Gradient	G
Paint Bucket	G
Bur	R
Burn	O
Dodge	O
Path Selection	A
Text	T
Paths	P
Rectangle	U
Notes	N
Eyedropper	I
Hand	H
Zoom	Z

OTHER

Open an image	Ctrl O
Close an image	Ctrl W
Save an image	Ctrl S
New blank document	Ctrl N
Undo	Ctrl Z
Copy	Ctrl C
Cut	Ctrl X
Paste	Ctrl V
Paste Into	Ctrl Shift V
Free Transform	Ctrl T
Levels	Ctrl L
Curves	Ctrl M
Colour Balance	Ctrl B
Hue & Saturation	Ctrl U
Invert	Ctrl I
New Layer	Ctrl Shift N
Bring Forwards	Ctrl]
Send Backwards	Ctrl [
Merge Layers	Ctrl E
Select All	Ctrl A
Deselect	Ctrl D
Inverse Selection	Ctrl Shift I
Feather Selection	Ctrl Shift D
Repeat last Filter	Ctrl F
Rulers	Ctrl R
Default B&W	D
Print	Ctrl P
Revert Image	F12

The keyboard shortcut dialogue box allows you to search through the preset shortcuts and also to customize them.

HARDWARE
MAC OR PC?

Whether you are already a keen photographer wanting to switch to digital photography, or a beginner who wants to get the best out of their photographs, you may find that buying a computer or upgrading your existing machine is well worth the expense.

There are two main choices when buying a computer: Mac (Apple Macintosh) or PC. Each system has its advantages and disadvantages, and you need to carefully weigh the pros and cons of both. If it is your first computer, then there will be a steep learning curve as you learn not only about digital photography, but also how to use a computer.

The term PC stands for personal computer, and is slightly misleading in the Mac/PC debate. An Apple computer is still a PC – in fact the range has for a long time used

the PowerPC name, but for the sake of clarification and to conform to modern usage, a PC is a computer that operates using the Microsoft Windows family of operating systems.

MAC

Apple Macintosh computers were one of the earliest desktop computers, and Apple were the first consumer manufacturers to adopt and develop the Graphical User Interface (GUI) invented by Rank Xerox, making computers easy to operate for non-programmers. In fact, Apple was the first company to use the 'window' system commercially as a way to open folders and software.

▲ *Apple Macintosh computers are renowned for their cutting-edge design.*

Apple's real breakthrough came in the early days of desktop publishing, as designers, printers and other creative or media companies began to switch to computers in the 1980s. At the time, Apple computers were ahead in the ability to process large graphic files. Today Apple continues to appeal to creative-minded people, including photographers, due to the ease of use of the operating system, the wide range of graphic software and the groundbreaking design of the computers themselves.

PC

▼ *A typical PC set-up.*

Microsoft Windows is the operating system of choice for the vast majority of computer users, especially in small offices and the home. Part of Microsoft's winning strategy has been its licensing policy. Rather than making computers, Microsoft concentrated on the software to make them work, with the operating system being included free with most new computers.

Microsoft has often been criticized for its software stability, but recent releases, such as XP and the new Vista, offer better performance. The fact also remains that most people use Windows and it is more compatible with peripherals and software.

WHICH ONE IS FOR YOU?

Ten years ago a Mac was the only choice for photography, but the Windows operating system is now a genuine contender and a PC tends to suit most people. Ultimately, choosing a computer is down to personal choice and how computer-literate you are.

MEMORY

There are two types of computer memory that you need to consider before buying or upgrading: RAM and the hard drive. In both cases, the more the better. But what is the difference and how much should you have?

RAM

RAM stands for Random Access Memory and is the computer's short term memory. RAM is used along with the processor to perform the complex mathematical calculations that are at the heart of computer operation.

Most modern computers should have at least 512 MB of RAM. Adding more, to achieve 1 or 2 GB, will increase the efficiency of your machine and make it work faster. The speed of RAM depends on the size of the file you are working with, the application you are working in and the action you are performing. In imaging, using layers rapidly increases the file size, and the larger the file size, the more

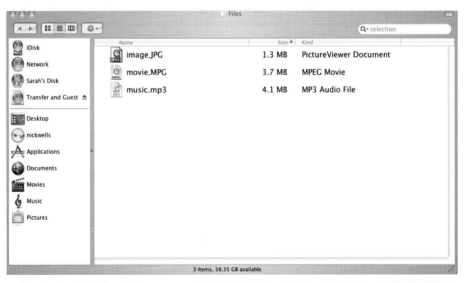

▲ The size column shows the relative memory each type of file uses.

Digital Camera Handbook

likely you are to run out of RAM. This means that the operations you perform will take longer, sometimes several minutes or even several hours. Alternatively the computer might freeze up altogether if the RAM is full and cannot cope with the task it is trying to perform.

RAM is also used up by other applications you may be accessing at the same time, notably the operating system, but also playing music through your computer, downloading files from the internet, etc., all of which will slow down your machine. Try to use memory more efficiently by quitting applications when you are not using them or flattening image files when you are happy with any work you have done. Always bear in mind that graphics and multimedia files such as videos and music use a lot of memory.

THE HARD DRIVE

The hard drive is essentially your storage area. Every bit of data that you save on your computer is stored on the hard drive, from the operating system and the applications you use to your files, including your pictures. This has caused many problems for computer manufacturers – as operating systems and software get more complex, they use more space on the hard drive, and file sizes are also increasing. In digital photography, for instance, as cameras get more powerful and provide more pixels per

picture, the need for more memory to store them is constantly increasing. Large video files, music files and other multimedia files also increase the need for storage space. A few years ago hard drive memory capacity was small and disks were used for extra storage, but hard drives are now getting bigger all the time – so much like RAM, the more you have, the better.

▲ *External hard drives can increase your memory capacity.*

PROCESSOR SPEED

▲ *Computer processors are becoming more sophisticated all the time.*

The first home computers had processors with a speed cycle of 8 Mhz – in other words, they were controlled by a clock that clicked to the next operation in 1/8,000,000 of a second. They had very little RAM and the instruction sets (permanently recorded mini-processes) were very simple. Their graphics were monochrome and unsophisticated.

A quarter of a century later and computers have processors that have 3.2 Ghz clocks (i.e. their clock cycles every 1/3,200,000,000 of a second). Ironically, this 400 times increase in clock speed doesn't necessarily mean that computers are any faster, as file sizes have more than kept up with the increase in computing speed. Software has also increased in size, needing more memory and more chip speed.

When looking at computer processors, it is easy to be drawn to the biggest numbers, but chip speed should not be the only consideration – you also need to think about the bus speed. The bus is the pathway by which all data comes in to and out of the processor. A fast chip with a slow bus runs at the speed of the slower component. Memory also has a maximum speed of transfer, so newer computers will have a memory speed of anything from 133 Mhz up to 750 Mhz.

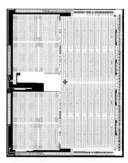

▲ *Chip speed and bus speed are important considerations.*

The computer, or CPU (Central Processing Unit) is the real thinking part of the computer. This is where the complex mathematical equations that are behind every change to your images are performed. Not content with having increasingly faster processors, manufacturers are now putting more than one processor into their computers. Computers are now available with dual processors or even quad processors that further boost the speed by parallel processing or multi threading, allowing several complex operations to be performed at the same time.

GRAPHICS AND VIDEO CARDS

Along with the processor, RAM and hard drive, digital imaging requires a fast video or graphics card. These are computer components dedicated to video and image rendering, i.e. converting the data for each pixel of an image and scaling the image to show the magnification you have chosen on your monitor. Each time you move your image the graphics card has to 're-draw' it.

The increase in 3D effects, from games and 3D rendering programmes has increased the need for even faster video processing. Some graphics cards can easily be upgraded while others are built in to the computer's motherboard and cannot be upgraded. Like other components, for digital imaging buy the fastest (i.e. the most expensive) you can afford. Otherwise the computer may be performing your manipulations in the blink of an eye, but it will take 30 seconds for you to see the results on screen. It doesn't sound like much, but in practice can be very frustrating.

▲ *When buying in a graphics card, invest in the most expensive one you can afford. A slow graphics card can be very frustrating.*

MONITORS & COLOUR CALIBRATION

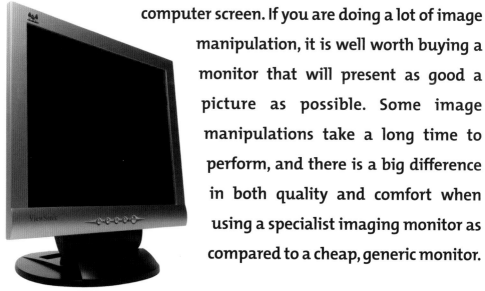

The first time you see a digital image is generally on your computer screen. If you are doing a lot of image manipulation, it is well worth buying a monitor that will present as good a picture as possible. Some image manipulations take a long time to perform, and there is a big difference in both quality and comfort when using a specialist imaging monitor as compared to a cheap, generic monitor.

There are various aspects to consider when choosing a good monitor, including type, size, resolution, brightness, contrast ratio, colour depth and the calibration it is capable of. There are two types of screen: CRT (Cathode Ray Tube) and LCD (Liquid Crystal Display). CRTs were the dominant technology for a long time, but now the superior power economy, smaller dimensions and significantly lighter weight of LCDs has seen them become popular, even with professional imagers.

The size of a screen is given in inches, and to a degree, the bigger the better. The size quoted on a screen is the physical measurement from one corner to an opposite corner, but this may not be the size of the image-showing screen. 19 inch screens, for example, may have a diagonal measurement of 18 inches that actually shows an image.

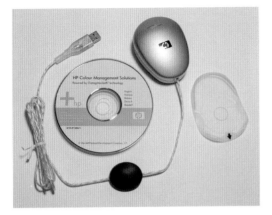
▼ *Colour calibration software can improve resolution.*

Resolution refers to how many blocks or phosphor groups each screen is made up of, in other words the maximum number of pixels it can display. 1,024 x 768 pixels is the minimum resolution you want. This is not just because of the size at which you can view images but also because the higher the screen resolution, the less room on your screen will be taken up by palettes and toolbars, and the more of your image you will be able to see when using an image manipulation program.

Monitor brightness is an absolute and is measured in candelas per metre squared. The contrast ratio is the difference in brightness between the brightest emission and the least bright. The brighter the screen the better, and as far as contrast goes, 300:1 is a good figure for an LCD screen. However to put this into context, the ratio between bright, direct sunlight and starlight is 100,000,000:1. You will find that 300:1 is rather easier on the eye, however. The colour depth refers to how many different shades a screen can show. Eight bit colour gives you 16.7 million colours; 10 bit gives you 1.1 billion different shades and so on. An eight bit colour depth is normally enough, though, as most images captured are in eight bit colour to begin with.

The effective management of colour in digital imaging is not something that can be covered in just one chapter, but there are accessories you can buy to make the task much more easy. Clip-on colour calibrators, for instance, compare the colours the screen thinks it is displaying with those it actually is, allowing you to fine tune the colour management of your screen and therefore help to colour manage the whole image manipulation process.

▲ *Clip-on colour calibrators improve colour management.*

CONNECTIONS

After you have taken a picture with your camera you need to transfer it to your computer, and then pass that picture to your printer. In order to connect these different devices you will need cables, and there are several options.

SERIAL CABLES

Serial cables and SCSI (Small Computer Systems Interface) were once the preferred choice of connections for computers. For their time they were fast enough, but the computer had to be turned off and on again before they could be connected or disconnected. Times have changed, however, and there is now a new series of interfaces that most peripherals use. Each has its own set of uses but the main thing to check before buying a peripheral of any kind is that your computer can actually connect to it.

USB

The first replacement for SCSI was the USB (Universal Serial Bus) connection – now the most common way of connecting devices to a computer. Many cameras still use USB 1.1, which offers a data transfer rate of 12 megabits per second. This is slower than SCSI, but there are many advantages to USB. Every PC now made has a USB port, making it truly universal. USB cables are also 'hot swappable', meaning that you can swap devices without turning off the computer. In addition, USB cables can, for low drain devices, supply power to peripherals.

▲ A USB cable (top) and a firewire connection (bottom).

Digital Camera Handbook

In 2001 the standard was upgraded to USB 2.0 and many more computers, printers, scanners and cameras now offer faster data transfer rates. It is worth bearing in mind however that USB now comes in a number of different types, namely USB, Hi-Speed USB and Full-Speed USB 2.0. Mice and keyboards use USB and only require a transfer rate of 1.5 Mbits (1.5 million bits of data per second). For non-keyboard/mice products USB offers the Full-Speed option (i.e. 12 Mbits per second), while High-Speed has a possible maximum transfer rate of 480 Mbits per second. These are theoretical maximums, however, and you will rarely get that high a rate of transfer.

USB 2.0 and 1.1 devices are compatible with USB 2.0 and 1.1 computers, but the slower transfer rate will apply where two standards are mixed.

FIREWIRE

Firewire appeared around the same time as USB 1.1 but offered faster transfer rates of up to 400 megabits per second. Although overtaken by USB 2.0, Firewire 800 was then released which doubles the rate. However, few cameras use Firewire with the exception of some high end models, usually digital SLRs. While the theoretical transfer rates may not differ too greatly, Firewire will generally outperform USB 2.0 in practice.

WI-FI AND BLUETOOTH

It is not always desirable to have cables cluttering up a desk, and wireless standards are becoming increasingly popular. The two main types of wireless communication are Wi-Fi and Bluetooth. Only a couple of cameras from Sony have so far used Bluetooth, but many camera phones use it as standard to transfer images between phones, computers and printers. This suits the small files produced by most phones, but the transfer rate is unsuitable for larger image files.

Wi-Fi (known as Airport on Apple Macs) on the other hand looks to be the future for cameras, with models in 2005 from Kodak, Nikon and Canon. The Kodak Easyshare One, for instance, transfers files across your home wireless network and also across the internet via Wi-Fi hotspots. This allows you to upload pictures directly to the Kodak website or email pictures to family and friends.

PORTABLE STORAGE

With ever increasing amounts of digital data, the importance of backing up your files, especially your photographs, has never been greater. Backing up your pictures means that if your hard drive crashes or your computer is stolen or damaged, you will not lose your memories and your photographs will stay safe.

There are several ways to back up your pictures. The easiest and most obvious is to print them, but digital photography has meant that we sometimes only print out a few pictures from a set, and even so prints can get lost or torn. There are other options, however.

DISKS

Most computers now have CD or even DVD burners that can copy data (in this case, image files) from the hard drive and 'write' it on to a disk, which you can then keep safe somewhere else. It is well worth getting into the habit of copying your pictures to a CD or DVD every time you download them. If you don't have a built-in CD burner, many companies make external units that attach to your computer via a USB cable. Some even have card slots so you can bypass the computer completely and copy straight to CD. You can also, of course, play music CDs or watch films on the DVD versions.

▲ *Compact disks and DVDs are a vital part of digital photography.*

HARD DRIVE

As your photographic collection increases, which it will do surprisingly quickly, you may find that your hard drive is filling up and you have no space left to store anything. In this situation you can either install a new internal hard drive, or even more easily, add an external hard drive. This will at least double your storage, and you can also disconnect the hard drive and swap between computers if you need to. It is still wise to make back-up disks though, just in case the hard drive fails.

PORTABLE HARD DRIVE

If you take a lot of photographs in one go, or are travelling for any length of time, you could use a portable storage device to copy files from your camera's memory card as you go. There are many types of portable hard drive available, and they usually have a

▲ *Portable hard drives are now available in pocket-sized versions.*

small screen built in so that you can view your pictures as you upload them, using built-in card slots. Many have the added advantage of built-in MP3 players and video viewers, allowing you to listen to music or watch films. They also often connect to TVs so that you can view your pictures on a larger screen without a computer. When you return home you can then download the files to your PC. Don't forget to back up to a disk as well though, as such devices do carry the risk of failing unexpectedly.

▶ *USB 'keys' can hold up to 16 GB of data, and even attach to your keyring.*

TAPE DRIVES

Those who want to get really serious about backing up can buy magnetic tape drives that come with software that automatically backs up your computer's hard drive each night. This is a very useful system, as it also stores your personal settings and all your applications as well as your picture data.

TYPES OF PRINTER

As well as the method by which a printer converts the digital data into a physical image (inkjet or dye-sub), printers can also be categorized in terms of their size and their additional functions.

Photo printers come in a wide variety of configurations. The first variable is the maximum size of print you wish to get from your digital images. Some printers are designed so that they can only produce 15 x 10 cm (6 x 4 in) prints, known as enprints. Whilst it might seem strange to pay nearly the same for a printer that can only produce enprints as for one that can produce A4-sized images, the usual difference between them is that the enprint printer does not require the use of a computer in order to access the images held by your camera. It also takes up much less space on a desktop.

There are a number of different versions of this sort of printer, and they all connect directly to a camera or its memory card. This connection might be via a wire (normally a USB cable), a memory card reader built into the printer, or via a wireless or Bluetooth (another wireless standard) connection. Bluetooth is generally found on printers that are designed to work with mobile phones as well as 'normal' digital cameras. In virtually all cases, printers designed to work directly with a camera or memory card have a screen so that you can preview and select your images. Some also offer the options of rudimentary image correction and cropping.

At the other end of the size scale is the poster printer. This is typically quoted as having a size of A3 or A3+. Machines of this size can produce printed images of up to 42 x 30 cm (16.5 x 12 in), but can produce 6 x 4 in prints as well. More sophisticated printers can print from a number of different input trays and can even print on to CDs and DVDs. Some models can print on both sides of the (appropriate) paper without your having to turn the sheet over manually in between.

One sector of the inkjet market that has really taken off in the last few years is the all-in-one (AIO). This is a combination of an inkjet printer and a flatbed scanner (see

Digital Camera Handbook

page 350) and they often have a fax machine and a photocopying facility as well. The benefits of these machines are that they take up less room than the individual components would, and they often cost less than the combined price of the individual devices. They are also set up to work together in a colour sense. The downside of this all-in-one approach is that each aspect of the AIO's performance is probably going to be less good than a dedicated individual machine would be. More recent AIOs have incorporated a CD burner so that you can download and print your images without a computer.

▼ *All-in-one printers have become very popular.*

HOW SCANNERS WORK: FLATBED

▲ Flatbed scanners are very straightforward to use.

Flatbed scanners, as their name implies, are horizontal scanners where the lens array, scan head and light source sit underneath a glass panel on which the item to be scanned is placed. The scanning head is as wide as the glass panel, but will typically have fewer lines of sensors on it than a dedicated film scanner would.

Some flatbed scanners are confined to performing reflective scans, where the light shines through the glass, reflects off a strip of the print to be scanned and that section of the print image is captured by the sensor.

▲ CIS scanners tend to be neat and slim.

Flatbed scanners have one of two types of sensor. The least expensive will have a sensor known as a CIS (Contact Image Sensor), whilst more expensive ones will have CCD arrays much like film scanners. The main practical difference between the two as regards reflective scans is that CIS scanners cannot scan three dimensional objects such as coins, as the system does not allow for any depth of field beyond the glass panel. Another difference is that CIS sensors tend to be slimmer in size thanks to the nature of their construction.

▲ *Scanners can be combined with printers.*

As well as reflective scanning, some flatbed scanners also have the ability to perform scanning of transparent objects – known as transmissive scanning. In order to be able to do this, the flatbed scanner must either have a second light source that can sit in a lid on top of the subject to be scanned, or a separate drawer beneath the scanning array (where the subject to be scanned sits) and a further light source beneath that drawer. In the former case, when a transmissive scan is performed, the light underneath the glass panel is turned off and the one above comes into action. With the separate scanning drawer system, the optical path of the scanning array has to be changed (normally by means of mirrors) with, once again, the light source changing to the one on the other side of the transparent object coming on, and the light associated with the scanning array being switched off.

Typical levels of resolution for flatbed scanners range from 1,200 lines per inch to 4,800 for the higher quality (and higher priced) scanners. You may occasionally see scanners advertising 9,600 x 9,600 ppi scans but this is an interpolated figure. Interpolation in scanning works just as it does in digital cameras. A portion of the image is real data, but the rest is merely made up by the scanner. Just as in digital cameras, using interpolation is not to be recommended.

When choosing a flatbed scanner it is worth going for one with a fast connection to your computer (either USB 2.0 or Firewire). It is also worth checking the colour depth at which it converts its data. A scanner with 12 or 14 bit colour will deliver many thousands more subtle colour tones than an 8 bit scanner. Remember, though, that the higher the resolution and the greater the colour depth, the bigger the files will be and the longer it will take to scan images in.

▶ *Some scanners can scan three dimensional objects.*

CAMERA ACCESSORIES

LENSES: WIDEANGLE/TELEPHOTO

The quality of lens that you use on your digital camera will affect and possibly limit the quality of images that your camera can produce. If you own a digital SLR, you will be able to buy additional lenses and expand the range of your photography.

▲ A wideangle photograph.

Cameras with fixed (i.e. permanently attached) lenses can be made to be more flexible with the addition of supplementary lenses, but your camera needs to have a filter ring or a special adaptor in order to be able to take advantage of these (see page 356 for more on supplementary lenses). There are two types of lens: fixed focal length and zooms. Zoom lenses are covered in more detail on page 354.

FIXED FOCAL LENGTH LENSES

Focal length is a scientific measurement of the distance between two key points in the optical train of a lens. It is meaningless when quoted alone, but when it is used in conjunction with the size of the image area (in practical terms, the size of the sensor), it gives you information about how much a lens will magnify an image and also how much of a scene it can fit in.

It is usual to see two figures quoted: the actual focal length, and what focal length would be required to get the same image magnification if the sensor were the size of a 35 mm film frame. So a digital SLR lens may have an actual focal length of

▲ Wideangle lenses literally give a wide angle of view.

12 mm, but has a 35 mm equivalent of 18 mm. These equivalents are quoted so that you can compare lenses between different types of digital camera lens from different manufacturers. Fixed focal length lenses come in one of three main forms, with either short, medium or long focal lengths.

The first of these is known as a wideangle lens, as it gives you a wide angle of view (and consequently a small image magnification). A medium focal length lens is often known as a standard lens (as this used to be the lens that came as standard with a new SLR) and

▲ *A telephoto lens.*

will have a focal length of about 50 mm. A telephoto is a higher magnification lens and as the literal translation of its name (far light) implies, it enables you to take pictures of objects far away.

▲ *Tekephoto lenses have higher magnification.*

Fixed focal length lenses have several advantages. They are less complex to design and build than zoom lenses, and it is therefore cheaper to build a really good fixed focal length lens than it is to build an equivalently good zoom lens. There is also the issue of the maximum aperture. The maximum aperture of the lens determines the maximum amount of light it will let through to the viewfinder and the sensor. A big (known as fast) aperture allows more light through and thus makes

it easier to see through an optical viewfinder and check focus and composition, which is particularly useful with wideangle lenses. It also allows you to blur backgrounds more easily, which is useful for telephoto lenses. Finally it allows faster maximum shutter speeds to be used, which is useful for any lens.

▲ *Far away detail becomes clear with a telephoto.*

LENSES: ZOOM

At one time zoom lenses were an expensive curiosity. Now they are by far the most popular kind of lens found in photography – whether on compact digicams or on digital SLRs.

The focal length of a zoom lens can be varied in order to aid composition. In theory, a zoom lens is one that does not require refocusing after its focal length has been changed, while a varifocal is one where you do need to refocus. In practice, whilst many zoom lenses do need refocusing, this job is taken care of by autofocus systems, so it may not be obvious which type of zoom lens you have.

Like fixed focal length lenses, the focal length of zoom lenses determines their image magnification and angle of view. They are always shown as two figures: the minimum and the maximum focal length. For example, 28–70 mm describes a zoom with a minimum focal length of 28 mm and a maximum of 70 mm. This kind of lens is either known as a wideangle zoom (as its minimum focal length is a wideangle one) or a standard zoom, as its focal length range includes 50 mm. You might also see this kind of lens described as a 3x zoom, as its maximum focal length divided by its minimum focal length is about three. A 35–420 mm lens would therefore be known as a 12x (420 divided by 35 = 12). This is known as a telezoom (as it includes telephoto lengths) or as a superzoom as its zoom ratio is over 6x. You are unlikely to find a lens of this kind as a digital SLR lens, as their sensors are bigger and this would be a huge piece of glass to carry around.

▲ *Zoom lenses are a very popular accessory.*

▲ *This first image shows Big Ben, London, in the distance behind a statue.*

It is also possible (although not always advisable) to use lenses designed for film SLRs on digital cameras. There are two reasons why it is not recommended to use film camera lenses on some digital SLRs. Firstly there is the issue of sensor size. Digital cameras are (with some exceptions) smaller than the 24 x 36 mm frame of 35 mm film. This means that the focal length quoted on the lens will not be accurate. For example, a film lens with a nominal 28–70 mm focal length may have the effect of a 42–105 mm lens when fitted to a camera with a sensor smaller than 24 x 36 mm.

The second reason for taking care before using film lenses is the manner in which digital cameras work. Every CCD element on the sensor has a tiny lens on it, and these lenses work best when hit head-on by the light. Film camera lenses may not be configured to deliver light in that manner.

Like fixed focal length lenses, different zoom types are useful for different kinds of photography. It is therefore useful to have a range of different focal lengths available. The less ambitious the zoom range the easier it is to make a good lens, but bear in mind that you will have to buy more lenses to cover the same focal length range as a superzoom.

▶ *The second image (left) and the third image (right) show the difference a zoom lens can make.*

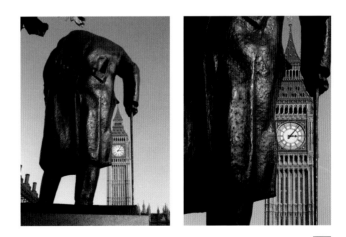

MACRO ACCESSORIES

Digital cameras are uniquely well placed to take macro pictures. This is because their small sensors require short focal length lenses, and that means they can focus much more closely than larger formats like 35 mm. While compact digital cameras can use accessory lenses to improve their minimum focusing distance, they often do not need them.

It is digital SLRs (or any cameras with a larger than average sensor) that benefit from having a macro lens. Alternatively, if you don't want to buy a macro lens, you can buy a close-up supplementary lens. This screws on to the main filter thread of your lens and changes its minimum focusing distance. This allows you to focus more closely than with the camera's lens alone.

▲ *A macro lens is a great accessory for a digital SLR camera. Although expensive, the results can be spectacular.*

Sometimes simply getting close to a subject is not all you want, and it is possible to buy macro lenses in a variety of different focal lengths. The wider angle lenses allow you to get close to your subject, while the longer focal length lenses allow you to keep your distance. These are particularly useful when it comes to wildlife photography, to avoid both scaring your subject off and getting too close to dangerous or aggressive animals.

Digital Camera Handbook

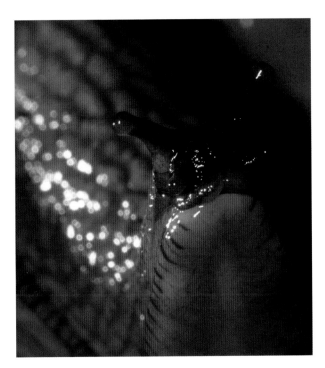

▲ *The level of detail achieved with a macro lens is extraordinary.*

It is good photographic technique to have a little distance between you and your subject, partly because the further away you are the easier it is to focus. In addition, and more importantly with regard to the quality of your images, if you are very close to a subject there is a good chance that either you, your camera, the lens or all three will be interfering with the light – either blocking it out or casting obvious shadows across the subject. Lighting in general can be a problem with macro work, and it is worth thinking about purchasing a few accessories to make it more straightforward. For instance, you can buy light tents that give you all-around soft light to illuminate your subject.

Flash is covered in more detail over the next few pages, but it is worth mentioning that a macro flash unit is well worth investing in. One of the best of these is a unit known as a ring flash. This is, as its name implies, a flash in the shape of a ring, the hole of which you shoot the image through. As the light comes from all around the subject, it creates a gentle all-over illumination. Some macro flash units have four flash tubes that you can individually turn on and off so as to have sidelighting on one side alone. This creates a shadow that helps to define the subject in terms of depth.

For very small subjects, you can get moveable clamps that will hold your subject steady while you organize your camera and lighting around it. You can also buy combined lighting and camera supports that allow you to hold the subject and camera in perfect position while you change the lighting around them.

Section   Three: Resources

FLASHGUNS

One of the greatest limitations in digital photography is the fact that digital cameras of all kinds have inadequate flash output. Go more than three metres away from your subject or close down your aperture for greater depth of field, and the built-in flash on a digital camera will not be effective. It is not that the technology to

▲ A hotshoe flashgun.

▲ A cord-connected flashgun.

build a decent flash does not exist, it is rather that the power required to fully charge a decent flash unit's capacitor would make the useful working life of the super slim lithium-ion cells significantly shorter than most users would want.

For those cameras where the manufacturers think that the likely users will want to have an additional option, in the shape of an accessory flashgun, you will find one of three connections on it. These are a power cord (PC) socket, a dedicated flash cord socket or a hotshoe. There are two types of hotshoe – the standard hotshoe, which will have a single central contact, or a dedicated hotshoe, which will have a series of additional contacts through which the camera can communicate with the flashgun. Some digital cameras have a system whereby their built-in flash units emit a coded

Digital Camera Handbook

CAMERA ACCESSORIES

series of pulses that dedicated units can obey wirelessly, avoiding the need for any wired connection between the camera and flashgun.

Those cameras with TTL (though the lens) flash metering can emit a flash to tell the unit to start the exposure, and as soon as the on-board metering system deems the sensor to have received enough exposure, fires again to tell it to stop. These pulses and the flash itself may be of the order of 1/10,000 second, so you may or may not see them as anything other than a single flash.

It is possible to buy accessory flashguns even if you have no way of connecting the camera to the flash unit. These units are known as slave flashes. However, it is worth checking very carefully what kind of flash your digital camera emits, as some cameras fire out the flash to aid autofocusing and others fire out one or two pre-flashes to either conquer red eye or to determine the correct exposure. Whichever system you choose, ensure that the slave will actually fire while the camera's shutter is open rather than before.

As well as doing everything automatically, external flashguns also allow you to operate manually. In terms of flash, the exposure calculation is a simple one. Simply set the shutter speed to the camera's flash synchronization speed (usually 1/60th, 1/125th or 1/250th second) or slower, and, using the guide number (GN) of the flashgun to help, choose an

▲ Flashguns are availble in all shapes and sizes.

appropriate aperture. Say, for example, you have a flashgun with a guide number of 20 and a subject 5 m away, then you can determine the correct aperture with the equation f = GN/D (where f = flash, GN = guide number and D = distance). In this example, therefore, f = 20/5 = f/4. A flash with a GN of 30 at the same subject distance would need an aperture of 30/5 = f/6 (or more practically f/5.6).

STUDIO FLASH, REFLECTORS & OTHER LIGHTING ACCESSORIES

▼ *Optional external battery units offer extra power.*

For subjects that can be shot indoors, a portable flashgun is not necessarily the best option. Sometimes you may want to exert more control than even a sophisticated TTL flashgun can give you.

Studio flash units are normally mains powered, which means (in comparison to battery operated units) limitless power. Studio units are normally used in groups, which means an entirely different approach to lighting a subject from the one most of us are used to – namely the solitary influence of sunlight. With studio flash you can put units in front, to the side, behind, above or even beneath a subject to get the lighting effect that you want. More than this, you can change the relative power of the units – either by moving the flash heads or by setting various flash heads to different power settings.

As well as the quantity of light thrown on to a subject, you can also change the quality of light that illuminates your subject. Lights can be fired through soft-boxes – huge, pyramid-shaped accessories with a diffusing screen of white material at the base of the pyramid and the light source at the apex. These make the light source

▲ *Studio flash units are endlessly adaptable.*

Digital Camera Handbook

bigger and create less in the way of shadows. Light can also be thrown backwards into silvered brollies – literally umbrella-shaped reflectors that fold up for easy storage. These reflectors are also available in a golden colour, to give warmth to portraits where skin-tones would otherwise be pale given the high light levels.

▲ *Soft-boxes diffuse the light and reduce shadows.*

For harsher lighting you can use a snoot – a cone-shaped metal accessory that forces the light to come out through the thinner end of the cone for a concentrated beam. Alternatively use gobos – disks that throw shapes of light on to the background for a speckled effect, or project a logo or recognizable shape on to it.

There are thousands of background designs, from pure white, via out of focus neutral coloured blobs that make the sharp reproduction of the portrait subject seem even sharper, through to pure black velvet or velveteen backgrounds, which reflect no light and isolate the subject to great effect.

As well as these options, you can now buy special studio kits that allow you to shoot products for internet selling sites and special macro outfits that contain all you need to produce perfect, shadow-less lighting on smaller subjects. When you have a flexible studio set up with an array of lights, reflectors and backgrounds, you can shoot the same subject a dozen times and come out with a dozen entirely different results. It can take a lifetime to master all the different possible studio techniques, but you can easily pick up two or three basic set-ups in no time at all. These will be enough to produce professional looking portraits irrespective of what the weather is doing outside, and with no worries about shooting before the sun disappears for the day.

▶ *A snoot gives a concentrated beam for harsher light.*

Section Three: Resources

TRIPODS & CAMERA SUPPORTS

One of the recurring problems of photography in general, and digital photography in particular, is the issue of shooting when light levels are low. Sometimes you don't want to have to increase CCD sensitivity or use an artificial light source. So how do you go about capturing sharp images when you know that the shutter speed is slower than you can safely hand-hold?

▲ Tripods for digital cameras are very compact.   ▲ A tripod will ensure sharp images.

The answer lies in the small threaded socket that sits at the base of your digital camera – the tripod socket. A tripod is a three-legged device that can stand without wobbling on any surface, no matter how uneven it is. Tripods normally feature adjustable legs to ensure that as well as standing immobile on any surface, their head (the part that screws into the bottom of the camera) is parallel to the floor, or indeed is at whichever angle you want it to be. As well as adjustable legs, most tripods have a central column that can be raised or lowered for fine adjustments of the shooting height without having to adjust all three legs.

Tripod heads come in all manner of designs. Some have built-in spirit levels to make sure you are level with the ground (useful for shooting panoramas). Others have pan and tilt heads that allow you to tilt the camera through 90 degrees for shooting in portrait format, or through 180 degrees to shoot at the floor, at the sky or to pan (rotate around the centre of the tripod). This means that you can rotate the camera to shoot in front of or behind you without having to pick the tripod up. Some tripods have ball and socket heads which allow both these movements at the same time, although it is harder to be as precise in either type of movement as it is on a pan/tilt. However, ball and socket heads do allow a much faster combination of pan and tilt movements.

▲ *Adjustable legs mean that you can shoot on any surface, no matter how uneven.*

Tripods come in all sizes, from pocket models that have limited functions but that will happily hold a compact digital camera, to huge models that allow you to shoot from well over head height. It used to be that the bigger the tripod, the heavier it was, but now manufacturers make carbon fibre tripods that weigh a fraction of their steel aluminium counterparts. The downside is that you may need to weigh them down to keep them still. Some tripods provide a hook under the tripod head to attach your camera bag, which will steady the tripod.

An alternative to a tripod is to make yourself part of a tripod by adding a monopod to your own two legs. A monopod is a pole of adjustable length that you press down on, through your camera, to give you more balance than standing on two legs alone, but at a quarter of the weight of a tripod. Monopods are the accessory of choice for pro sports photographers, as they allow rapid changing of composition from a sitting position whilst still hugely reducing unwanted camera movement.

▶ *Pan and tilt heads give you a much greater range of movement.*

FILTERS & FILTER HOLDERS

▲ Optical filters retain pixel data.

You might think that the era of camera filters was long past. Many cameras now have filters built in, and even if not, there are many opportunities to influence and manipulate your images once they are on the computer.

Filters are still useful, however. Every manipulation performed on a digital image file results in some image data being lost. When you capture an image using a filter over the lens, you may have a manipulated image but it will be one in which all the pixel data is present. However advanced cameras get, there is still more usable image data in an optically filtered shot than in an electronically filtered shot.

There are four basic types of filter: exposure adjustment, hue adjustment, reflection/saturation adjustment and graduated filters.

EXPOSURE ADJUSTMENT

▼ Filters don't have to be expensive.

The first type of exposure adjustment filter that it is worth fitting to your camera comes under a generic heading of exposure control. These reduce or eliminate the invisible UV rays that come with bright, sunny days. UV rays have no effect on the image itself, but they can influence meters and cause underexposure.

Digital Camera Handbook
Digital Camera Handbook

Using this kind of filter can prevent underexposure in extreme circumstances. They are also a physical barrier between your lens and the outside world. A scratched or broken filter is cheaper to replace than a ruined lens – especially if the lens is built in to the camera.

The second kind of exposure adjustment is a neutral density filter, which reduces the amount of light that comes through the lens. One of the problems with the small size of digital camera sensors is that they have increased depth of field in comparison to film cameras. To get around this, you should shoot with as wide an aperture as possible. Even with the camera's ISO set to its minimum value, this may still be out of range of your available shutter speeds on a very bright day. In other words, an image would be overexposed if you used a wide aperture and the shortest shutter speed available was still slower than the meter recommended. The solution is a neutral density filter. These are also helpful when you want to use a slow shutter speed but there is too much light. For example, you might want to capture the movement of a stream or the sea as gentle, blurred water to give the impression of movement while the rest of the scene was captured sharply. A neutral density filter can capture this effect.

HUE ADJUSTMENT

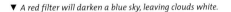

▼ A red filter will darken a blue sky, leaving clouds white.

Changing the colour of an image is a common use for filters. With digital imaging, colour changing is achieved much more easily with the hue controls in Photoshop or similar image manipulation programs. However, filters also give you the option of changing how the chip perceives and records the colours

in a scene. This is particularly useful when you want to shoot images that are going to be reproduced in black and white. Using a yellow or red filter on a digital camera where there are blue skies will darken the sky whilst leaving clouds fluffy and white (once the image has been converted to black and white). Using a green filter will cause leaves and grass to be reproduced in a relatively lighter hue.

▲ *A polarizing lens has several uses.*

REFLECTION/SATURATION ADJUSTMENT

Whilst other filters can have their effects partially duplicated by post-processing, the filter with the most profound change is the polarizer. Light is plane polarized – in other words, its waves vibrate along a specific angled plane – by the sky and also by any non-metallic object it is reflected from, such as glass or water. A polarizing filter does this to a greater degree, only allowing waves in a particular plane to pass through it. In image terms, this means that any light that is plane polarized at perpendicular angles to the filter is not allowed to pass through it. Therefore you can eliminate, or at least very much reduce, distracting reflections from windows, puddles, lakes or other wet and reflective surfaces. In addition, as the sky also polarizes light, a polarizer can be made to reduce the amount of light passing through the lens from the sky, deepening the colour of a blue sky on a sunny day, for instance. Polarizers are mounted on rotating rings that allow you to see the effect of the filter on the LCD screen before choosing the appropriate angle for your shot.

Another less-known use for polarizers is to increase the amount of reflection in an image. This is done by first rotating the filter to where it minimizes reflection, and then turning it through a further 90 degrees. By doing this (aligning the plane of polarization of the filter to the reflective surface) you allow in all the reflected light from that surface, but reduce the amount of light coming from everywhere else in the scene. As the metering system of the camera is reading the light coming through the filter, it still gives you the correct exposure.

▶ *Most filters screw on to the lens.*

GRADUATED FILTERS

Sometimes you do not want to give the same exposure or the same colour shift to the whole of a scene. Graduated filters assist here by applying whatever hue or neutral density factor to only half of the scene, and the point at which they stop is, as the name suggests, a graduated one. This means you can use a filter to reduce the amount of light coming into the sensor from the sky, for example, whilst allowing the much lower light levels to pass undiminished through the clear portion of the filter. This gives the sensor a much easier contrast range to deal with and retains detail in both the highlight and shadow areas.

Graduated filters are square or rectangular and held in a filter holder in front of the lens that allows you to slide them up and down to get the right position. Even if you have a sloping horizon, the filter holder can be rotated and the filter slid up and down to match the orientation and position of the filter to that of the horizon.

▼ *Graduated filters prevent the same exposure being given to the whole of a scene. They also help to retain detail.*

CAMERA BAGS

Looking after your digital camera is obviously sensible, but you should also be able to carry it around with you and take pictures whenever you want. A good camera bag will allow you to do both in comfort and security.

There are hundreds of different styles and designs of bags, meaning that it can be difficult to establish which one is right for you. Bear in mind that you may need room not just for your camera, but also a spare memory card, batteries and perhaps the charger too if you are going away rather than merely going out. You may also want to carry some of the accessories mentioned in this chapter. Rather than having two camera bags – one for day trips and one for longer breaks – it is better that you keep everything in one bag so that you are able to lay your hands on it at a moment's notice.

▲ *Whether you want a bag that holds all your equipment or one that is neat and compact, there is something available for everyone.*

There are two factors to bear in mind when choosing a bag: protection and accessibility. Protection encompasses protection against the elements (dust and sand, water and extremes of heat), protection against shocks (bumping into things or the bag being dropped) and protection against theft. The latter is a case of both how securely a bag is attached to you and appearance. A bag that is obviously a camera bag, or looks as if it may contain something more valuable than a standard

▲ *Multiple zips and pockets are useful.*

digital camera, will increase the chances of it being targeted by thieves.

In terms of accessibility, you should note how many points of access there are to different compartments. Some bags allow you to put the bag flat on the ground and instantly have access to everything inside it, and have separate zipped or Velcro-closing side access points that allow you to access one or more of these compartments without having to open everything up to the elements. Some models have hinged or separately zipped additional protective flaps over their compartments to provide maximum protection for travelling, but easier and quicker access when the bag is in use.

Finally, you should note how comfortable a bag is likely to be to carry around for any length of time. Purchasing a bag that will carry all your gear is obviously vital, but try to choose one that gives a number of options as to how it can be carried and that spreads the weight over both shoulders. Anyone who has been involved in camera testing or professional photography for a couple of decades will have some curvature of the spine from carrying 30–40 kg of kit in older, over-one-shoulder bags. Newer bags have better load-spreading on their shoulder straps, second contact points (or additional straps) to avoid loading all the weight on one side, and waist straps to prevent bags from swinging out and unbalancing you. Even if you don't carry more than a single compact and a few bits and pieces, a properly designed bag will be more comfortable, afford much more protection and last longer than one chosen simply for its looks.

▶ *Rucksack-style bags are practical and comfortable.*

MAINTENANCE

Digital cameras are very much like cars in terms of how you can best ensure their long term survival. They work better with a little maintenance than with none, but tinkering is not advised.

It is quite easy to break a digital camera, or at least render it useless, which is not quite the same thing. Dropping a camera repeatedly can lead to problems such as the shutter release button working loose and even falling out, while sticky sliding lens caps are another common problem

▲ *Take care at the beach – sand and seawater are bad news for cameras.*

resulting from too much wear and tear. If your lens cap doesn't get out of the way of the front element of the lens, you cannot take pictures. This kind of thing often happens when cameras are incorrectly stored (in a tight trouser pocket, rather than on a strap or in its own bag), or used in adverse situations – in a sandstorm at the beach, for instance, or by children with sticky fingers. Sand and seawater in particular can be fatal to a digital camera. If sand gets into your lens it will cause trouble sooner or later, and if seawater gets into your electronics you will probably already have lost the use of your camera.

Regular maintenance can help you, however. If you get into a sensible cleaning routine at the end of a day's shoot, you can avoid these camera disasters. Cleaning includes checking that there is no sand or moisture in your camera bag, either. There is no point in cleaning the camera and then putting it into an even more hostile environment that you have used it in.

▼ A blower brush and lubricant are useful accessories.

First, blow any extraneous matter off the camera before you start cleaning. Pay special attention to the lens barrel, and in the event of a digital SLR, to the lens mount and mirror box. Always hold the camera so that you are blowing dust or dirt down and off rather than up and into the camera. Using a blower brush means that you won't be blowing small amounts of saliva on to your camera.

For the lens and, specifically, the front element, first brush, then blow and only then, and with a special lens cleaning cloth, sweep the lens radially (down) rather than in a circular motion. Give any hard matter a chance to fall off rather than being ground in.

Finally, always make sure that if your camera is stored somewhere other than on your person for a long period, that the batteries are kept outside. Batteries left too long can leak and corrode the contacts, and equally importantly the on/off switch may get accidentally pressed and cause the camera to open in a confined space, damaging the lens irreparably.

▲ Use a specialist lens cleaning kit.

MEDIA CARDS

Media, or memory cards are a vital part of your digital imaging kit. No free memory space means no digital images. However, whilst prices for accessory memory cards have come down rapidly over the last few years, it is not the case that all memory cards are the

▲ *Memory cards are an integral part of digital photography.*

same. The quality of flash memory chips used to store the data on the memory cards varies greatly. It is a simple equation: the more you pay for your memory cards, the higher the standard of flash memory that will have been used in it. Higher quality means that it will last longer and, on average, better cards will have much fewer catastrophic data loss incidents (i.e. losing all the pictures on a card) than cheaper generic cards.

Higher priced cards also deliver a much better speed of data storage and transfer compared with cheaper cards. Faster read/write times mean that you can take pictures more quickly (particularly in close succession, and when using bigger file formats such as RAW or TIFF), and also view the images on your camera more speedily. Another advantage of improved data transfer speeds is that it takes less time to transfer data from your memory card after it has been removed from the camera. This means uploading to your computer more quickly, and faster printing if you are using a computer-less enprint printer (see page 348).

Along with data storage and transfer rates, the capacity and type of memory card also massively influence their cost. Older established card types such as SD/MMC (Secure Digital/ MultiMedia Card) or CF (Compact Flash) are likely to be cheaper than newer or more rarely used types such as Memory Stick (MS) in any one of its four forms and xD picture cards. It is worth remembering that if you have bought, for example, a second hand digital camera, it may not be able to use the newer, large capacity memory cards.

If you are wondering whether it is better to have one very large capacity memory card or rather to buy a number of smaller capacity cards, you should work on the rule that it is always better to have a back-up. Memory cards are not infallible and can

corrupt, so it always better to have two cards than one. You may still lose your photographs from the failed card, but at least you can carry on shooting.

There are programs available that can attempt to recover the data on a memory card. It is often the catalogue

▲ Even large capacity cards are tiny in size.

or directory file (the system that tells the computer where the picture data is stored on the card) that has corrupted, rather than the pictures themselves. However that is not always the case, so a back-up is always recommended. Always bear in mind that the fewer cards you have, the more times a catalogue file will be overwritten and therefore risk corruption.

MANUFACTURERS: HARDWARE & SOFTWARE

All the major camera, software and accessory manufacturers have websites, which are a source of useful information if you want to find out more about a specific product. Many camera manufacturers include support sections on their websites from which you can download a firmware update or a manual, as well as access customer support numbers. The sites listed below are international, so you may need to find the section of the site specific to where you live.

ACD Systems
www.acdsystems.com
Image management software

Adobe
www.adobe.com
Picture editing and image management software

Apple
www.apple.com
Computers, photo storage, image management software and viewing devices

Belkin
www.belkin.com
Card readers, flash drives, notebooks, mobile phone and computer accessories

BenQ
www.benq.com
Digital compacts, mobile phones, laptops and computer accessories

Canon
www.canon.com
Digital compacts, digital SLRs, lenses, flashguns, printers, all-in-one printing devices, scanners, consumables and camera accessories

Casio
www.exilim.com
Digital compacts and camera accessories

Corel
www.corel.com
Picture editing and image management software

Delkin
www.delkin.com
Flash memory cards, card readers, DVD burners, DVDs and memory card adaptors

Epson
www.epson.com
Digital compacts, printers, all-in-one printing devices, flatbed scanners, picture viewers and consumables

Extensis
www.extensis.com
Image management software and Photoshop plug-ins

Fujifilm
www.fujifilm.com
Digital compacts, digital SLRs, memory cards, printers and camera accessories

Hama
www.hama.com
Camera bags, computers, memory cards, card readers and digital camera accessories

Hasselblad
www.hasselblad.com
Digital backs, medium-format cameras, lenses, camera accessories and film scanners

Hewlett-Packard (HP)
www.hp.com/uk
Digital camera, printers, scanners, all-in-one printing devices and consumables

Iomega
www.iomega.com
Hard drives, DVD writers and USB drives

iView
www.iviewmultimedia.com
Image management software

Kingston
www.kingston.com
Flash memory cards, computer memory and flash drives

Kodak
www.kodak.com
Digital compacts, printers, picture viewers, camera accessories and consumables

Konica Minolta
www.konicaminolta.com
Digital compacts, digital SLRs, lenses, camera accessories and film scanners

Leica
www.leica-camera.com
Digital compacts, lenses and camera accessories

Lexar
www.lexar.com
Flash memory cards, card readers, USB flash drives and software

Lexmark
www.lexmark.com
Printers, all-in-one printing devices and consumables

Lowepro
www.lowepro.com
Hard cases, camera bags and pouches

Manfrotto
www.manfrotto.com
Tripods and lighting support

Microsoft
www.microsoft.com
Home computer and image editing software and computer accessories

Microtek
www.microtek.com
Digital compacts, film scanners and flatbed scanners

Nik Multimedia
www.nikmultimedia.com
Software and filters

Nikon
www.nikon.com
Digital compacts, digital SLRs, portable storage devices, lenses, flash guns and camera accessories

Nokia
www.nokia.com
Digital camera phones

Olympus
www.olympus.com
Digital compacts, digital SLRs, lenses, printers and camera accessories

Panasonic
www.panasonic.com
Digital compacts, camera accessories, memory cards and computers

Pentax
www.pentax.com
Digital compacts, digital SLRs, lenses and camera accessories

PixelGenius
www.pixelgenius.com
Software and plug-ins

Ricoh
www.ricohpmmc.com
Digital compacts, camera accessories, CD writers and storage media

Rollei
www.rollei.de
Digital compacts

Roxio
www.roxio.com
Image management, editing and burning software

Samsung
www.samsungcamera.com
Digital cameras and accessories

SanDisk
www.sandisk.com
Flash memory cards, card readers and photo viewers

Sanyo
www.sanyo.com
Digital cameras, camera accessories and printers

Sigma
www.sigma-imaging-uk.com
Digital SLRs, lenses and camera accessories

Sony
www.sony.com
Digital compacts, camera accessories, memory cards, printers and computers

Sony Ericsson
www.sonyericsson.com
Camera phones

Tamron
www.tamron.com
Lenses

Trust
www.trust.com
Digital compacts and computer accessories

Wacom
www.wacom.com
Graphics tablets

ULead
www.ulead.com
Image management and photo editing software

Umax
www.umax.com
Card readers, film scanners and flatbed scanners

Vosonic
www.vosonic.com
Portable storage devices

MAKING USE OF THE INTERNET

Whether it is news, views or online printing, the Internet is packed with useful information about digital photography. Many websites boast discussion forums and online galleries where you can display your photographs. Others offer printing facilities at competitive prices so shop around to ensure you get the best price. Some sites even offer free prints or online storage if you sign up, but beware of hidden costs.

www.amateurphotographer.com
The UK's longest running photographic magazine has a strong online presence with regularly updated news pages, forums and reader photos.

www.bonusprint.com
Reasonably priced digital processing on a wide range of conventional, traditional and digital print paper sizes, with price reductions for buying in bulk. Bonusprint can also print on to a range of other media including mugs, cards, photo books and t-shirts.

www.bootsdigitalphotocentre.com
It doesn't offer the print size choice as some print providers and is not particularly cheap, but by registering at Boots online you can get 100 MB of storage and share your albums with family and friends.

www.cnet.com
Probably the leading resource on the Internet for all things gadget related, CNET includes the latest technological news and reviews of cameras, camcorders and computer accessories.

www.colorama.co.uk
While the website layout isn't as straightforward as some print providers, prices at Colorama are reasonable, and there are a varied selection of gift options on to which you can print.

www.colourmailer.co.uk
Based in Switzerland, Colour Mailer offers photo printing and enlargements at mid-range prices. It is extremely simple to use, offering easy and advanced upload options, enabling photos to be transferred individually by downloading a small piece of software.

www.dcresource.com
Featuring reviews, news and previews of digital cameras. The buyers guide contains a list of models picked by the editor to suit a range of different budgets, including compacts and SLRs.

www.dcviews.com
As well as the latest camera news, if you are looking for advice on a specific camera Digital Camera Views is worth a visit, with links to professional online reviews and forum discussions.

www.dpreview.com
Extensive digital compact and SLR reviews with some of the most detailed digital camera information on the Internet, extremely lively forums and up-to-date news.

www.ephotozine.com
While a good source for the latest news, undoubtedly the highlights of ephotozine are the reader galleries and portfolios, which have the feel of a real online community.

www.imaging-resource.net
From news, camera reviews and photo galleries, to forums and useful lessons on photographic technique, Imaging Resource contains a little bit of everything.

www.jessopsphotoexpress.com
High street photography retailer Jessops has a user-friendly website, offering prints at a range of different sizes and gift formats at mid-range prices. By registering you can store your photographs in an online album.

www.klick.co.uk
Klick offers a fairly limited range of print sizes and there are no options to print on gifts. However this colourful website is easy to operate and reasonably priced.

www.kodakgallery.com
The Kodak EasyShare Gallery offers a good selection of printing sizes at reasonable prices as well as photo books and cards. The layout is straightforward and there is free online photo storage for registered members.

www.luminous-landscape.com
With emphasis on the genre of landscape photography, Luminous Landscape has some great essays along with reviews, news and tutorials.

www.megapixel.net
Although the reviews are not as comprehensive as some, megapixel.net contains camera reviews and a wide selection of in-depth articles on camera basics, photography tips and peripherals.

www.outbackphoto.com
Aimed at serious and professional photo-graphers, Digital Outback Photo contains reviews of the latest SLRs, digital backs and printers and a useful selection of articles including colour management and workflow.

www.pbase.com
One of the foremost sites for photo sharing on the Internet. For a yearly fee you can obtain 300 MB of storage and create your own gallery.

www.peak-imaging.co.uk
Frequently the choice of professional photographers, Peak Imaging has a reputation for producing quality prints. You can order digital prints by downloading a piece of software, but it is expensive and doesn't offer any gift printing options.

www.photobox.com
As well as having a superb online gallery, Photobox frequently wins awards for its photo printing service. Prices are reasonable and you can print on to a wide range of paper sizes as well as an extensive selection of gift products.

www.photo-i.co.uk
This printing-orientated site has in-depth printer reviews and news and is well worth a visit if you are thinking of investing in a printer.

http://photos.fotango.com
Fotango offers a wide range of print sizes and some rather unusual gift options. You can display your photographs in the public gallery, but it is expensive compared to other online print services.

www.pixum.co.uk
German based company Pixum offers a dazzling array of print services including posters, teddy bears and cards, as well as a range of different paper sizes. You can choose to upload your pictures using online and offline options.

www.pocket-lint.co.uk
News and reviews on the latest 'gadgets, gear and gizmos', including software, phones, and digital cameras, presented in a user-friendly format.

www.photoshopnews.com
A site for Photoshop aficionados, containing – as the name suggests – the latest news on Photoshop, as well as a good selection of links.

www.robgalbraith.com
Run by photojournalist Rob Galbraith, it contains news, forums and links. The CompactFlash performance database is excellent, collating read and write speeds of memory cards when used with digital SLRs.

www.shutterbug.net
Accompanying the US photography magazine, Shutterbug is packed with information including news, forums, book reviews and some useful features on photographic technique that are regularly updated.

www.snapfish.com
A service of printing giant HP, Snapfish offers some of the cheapest prices on the Internet, printing on to a range of paper sizes and gift formats. Users can take advantage of unlimited free storage.

www.steves-digicams.com
This US-based site contains extremely detailed reviews of masses of digital cameras (past and present), printers and accessories.

www.whatdigitalcamera.com
The website for one of Britain's best-selling digital photography magazines containing regularly updated news, test pictures from the latest issue, downloadable tutorials and reader photographs.

BIBLIOGRAPHY

Ang, Tom, *Digital Photography: An Introduction*, Dorling Kindersley, 2003

Ang, Tom, *Digital Photographer's Handbook*, Dorling Kinderlsey, 2004

Busch, David, *Digital SLR Cameras for Dummies*, Hungry Minds Inc., 2005

Freeman, Michael, *The Digital SLR Handbook*, Ilex, 2005

Freeman, Michael, *The Complete Guide to Digital Photography*, Thames & Hudson, 2003

Freeman, Michael, *Close-Up Photography: The Definitive Guide for Serious Digital Photographers*, Ilex, 2004

Freeman, Michael, *Black and White: The Definitive Guide for Serious Digital Photographers*, Ilex, 2005

Gartside, Tim, *Digital Night and Low Light Photography*, Ilex, 2006

Johnson, Dave, *How to Do Everything with Your Digital Camera*, Osborne McGraw-Hill, 2005

Johnson, Harald, *Mastering Digital Printing*, Premier Press, 2004

Lacey, Joël, *The Complete Guide To Digital Imaging*, Thames & Hudson, 2002

Lacey, Joël, *The Digital Darkroom: A Complete Guide to Image Processing for Digital Photographers*, RotoVision, 2004

Lacey, Joël & Henshall, John, *Going Digital: Wedding and Portrait Photography*, RotoVision, 2003

Peterson, Bryan, *Understanding Digital Photography: Techniques for Getting Great Pictures*, Amphoto Books, 2005

Peterson, Bryan, *Understanding Exposure: How to Shoot Great Photographs with a Film or Digital Camera*, Amphoto Books, 2004

Rouse, Andy, *Digital SLR Handbook*, Guild of Master Craftsman Publications, 2005

Weston, Chris, *Mastering Your Digital SLR: How to Get the Most Out of Your Digital Camera*, RotoVision, 2005

Weston, Chris, *Digital Wildlife Photography*, Guild of Master Craftsman Publications, 2005

PICTURE CREDITS

All images courtesy of Alan McFaden, Nigel Atherton (www.nigelatherton.com), Hannah Bouckley, Ian Burley (www.dpnow.com), Steve Crabb, James Goulding, Jamie Harrison, Nick Wells and Andrew Harris (www.andrewharrisphotography.co.uk).

AUTHORS

Nigel Atherton is currently the Editor of *What Digital Camera*, the UK's oldest digital photography magazine. Originally from Bath, Somerset, Nigel became interested in photography during his last year at school. After a year assisting a local photographer he studied photography, film and TV production at Plymouth College of Art and Design. In 1984 he became a cruise ship photographer, during which time he visited around 40 countries and supplied travel photography to a major stock library. On returning to the UK in 1990, Nigel worked as a ballistics and weapons photographer for the Ministry of Defence, then as technical helpline manager for a major camera manufacturer before continuing his photographic education at the University of Westminster. He joined *Amateur Photographer* magazine as a technique writer in 1994, and was Features Editor from 1998 to 2001. After spending a year publishing photography books he became Editor of *What Digital Camera* in 2002. He lives in Brighton with his wife and two children.

Hannah Bouckley has been a keen photographer since she was a child and has continued to enjoy taking pictures ever since. She discovered Photoshop while studying for a Media Production degree at Bournemouth University, where she gained a 2:1. On graduating she contributed to a range of photographic titles, including *Digital Photography Made Easy*, *Digital Photographer* and *Digital Camera Buyer*, before moving to *What Digital Camera*, the UK's original digital photography magazine, in 2005. She is currently Reviews Editor on *T3* magazine, a role that puts her in the enviable position of trying out the latest digital cameras.

Ian Burley was hooked on photography by the age of ten and, from then on, regularly badgered his parents to buy him a darkroom. Later, Ian ran the school photographic society and spent summer holidays helping out at the local camera store. After studying computer science at degree level in the early 80s, Ian went back to the same camera store and was managing it within a year. He later managed the company's flagship store in north London, winning the Amateur Photographer Dealer of the Year Award in the process. By the mid-80s Ian had settled into a longer term career as an IT journalist. The advent of digital imaging neatly married Ian's passion for photography and IT skills. Since 2000 his writing has been primarily in the field of digital photography, and in 2001 he launched his Digital Photography Now website (www.dpnow.com). Ian thinks his two young daughters are probably the most photographed kids in the world, though some of his colleagues who also contributed to this book just might disagree.

Steve Crabb studied photography at Bournemouth & Poole College of Art in 1986. He has worked in the media industry for nearly twenty years and has produced Photoshop work for clients such as Yahoo, The Body Shop and the Football Association. He is currently the Art and Tutorials Editor for *What Digital Camera* magazine and has co-authored several other books on digital photography and Adobe Photoshop.

Jamie Harrison has been a professional photographer and printer for over twenty years, working in most disciplines. His experience covers everything from social photography on cruise ships to weddings, advertising and corporate photography. As a black and white and colour printer, he has produced work for many commercial clients and was also the main printer for the British Film Institutes archive. In 1997 he discovered Adobe Photoshop and began working with Apple Macintosh computers and digital scans. He joined *Amateur Photographer* magazine soon after and began reviewing both film cameras and digital cameras. He is now Technical Editor of *What Digital Camera* and has tested most of the digital cameras released in the last three years, as well as writing tutorials on photography and Adobe Photoshop. Jamie has also appeared on TV and radio, and has written about photography and cameras for several national newspapers and magazines.

Joël Lacey is Editor of *What Camera?* magazine and has been writing on photography since 1981. He has been short-listed for the Periodical Publishers Association Specialist Writer of the Year award and is the former technical editor of *Amateur Photographer* magazine. Joël has written three books on digital photography including *The Complete Guide To Digital Imaging* (Thames & Hudson), *The Digital Darkroom: A Complete Guide to Image Processing for Digital Photographers* (RotoVision) and (with John Henshall) the award-winning *Going Digital: Wedding and Portrait Photography* (RotoVision). He currently lives in rural Dorset with his wife, his dog and a garden full of chickens.

INDEX

Digital Camera Handbook
Digital Camera Handbook